STAR WARS
REBEL HEIST

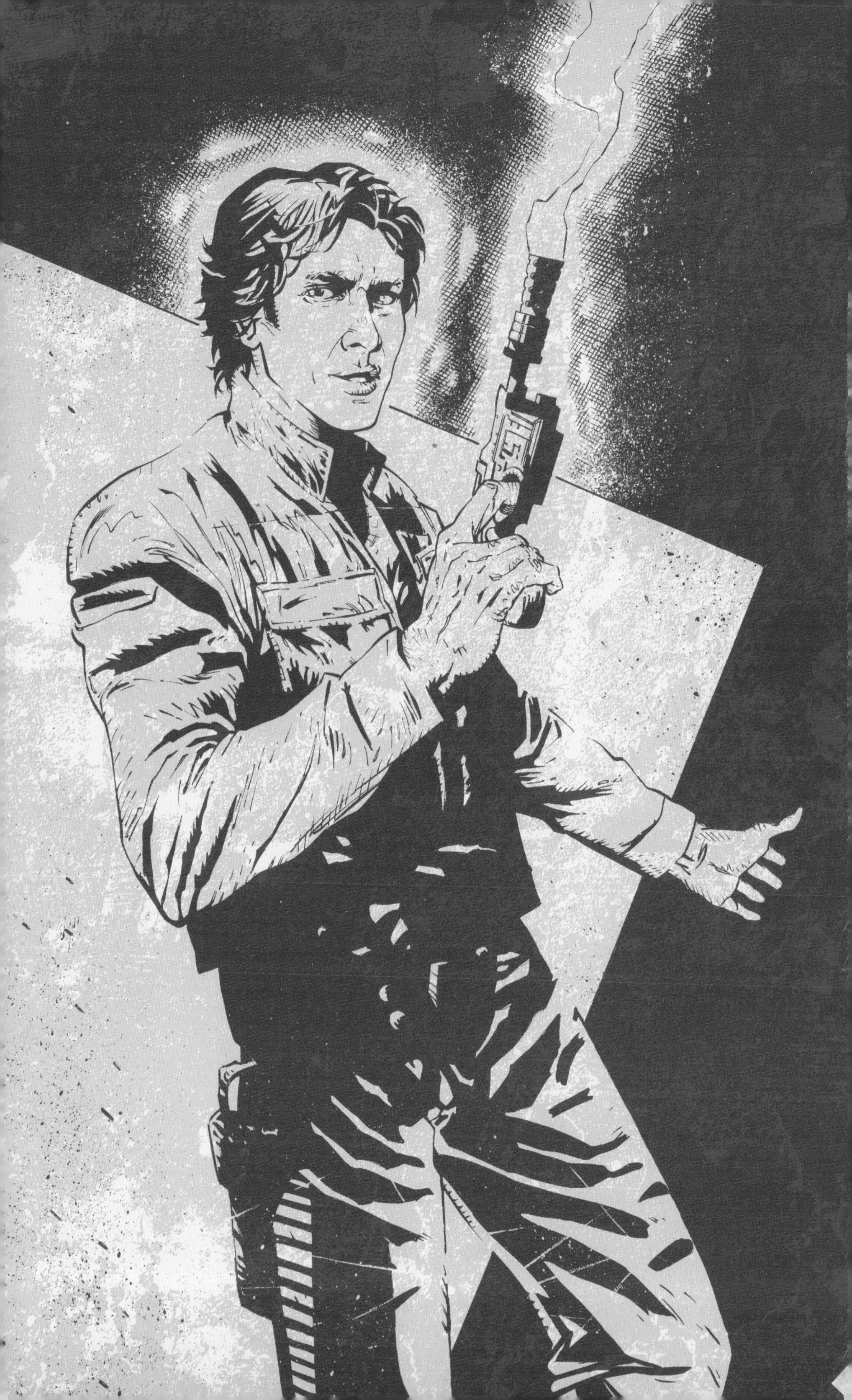

THE REBELLION

FROM THE BATTLE OF YAVIN TO FIVE YEARS AFTER

Open resistance begins to spread across the galaxy in protest of the Empire's tyranny. Rebel groups unite, and the Galactic Civil War begins. This era starts with the Rebel victory that secured the Death Star plans, and ends a year after the death of the Emperor high over the forest moon of Endor. This is the era in which the events in *A New Hope*, *The Empire Strikes Back*, and *Return of the Jedi* take place.

The events in this story take place sometime before the events in *Star Wars: Episode V—The Empire Strikes Back*.

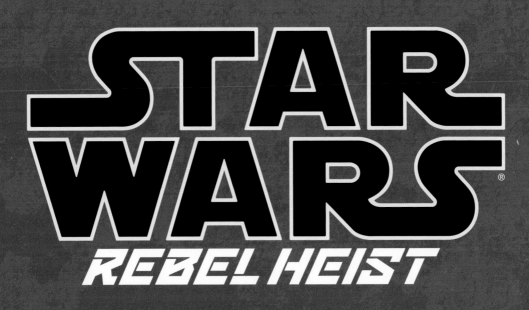

STAR WARS®
REBEL HEIST

SCRIPT
MATT KINDT

PENCILS
MARCO CASTIELLO

INKS
DAN PARSONS

COLORS
GABE ELTAEB

LETTERS
MICHAEL HEISLER

FRONT COVER ART
ADAM HUGHES

BACK COVER ART
MATT KINDT

DARK HORSE BOOKS
LUCAS BOOKS

PRESIDENT AND PUBLISHER
MIKE RICHARDSON

COLLECTION DESIGNER
JIMMY PRESLER

EDITOR
RANDY STRADLEY

ASSISTANT EDITOR
FREDDYE LINS

NEIL HANKERSON EXECUTIVE VICE PRESIDENT **TOM WEDDLE** CHIEF FINANCIAL OFFICER **RANDY STRADLEY** VICE PRESIDENT OF PUBLISHING **MICHAEL MARTENS** VICE PRESIDENT OF BOOK TRADE SALES **ANITA NELSON** VICE PRESIDENT OF BUSINESS AFFAIRS **SCOTT ALLIE** EDITOR IN CHIEF **MATT PARKINSON** VICE PRESIDENT OF MARKETING **DAVID SCROGGY** VICE PRESIDENT OF PRODUCT DEVELOPMENT **DALE LaFOUNTAIN** VICE PRESIDENT OF INFORMATION TECHNOLOGY **DARLENE VOGEL** SENIOR DIRECTOR OF PRINT, DESIGN, AND PRODUCTION **KEN LIZZI** GENERAL COUNSEL **DAVEY ESTRADA** EDITORIAL DIRECTOR **CHRIS WARNER** SENIOR BOOKS EDITOR **DIANA SCHUTZ** EXECUTIVE EDITOR **CARY GRAZZINI** DIRECTOR OF PRINT AND DEVELOPMENT **LIA RIBACCHI** ART DIRECTOR **CARA NIECE** DIRECTOR OF SCHEDULING **TIM WIESCH** DIRECTOR OF INTERNATIONAL LICENSING **MARK BERNARDI** DIRECTOR OF DIGITAL PUBLISHING

This volume collects issues one through four of the Dark Horse comic-book series
Star Wars: Rebel Heist, originally published April–July 2014.

Published by Dark Horse Books, a division of Dark Horse Comics, Inc.
10956 SE Main Street Milwaukie, OR 97222

DarkHorse.com StarWars.com
To find a comics shop in your area, call the Comic Shop Locator Service toll-free at 1-888-266-4226

Library of Congress Cataloging-in-Publication Data
Kindt, Matt, author.
Star wars : rebel heist / script, Matt Kindt ; pencils, Marco Castiello ; inks, Dan Parsons ; colors, Gabe Eltaeb ;
letters, Michael Heisler ; front cover art, Adam Hughes ; back cover art, Matt Kindt. -- First edition.
pages cm
Summary: ""Rebel Alliance recruits are teamed with heroes Han Solo, Princess Leia, Luke Skywalker,
and Chewbacca to pull off a heist right under the nose of the evil Empire"--Provided by publisher.
"This volume collects issues one through four of the Dark Horse comic-book series Star Wars:
Rebel Heist, originally published April-July 2014"--T.p. verso.
ISBN 978-1-61655-500-9 (paperback)
1. Graphic novels. [1. Graphic novels. 2. Science fiction.] I. Castiello, Marco, illustrator. II. Title.

PZ7.7.K58ST 2014
741.5'973--DC23

2014020043

FIRST EDITION: OCTOBER 2014
ISBN 978-1-61655-500-9

1 3 5 7 9 10 8 6 4 2
PRINTED IN CHINA

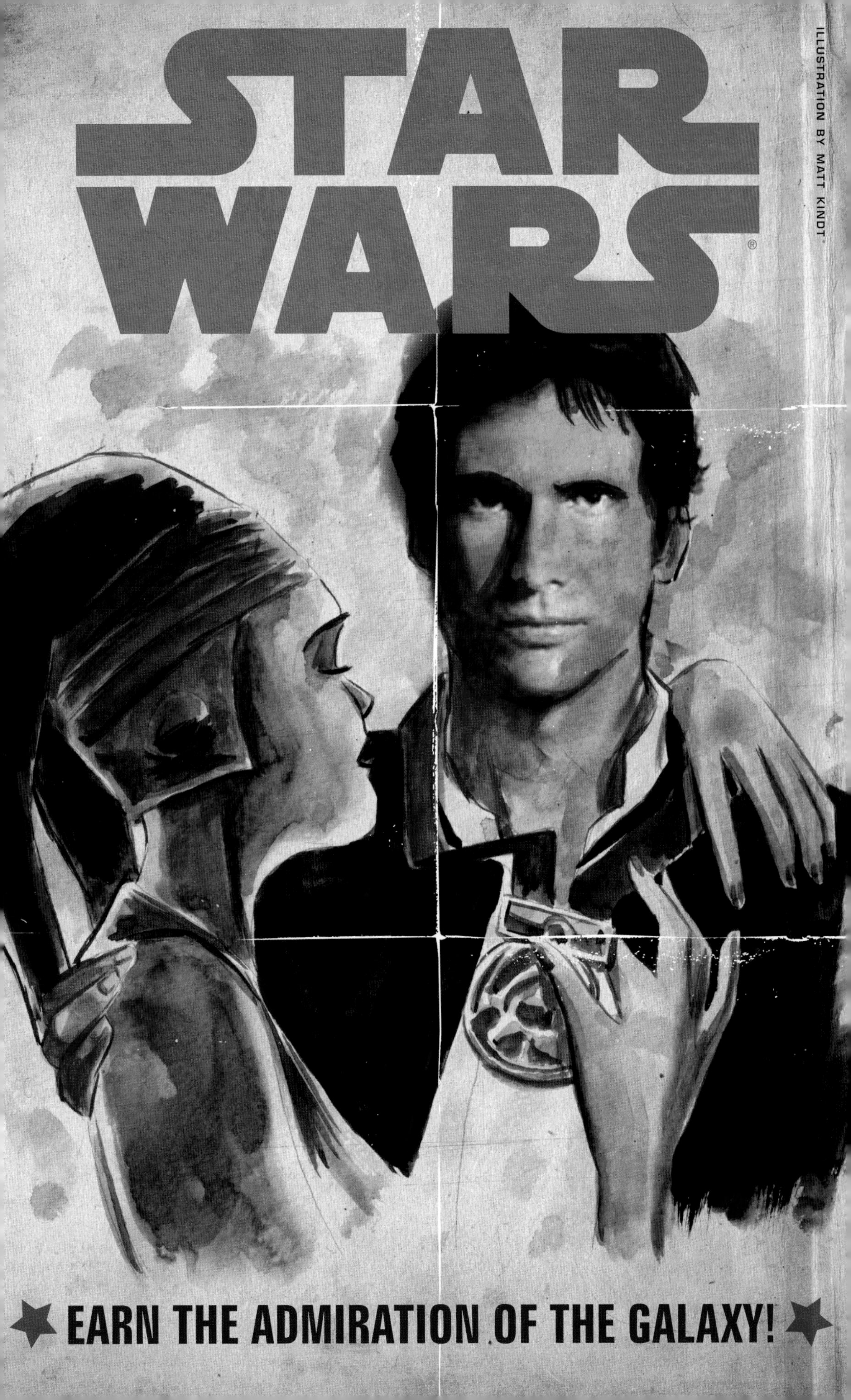
STAR WARS®
EARN THE ADMIRATION OF THE GALAXY!
ILLUSTRATION BY MATT KINDT

The Rebellion's victory at the Battle of Yavin
made heroes of Han Solo, Chewbacca, Princess
Leia, and Luke Skywalker. In the aftermath they
have become leaders within the Rebel Alliance—at
the forefront of its most dangerous missions.

But for the Alliance to remain strong, it must
bring on new recruits—and train those recruits
to be prepared for all the Empire might throw
at them. Sometimes it is even necessary to
drop recruits into the middle of a mission so
they can learn on the job . . . under fire.

In those situations, pairing them with
an experienced operative will allow them to
survive the mission and gain the confidence
to complete the next one on their own.
Or so the Alliance hopes . . .

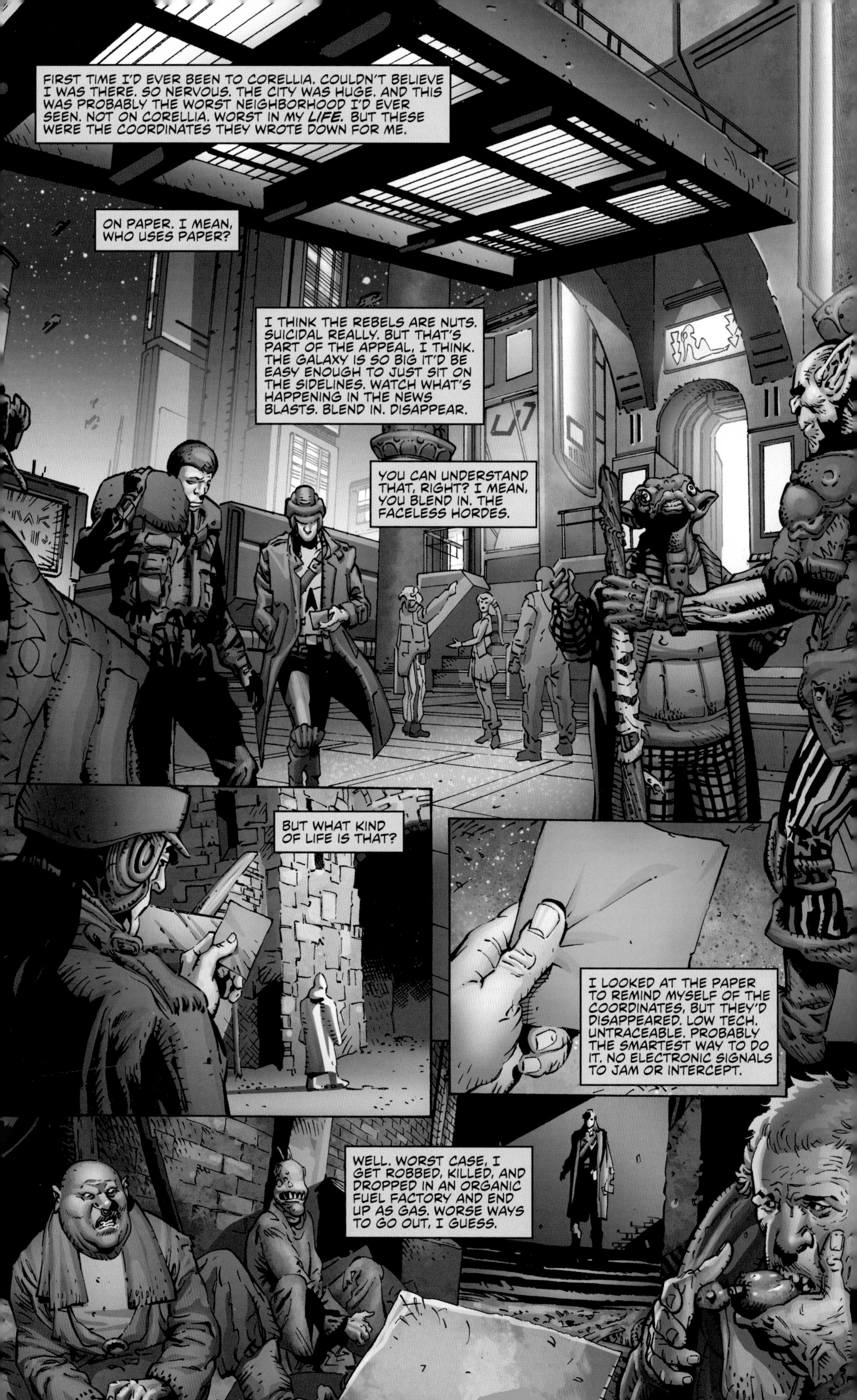
FIRST TIME I'D EVER BEEN TO CORELLIA. COULDN'T BELIEVE I WAS THERE. SO NERVOUS. THE CITY WAS HUGE. AND THIS WAS PROBABLY THE WORST NEIGHBORHOOD I'D EVER SEEN. NOT ON CORELLIA. WORST IN MY *LIFE.* BUT THESE WERE THE COORDINATES THEY WROTE DOWN FOR ME.
ON PAPER. I MEAN, WHO USES PAPER?
I THINK THE REBELS ARE NUTS. SUICIDAL REALLY. BUT THAT'S PART OF THE APPEAL, I THINK. THE GALAXY IS SO BIG IT'D BE EASY ENOUGH TO JUST SIT ON THE SIDELINES. WATCH WHAT'S HAPPENING IN THE NEWS BLASTS. BLEND IN. DISAPPEAR.
YOU CAN UNDERSTAND THAT, RIGHT? I MEAN, YOU BLEND IN. THE FACELESS HORDES.
BUT WHAT KIND OF LIFE IS THAT?
I LOOKED AT THE PAPER TO REMIND MYSELF OF THE COORDINATES, BUT THEY'D DISAPPEARED. LOW TECH. UNTRACEABLE. PROBABLY THE SMARTEST WAY TO DO IT. NO ELECTRONIC SIGNALS TO JAM OR INTERCEPT.
WELL. WORST CASE, I GET ROBBED, KILLED, AND DROPPED IN AN ORGANIC FUEL FACTORY AND END UP AS GAS. WORSE WAYS TO GO OUT, I GUESS.

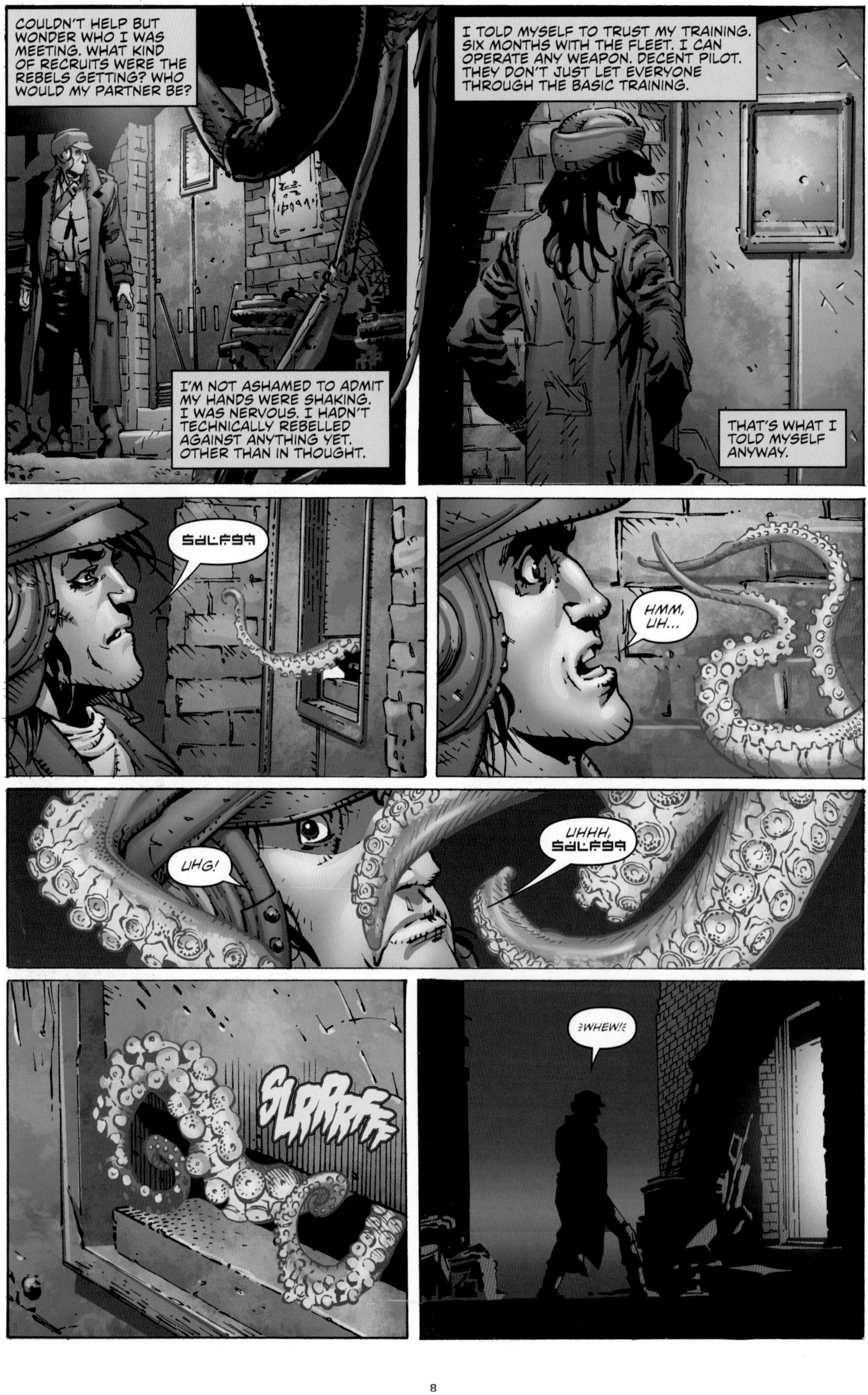
COULDN'T HELP BUT WONDER WHO I WAS MEETING. WHAT KIND OF RECRUITS WERE THE REBELS GETTING? WHO WOULD MY PARTNER BE?
I'M NOT ASHAMED TO ADMIT MY HANDS WERE SHAKING. I WAS NERVOUS. I HADN'T TECHNICALLY REBELLED AGAINST ANYTHING YET. OTHER THAN IN THOUGHT.
I TOLD MYSELF TO TRUST MY TRAINING. SIX MONTHS WITH THE FLEET. I CAN OPERATE ANY WEAPON. DECENT PILOT. THEY DON'T JUST LET EVERYONE THROUGH THE BASIC TRAINING.
THAT'S WHAT I TOLD MYSELF ANYWAY.
HMM, UH...
UHG!
UHHH,
SLRRFF
WHEW!

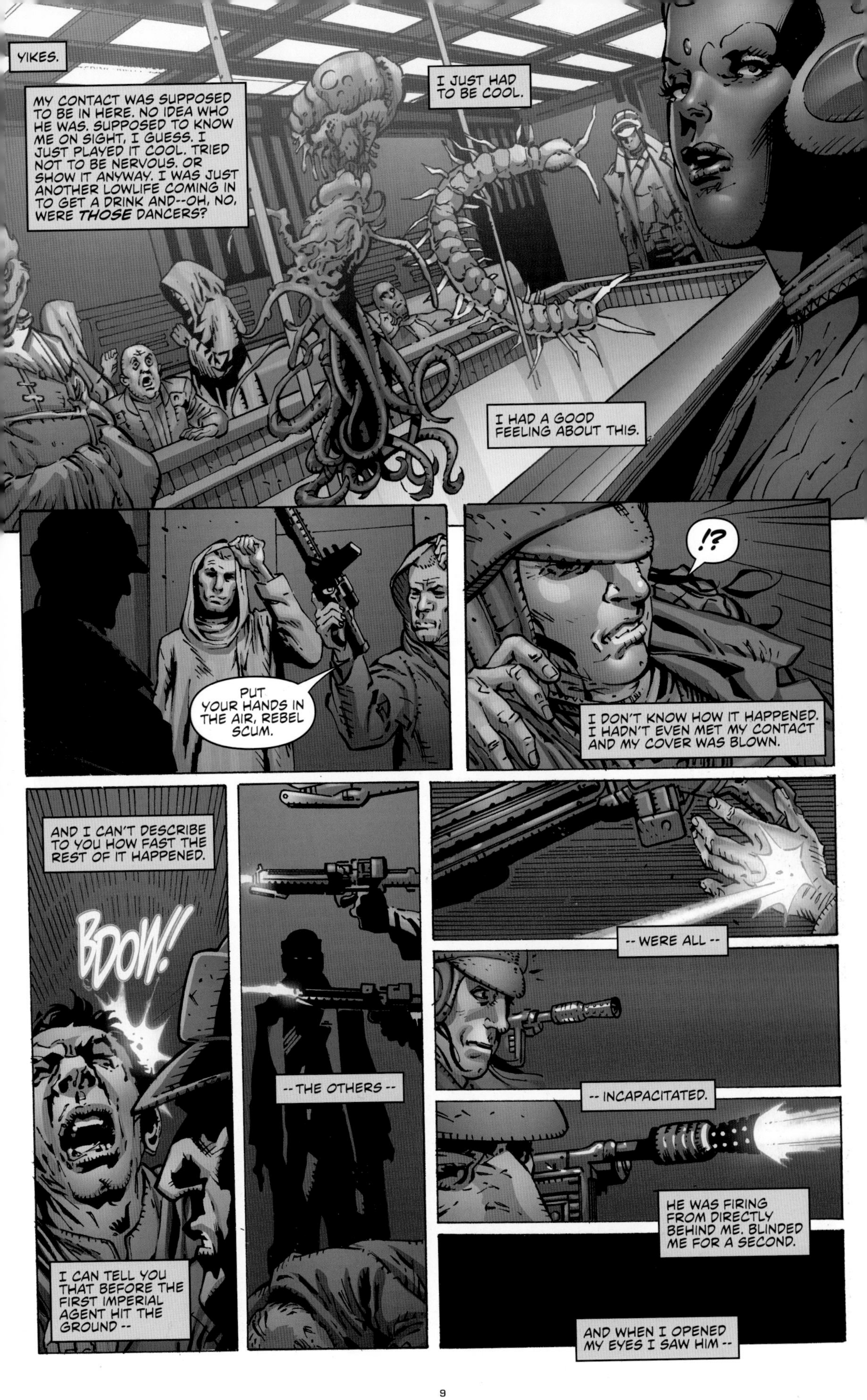
YIKES.
MY CONTACT WAS SUPPOSED TO BE IN HERE. NO IDEA WHO HE WAS. SUPPOSED TO KNOW ME ON SIGHT, I GUESS. I JUST PLAYED IT COOL. TRIED NOT TO BE NERVOUS. OR SHOW IT ANYWAY. I WAS JUST ANOTHER LOWLIFE COMING IN TO GET A DRINK AND--OH, NO, WERE *THOSE* DANCERS?
I JUST HAD TO BE COOL.
I HAD A GOOD FEELING ABOUT THIS.
PUT YOUR HANDS IN THE AIR, REBEL SCUM.
!?
I DON'T KNOW HOW IT HAPPENED. I HADN'T EVEN MET MY CONTACT AND MY COVER WAS BLOWN.
AND I CAN'T DESCRIBE TO YOU HOW FAST THE REST OF IT HAPPENED.
BDOW!!
I CAN TELL YOU THAT BEFORE THE FIRST IMPERIAL AGENT HIT THE GROUND --
-- THE OTHERS --
-- WERE ALL --
-- INCAPACITATED.
HE WAS FIRING FROM DIRECTLY BEHIND ME. BLINDED ME FOR A SECOND.
AND WHEN I OPENED MY EYES I SAW HIM --

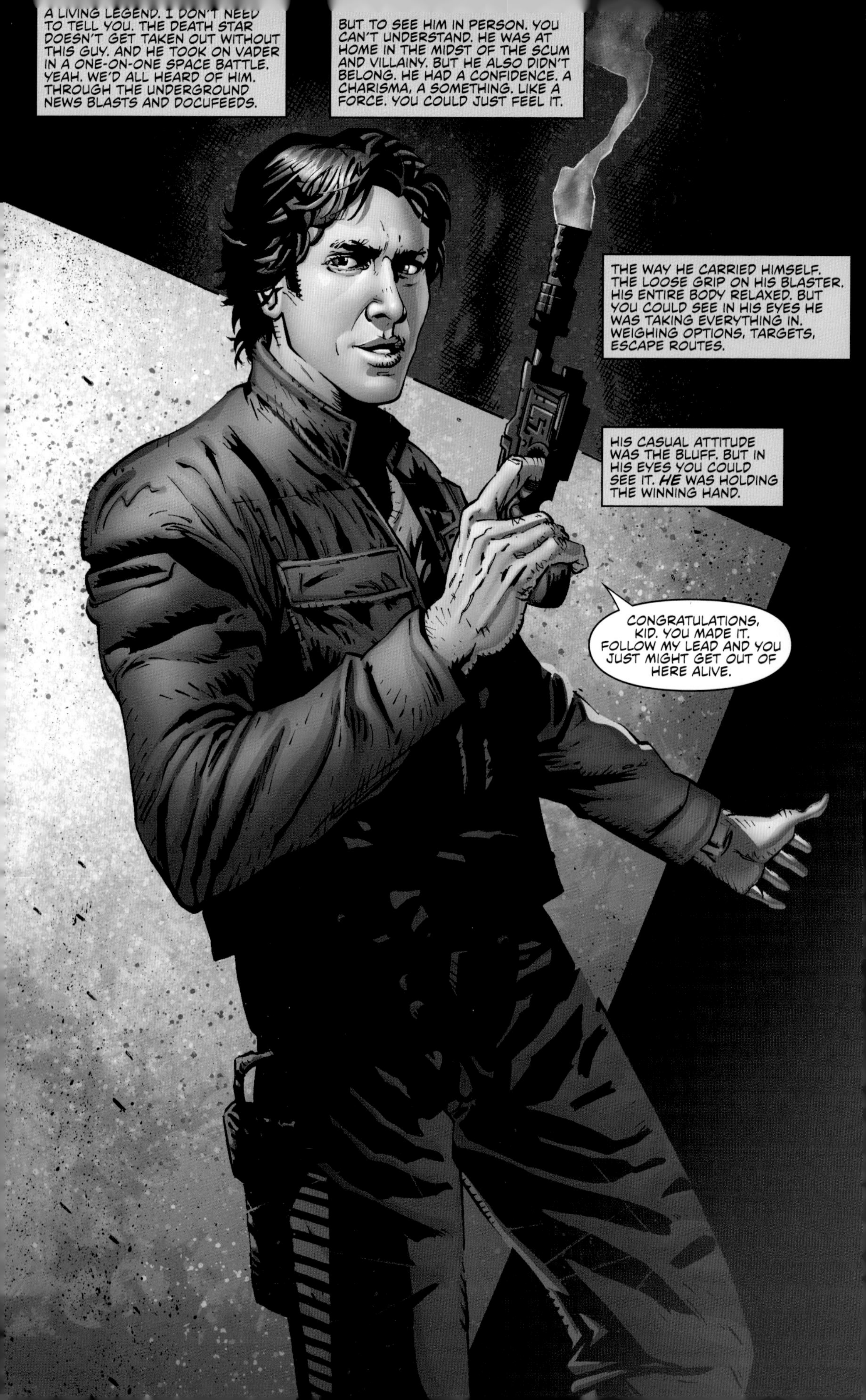
A LIVING LEGEND. I DON'T NEED TO TELL YOU. THE DEATH STAR DOESN'T GET TAKEN OUT WITHOUT THIS GUY. AND HE TOOK ON VADER IN A ONE-ON-ONE SPACE BATTLE. YEAH. WE'D ALL HEARD OF HIM. THROUGH THE UNDERGROUND NEWS BLASTS AND DOCUFEEDS.
BUT TO SEE HIM IN PERSON. YOU CAN'T UNDERSTAND. HE WAS AT HOME IN THE MIDST OF THE SCUM AND VILLAINY. BUT HE ALSO DIDN'T BELONG. HE HAD A CONFIDENCE. A CHARISMA, A SOMETHING. LIKE A FORCE. YOU COULD JUST FEEL IT.
THE WAY HE CARRIED HIMSELF. THE LOOSE GRIP ON HIS BLASTER. HIS ENTIRE BODY RELAXED. BUT YOU COULD SEE IN HIS EYES HE WAS TAKING EVERYTHING IN. WEIGHING OPTIONS, TARGETS, ESCAPE ROUTES.
HIS CASUAL ATTITUDE WAS THE BLUFF. BUT IN HIS EYES YOU COULD SEE IT. *HE* WAS HOLDING THE WINNING HAND.
CONGRATULATIONS, KID. YOU MADE IT. FOLLOW MY LEAD AND YOU JUST MIGHT GET OUT OF HERE ALIVE.

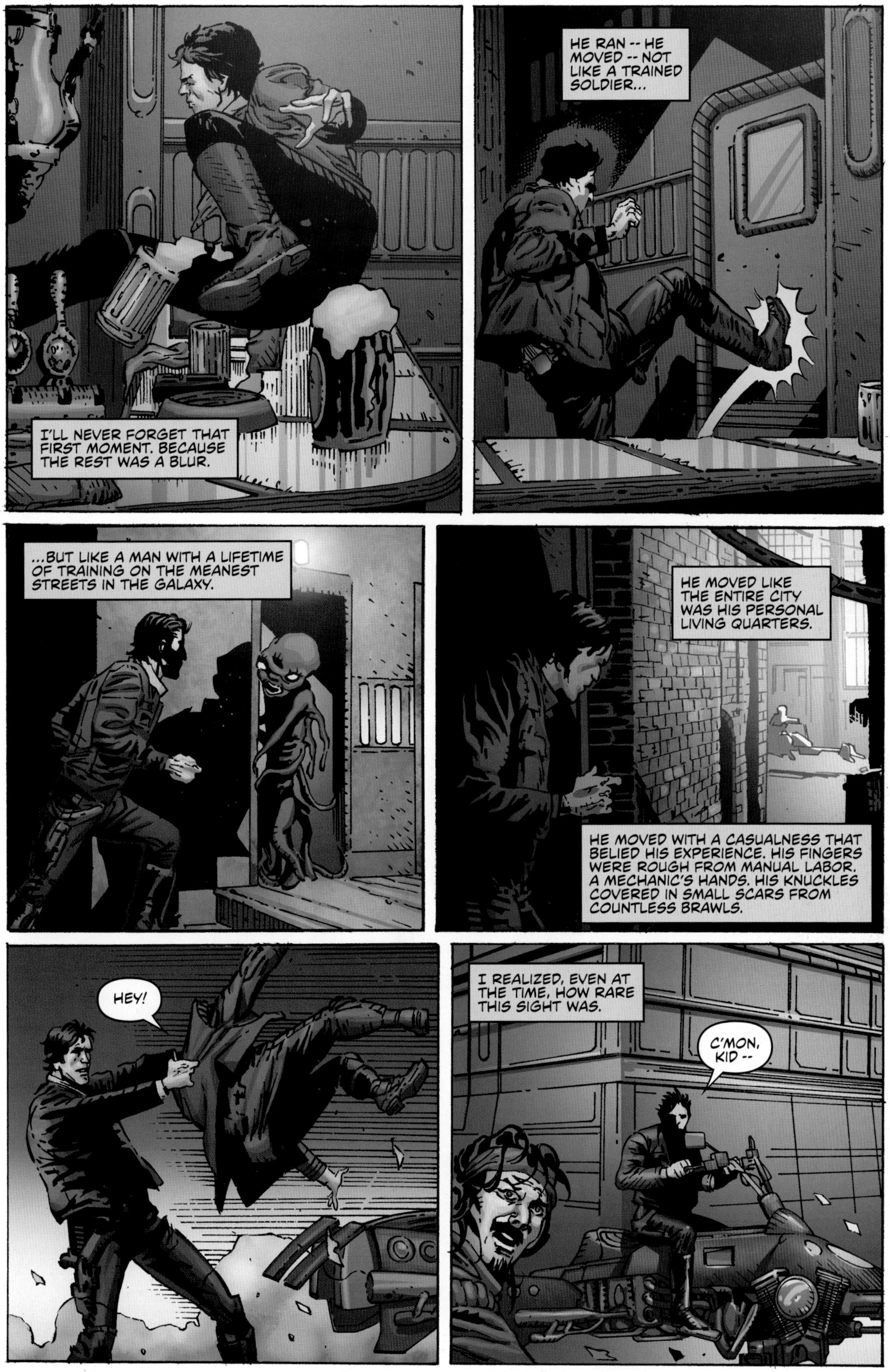
I'LL NEVER FORGET THAT FIRST MOMENT. BECAUSE THE REST WAS A BLUR.
HE RAN -- HE MOVED -- NOT LIKE A TRAINED SOLDIER...
...BUT LIKE A MAN WITH A LIFETIME OF TRAINING ON THE MEANEST STREETS IN THE GALAXY.
HE MOVED LIKE THE ENTIRE CITY WAS HIS PERSONAL LIVING QUARTERS.
HE MOVED WITH A CASUALNESS THAT BELIED HIS EXPERIENCE. HIS FINGERS WERE ROUGH FROM MANUAL LABOR. A MECHANIC'S HANDS. HIS KNUCKLES COVERED IN SMALL SCARS FROM COUNTLESS BRAWLS.
HEY!
I REALIZED, EVEN AT THE TIME, HOW RARE THIS SIGHT WAS.
C'MON, KID --

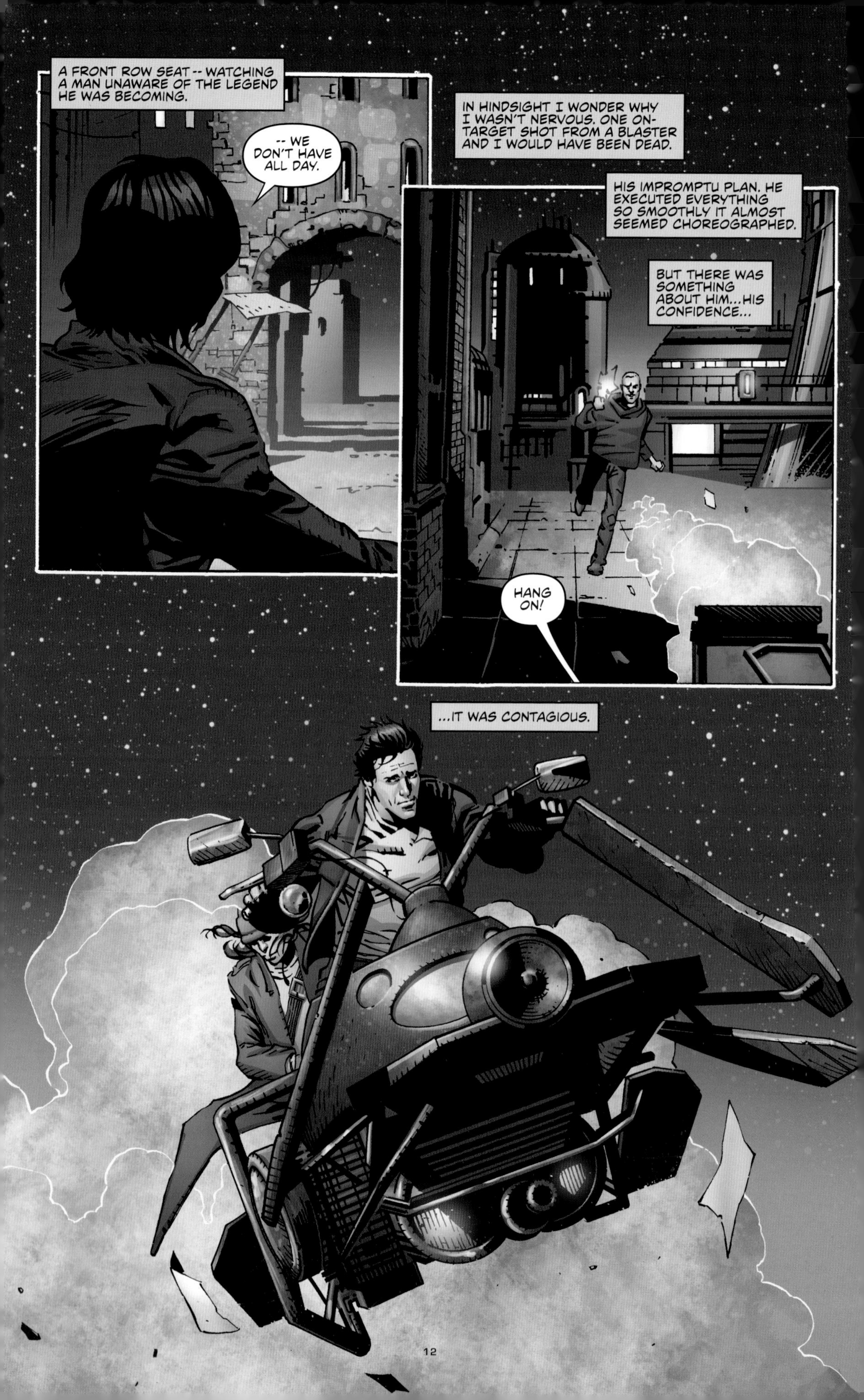
A FRONT ROW SEAT -- WATCHING A MAN UNAWARE OF THE LEGEND HE WAS BECOMING.
-- WE DON'T HAVE ALL DAY.
IN HINDSIGHT I WONDER WHY I WASN'T NERVOUS. ONE ON-TARGET SHOT FROM A BLASTER AND I WOULD HAVE BEEN DEAD.
HIS IMPROMPTU PLAN. HE EXECUTED EVERYTHING SO SMOOTHLY IT ALMOST SEEMED CHOREOGRAPHED.
BUT THERE WAS SOMETHING ABOUT HIM...HIS CONFIDENCE...
HANG ON!
...IT WAS CONTAGIOUS.

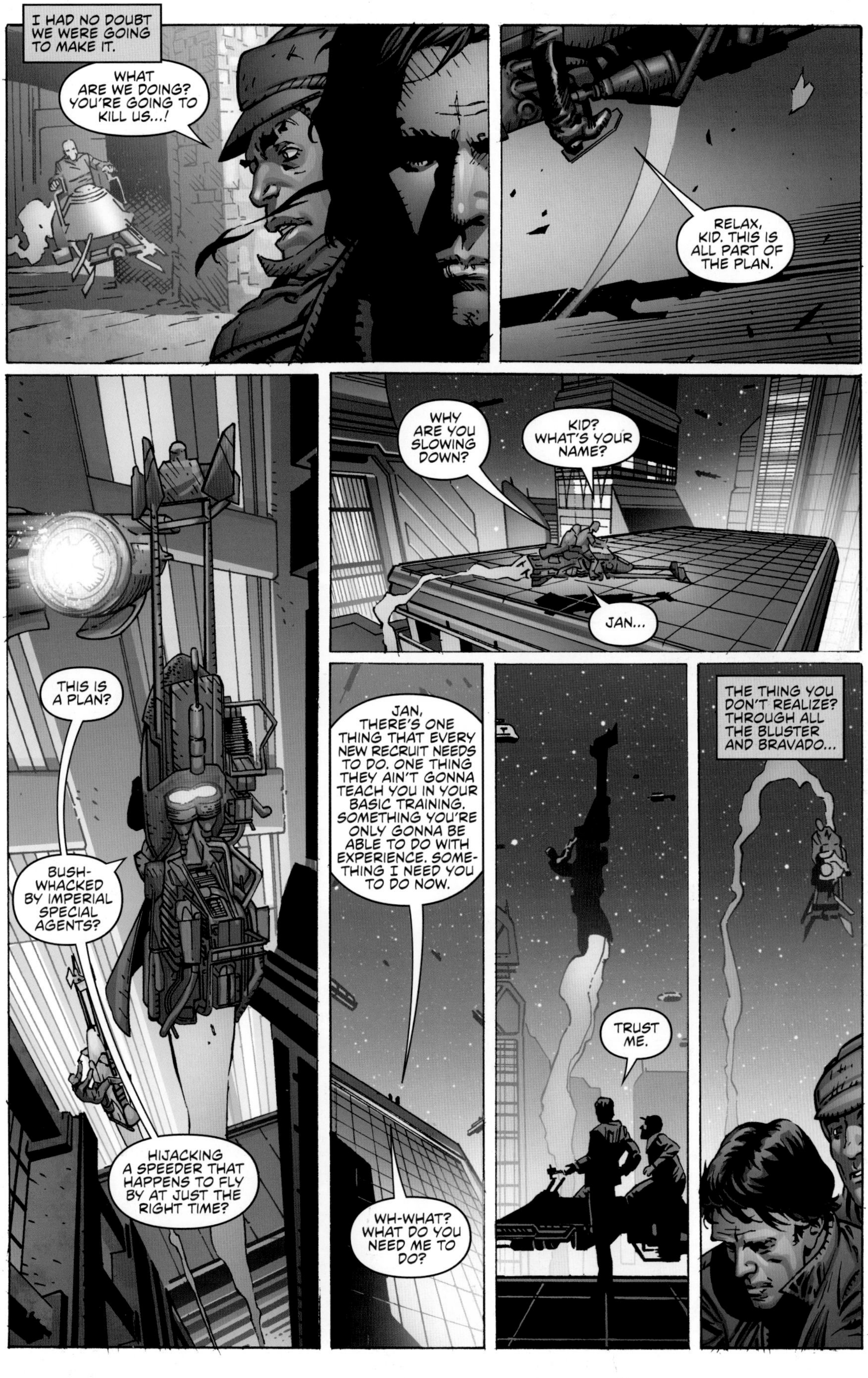
I HAD NO DOUBT WE WERE GOING TO MAKE IT.
WHAT ARE WE DOING? YOU'RE GOING TO KILL US...!
RELAX, KID. THIS IS ALL PART OF THE PLAN.
THIS IS A PLAN?
BUSH-WHACKED BY IMPERIAL SPECIAL AGENTS?
HIJACKING A SPEEDER THAT HAPPENS TO FLY BY AT JUST THE RIGHT TIME?
WHY ARE YOU SLOWING DOWN?
KID? WHAT'S YOUR NAME?
JAN...
JAN, THERE'S ONE THING THAT EVERY NEW RECRUIT NEEDS TO DO. ONE THING THEY AIN'T GONNA TEACH YOU IN YOUR BASIC TRAINING. SOMETHING YOU'RE ONLY GONNA BE ABLE TO DO WITH EXPERIENCE. SOME-THING I NEED YOU TO DO NOW.
WH-WHAT? WHAT DO YOU NEED ME TO DO?
TRUST ME.
THE THING YOU DON'T REALIZE? THROUGH ALL THE BLUSTER AND BRAVADO...

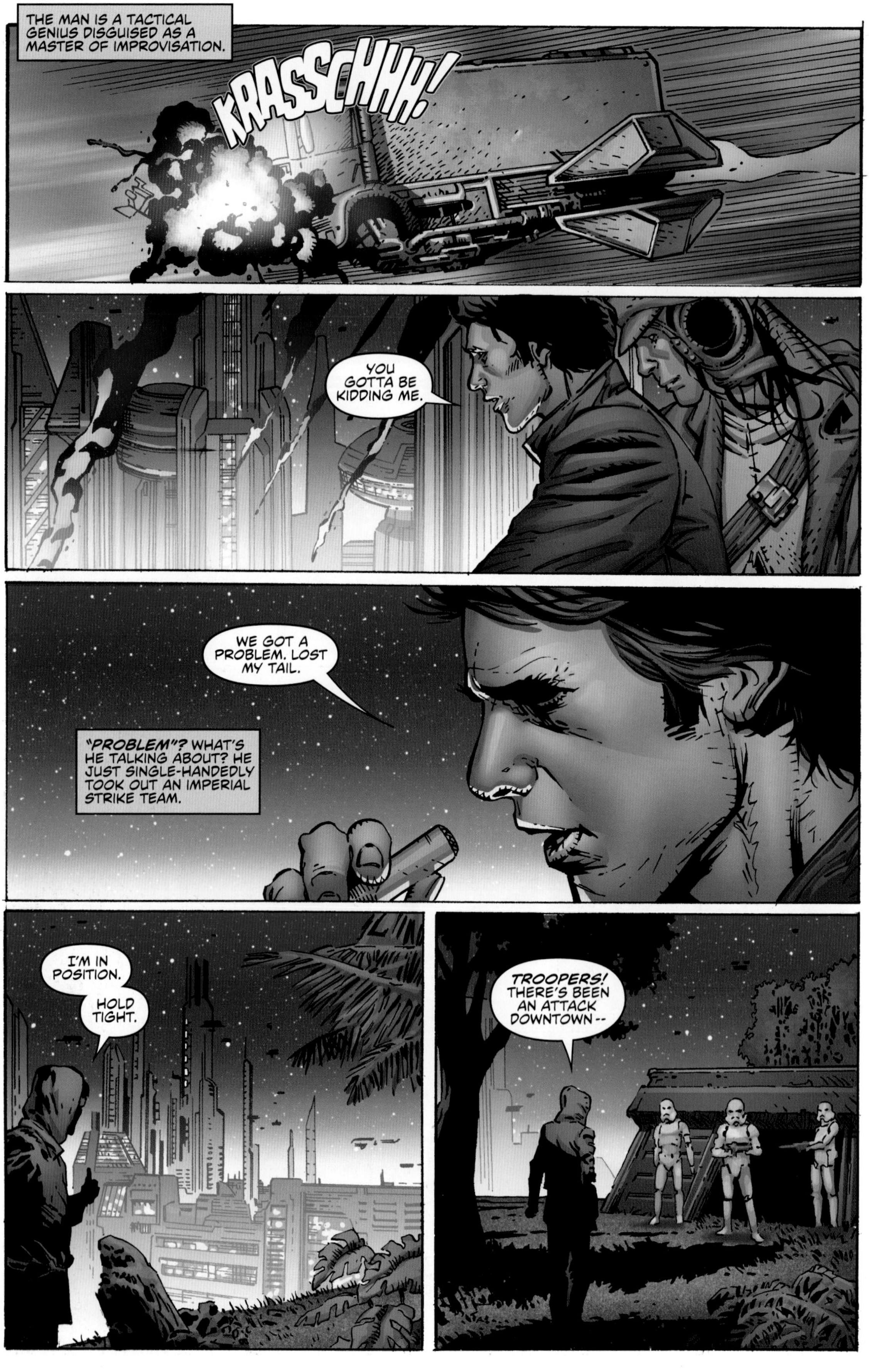
THE MAN IS A TACTICAL GENIUS DISGUISED AS A MASTER OF IMPROVISATION.
KRASSCHHH!
YOU GOTTA BE KIDDING ME.
WE GOT A PROBLEM. LOST MY TAIL.
"PROBLEM"? WHAT'S HE TALKING ABOUT? HE JUST SINGLE-HANDEDLY TOOK OUT AN IMPERIAL STRIKE TEAM.
I'M IN POSITION.
HOLD TIGHT.
TROOPERS! THERE'S BEEN AN ATTACK DOWNTOWN--

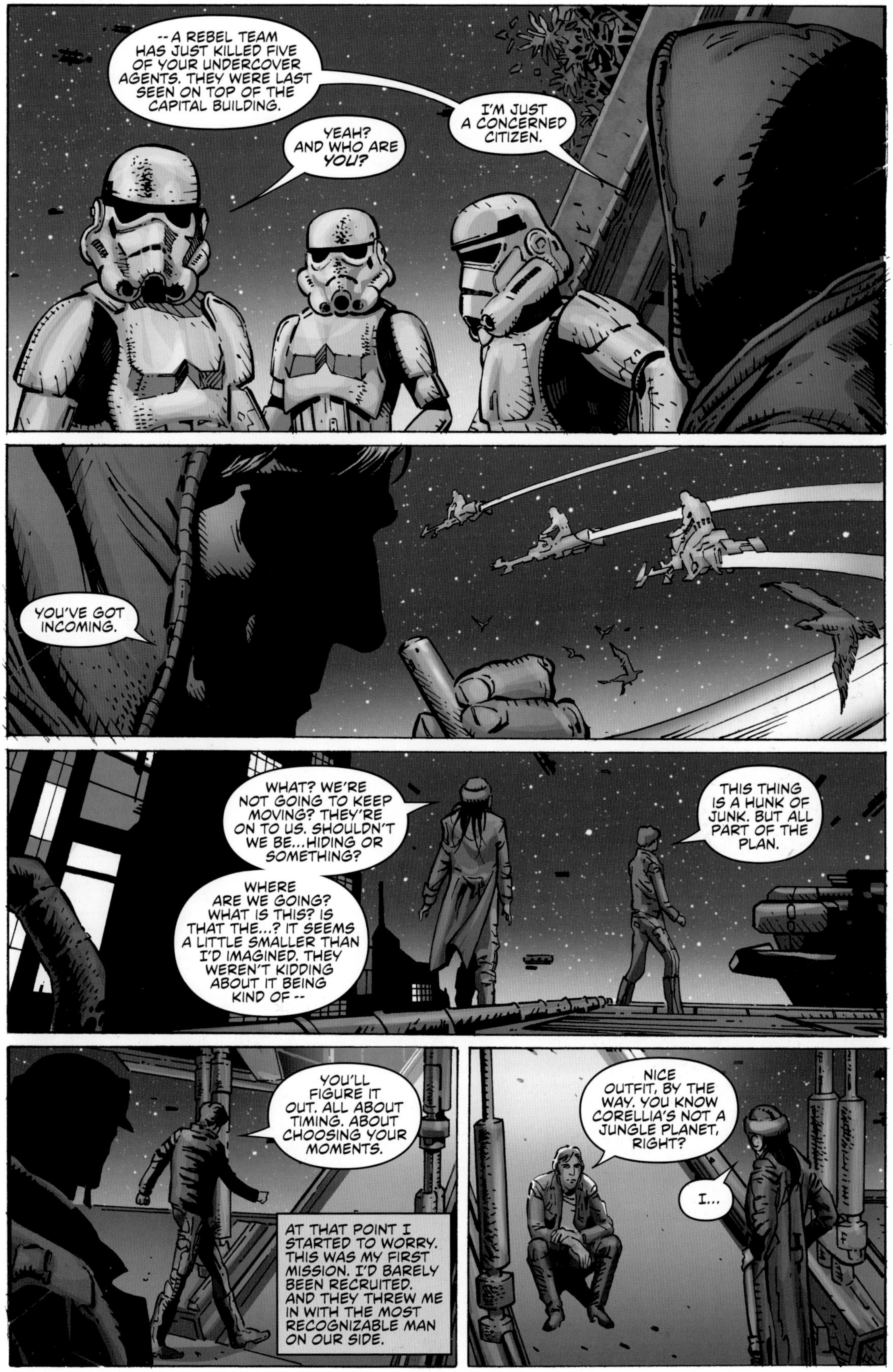
--A REBEL TEAM HAS JUST KILLED FIVE OF YOUR UNDERCOVER AGENTS. THEY WERE LAST SEEN ON TOP OF THE CAPITAL BUILDING.
YEAH? AND WHO ARE *YOU*?
I'M JUST A CONCERNED CITIZEN.
YOU'VE GOT INCOMING.
WHAT? WE'RE NOT GOING TO KEEP MOVING? THEY'RE ON TO US. SHOULDN'T WE BE...HIDING OR SOMETHING?
WHERE ARE WE GOING? WHAT IS THIS? IS THAT THE...? IT SEEMS A LITTLE SMALLER THAN I'D IMAGINED. THEY WEREN'T KIDDING ABOUT IT BEING KIND OF --
THIS THING IS A HUNK OF JUNK. BUT ALL PART OF THE PLAN.
YOU'LL FIGURE IT OUT. ALL ABOUT TIMING. ABOUT CHOOSING YOUR MOMENTS.
AT THAT POINT I STARTED TO WORRY. THIS WAS MY FIRST MISSION. I'D BARELY BEEN RECRUITED. AND THEY THREW ME IN WITH THE MOST RECOGNIZABLE MAN ON OUR SIDE.
NICE OUTFIT, BY THE WAY. YOU KNOW CORELLIA'S NOT A JUNGLE PLANET, RIGHT?
I...

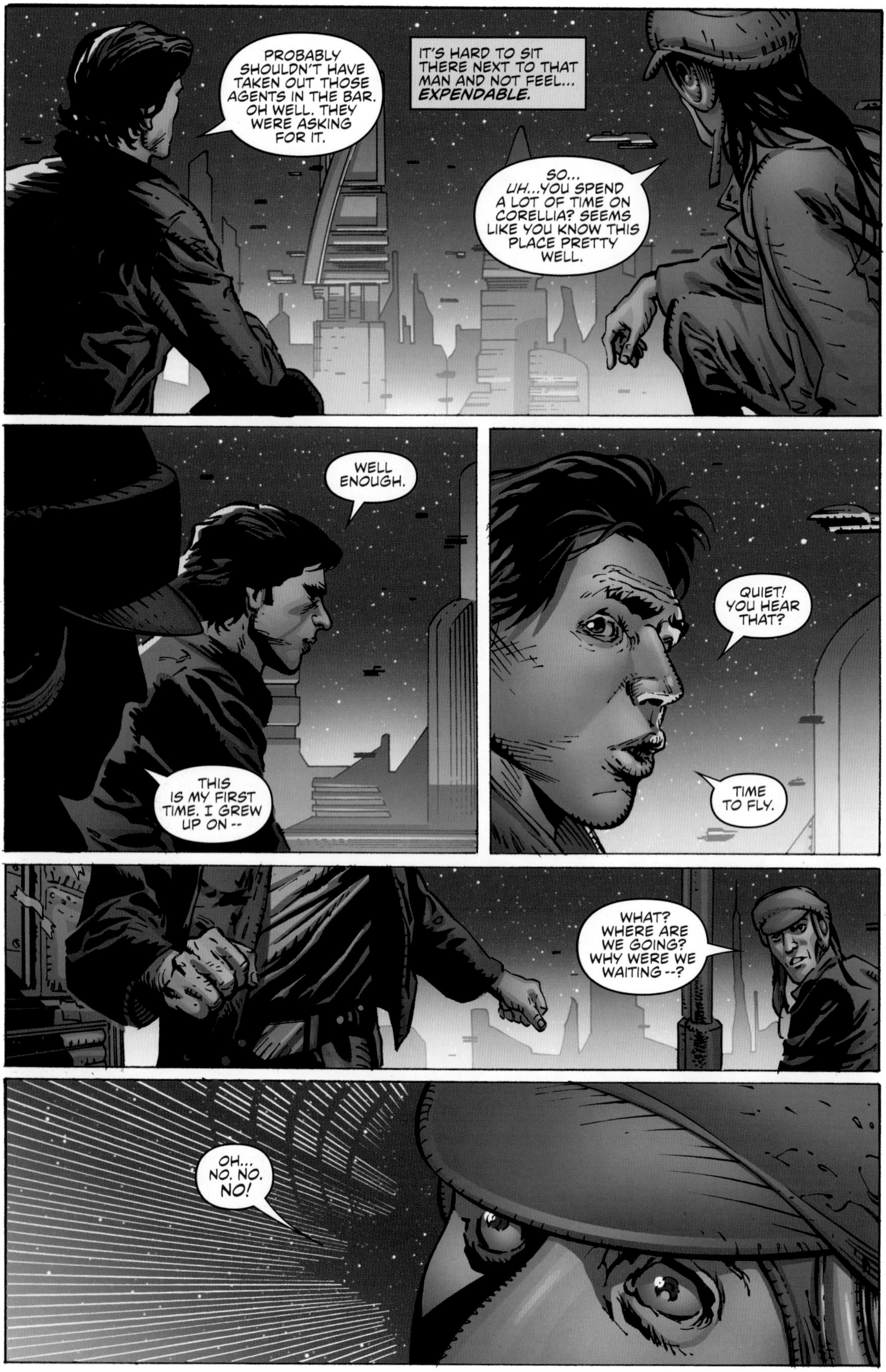
PROBABLY SHOULDN'T HAVE TAKEN OUT THOSE AGENTS IN THE BAR. OH WELL. THEY WERE ASKING FOR IT.
IT'S HARD TO SIT THERE NEXT TO THAT MAN AND NOT FEEL... EXPENDABLE.
SO... UH...YOU SPEND A LOT OF TIME ON CORELLIA? SEEMS LIKE YOU KNOW THIS PLACE PRETTY WELL.
WELL ENOUGH.
THIS IS MY FIRST TIME. I GREW UP ON --
QUIET! YOU HEAR THAT?
TIME TO FLY.
WHAT? WHERE ARE WE GOING? WHY WERE WE WAITING --?
OH... NO. NO. NO!

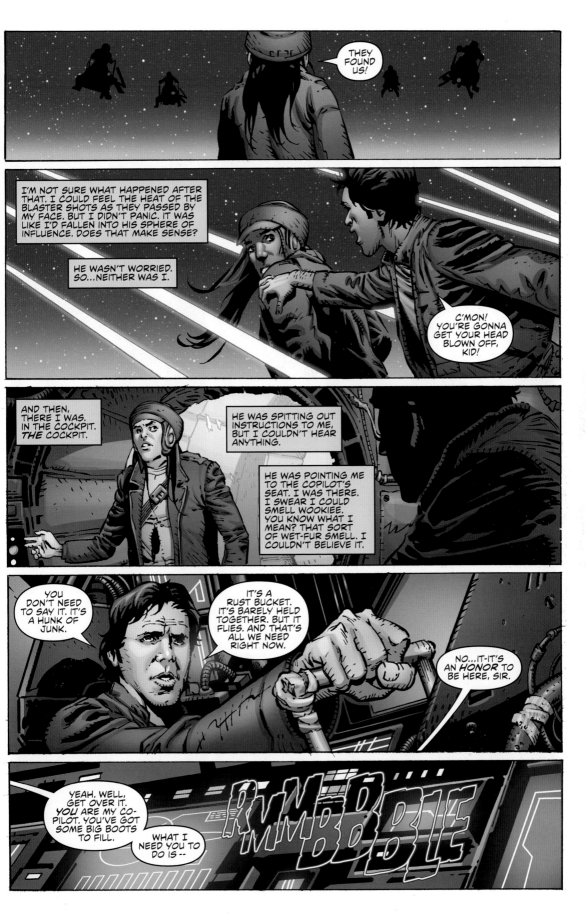

THEY FOUND US!

I'M NOT SURE WHAT HAPPENED AFTER THAT. I COULD FEEL THE HEAT OF THE BLASTER SHOTS AS THEY PASSED BY MY FACE. BUT I DIDN'T PANIC. IT WAS LIKE I'D FALLEN INTO HIS SPHERE OF INFLUENCE. DOES THAT MAKE SENSE?

HE WASN'T WORRIED. SO...NEITHER WAS I.

C'MON! YOU'RE GONNA GET YOUR HEAD BLOWN OFF, KID!

AND THEN, THERE I WAS. IN THE COCKPIT. *THE* COCKPIT.

HE WAS SPITTING OUT INSTRUCTIONS TO ME, BUT I COULDN'T HEAR ANYTHING.

HE WAS POINTING ME TO THE COPILOT'S SEAT. I WAS THERE. I SWEAR I COULD SMELL WOOKIEE. YOU KNOW WHAT I MEAN? THAT SORT OF WET-FUR SMELL. I COULDN'T BELIEVE IT.

YOU DON'T NEED TO SAY IT. IT'S A HUNK OF JUNK.

IT'S A RUST BUCKET. IT'S BARELY HELD TOGETHER. BUT IT FLIES. AND THAT'S ALL WE NEED RIGHT NOW.

NO...IT-IT'S AN *HONOR* TO BE HERE, SIR.

YEAH. WELL, GET OVER IT. *YOU* ARE MY CO-PILOT. YOU'VE GOT SOME BIG BOOTS TO FILL.

WHAT I NEED YOU TO DO IS --

RRMMBBBLE

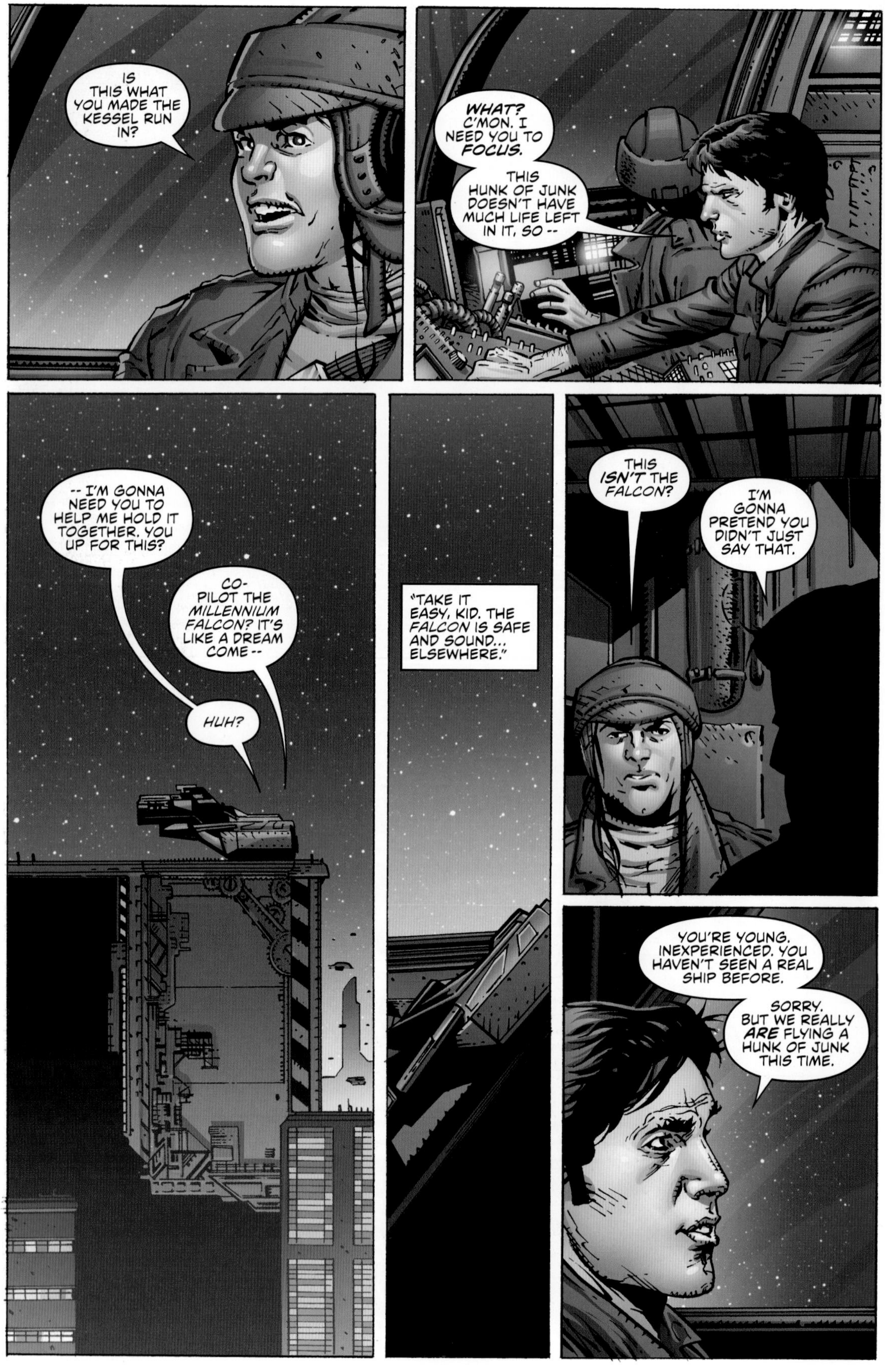
IS THIS WHAT YOU MADE THE KESSEL RUN IN?
WHAT? C'MON. I NEED YOU TO FOCUS.
THIS HUNK OF JUNK DOESN'T HAVE MUCH LIFE LEFT IN IT, SO --
-- I'M GONNA NEED YOU TO HELP ME HOLD IT TOGETHER. YOU UP FOR THIS?
CO-PILOT THE MILLENNIUM FALCON? IT'S LIKE A DREAM COME --
HUH?
"TAKE IT EASY, KID. THE FALCON IS SAFE AND SOUND... ELSEWHERE."
THIS ISN'T THE FALCON?
I'M GONNA PRETEND YOU DIDN'T JUST SAY THAT.
YOU'RE YOUNG. INEXPERIENCED. YOU HAVEN'T SEEN A REAL SHIP BEFORE.
SORRY. BUT WE REALLY ARE FLYING A HUNK OF JUNK THIS TIME.

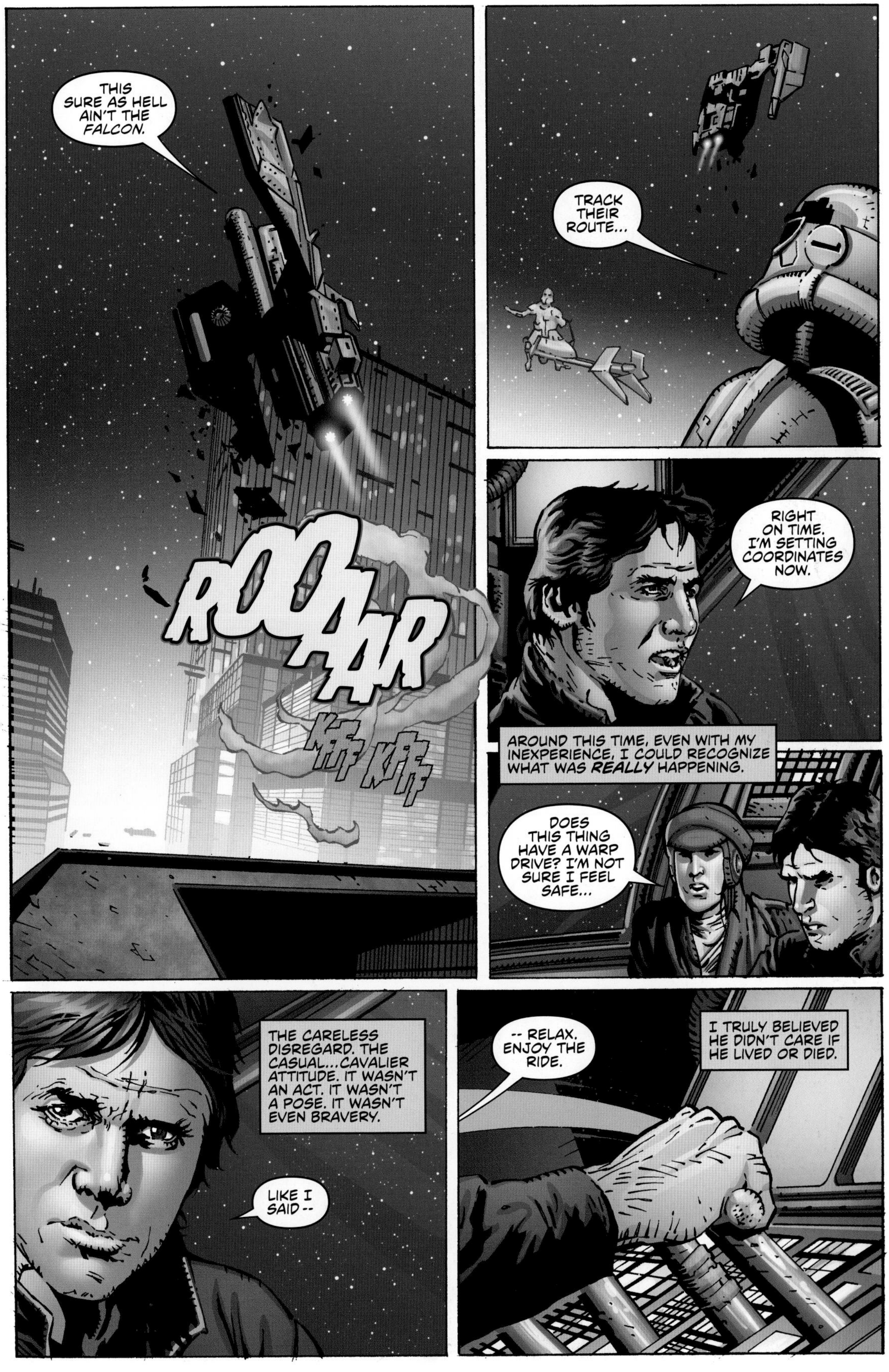

THIS SURE AS HELL AIN'T THE FALCON.
ROOOAAAR
KFF KFF
TRACK THEIR ROUTE...
RIGHT ON TIME. I'M SETTING COORDINATES NOW.
AROUND THIS TIME, EVEN WITH MY INEXPERIENCE, I COULD RECOGNIZE WHAT WAS REALLY HAPPENING.
DOES THIS THING HAVE A WARP DRIVE? I'M NOT SURE I FEEL SAFE...
THE CARELESS DISREGARD. THE CASUAL...CAVALIER ATTITUDE. IT WASN'T AN ACT. IT WASN'T A POSE. IT WASN'T EVEN BRAVERY.
LIKE I SAID --
-- RELAX. ENJOY THE RIDE.
I TRULY BELIEVED HE DIDN'T CARE IF HE LIVED OR DIED.

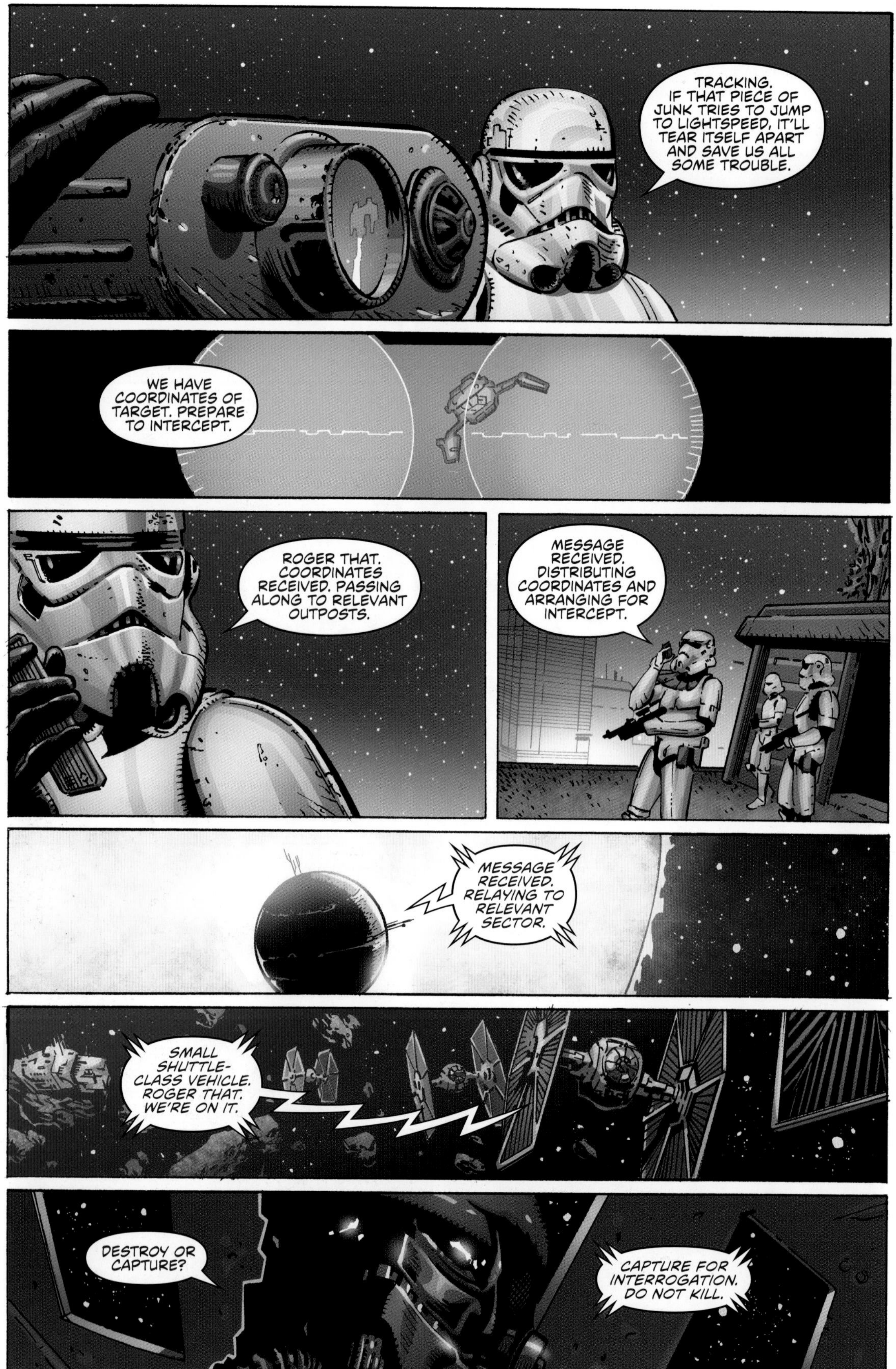
TRACKING. IF THAT PIECE OF JUNK TRIES TO JUMP TO LIGHTSPEED, IT'LL TEAR ITSELF APART AND SAVE US ALL SOME TROUBLE.
WE HAVE COORDINATES OF TARGET. PREPARE TO INTERCEPT.
ROGER THAT. COORDINATES RECEIVED. PASSING ALONG TO RELEVANT OUTPOSTS.
MESSAGE RECEIVED. DISTRIBUTING COORDINATES AND ARRANGING FOR INTERCEPT.
MESSAGE RECEIVED. RELAYING TO RELEVANT SECTOR.
SMALL SHUTTLE-CLASS VEHICLE. ROGER THAT. WE'RE ON IT.
DESTROY OR CAPTURE?
CAPTURE FOR INTERROGATION. DO NOT KILL.

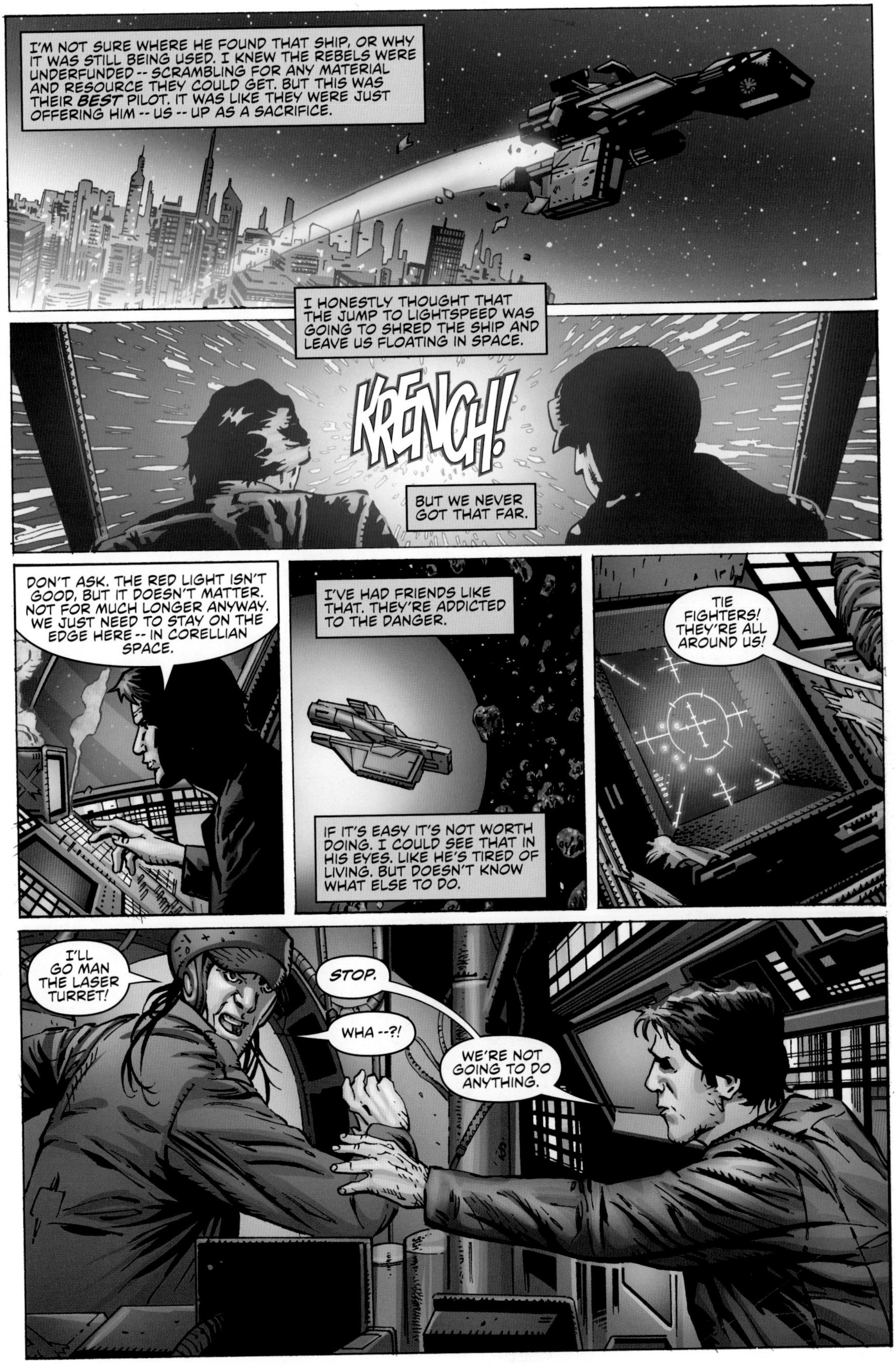
I'M NOT SURE WHERE HE FOUND THAT SHIP, OR WHY IT WAS STILL BEING USED. I KNEW THE REBELS WERE UNDERFUNDED -- SCRAMBLING FOR ANY MATERIAL AND RESOURCE THEY COULD GET. BUT THIS WAS THEIR BEST PILOT. IT WAS LIKE THEY WERE JUST OFFERING HIM -- US -- UP AS A SACRIFICE.
I HONESTLY THOUGHT THAT THE JUMP TO LIGHTSPEED WAS GOING TO SHRED THE SHIP AND LEAVE US FLOATING IN SPACE.
KRENCH!
BUT WE NEVER GOT THAT FAR.
DON'T ASK. THE RED LIGHT ISN'T GOOD, BUT IT DOESN'T MATTER. NOT FOR MUCH LONGER ANYWAY. WE JUST NEED TO STAY ON THE EDGE HERE -- IN CORELLIAN SPACE.
I'VE HAD FRIENDS LIKE THAT. THEY'RE ADDICTED TO THE DANGER.
IF IT'S EASY IT'S NOT WORTH DOING. I COULD SEE THAT IN HIS EYES. LIKE HE'S TIRED OF LIVING. BUT DOESN'T KNOW WHAT ELSE TO DO.
TIE FIGHTERS! THEY'RE ALL AROUND US!
I'LL GO MAN THE LASER TURRET!
STOP.
WHA --?!
WE'RE NOT GOING TO DO ANYTHING.

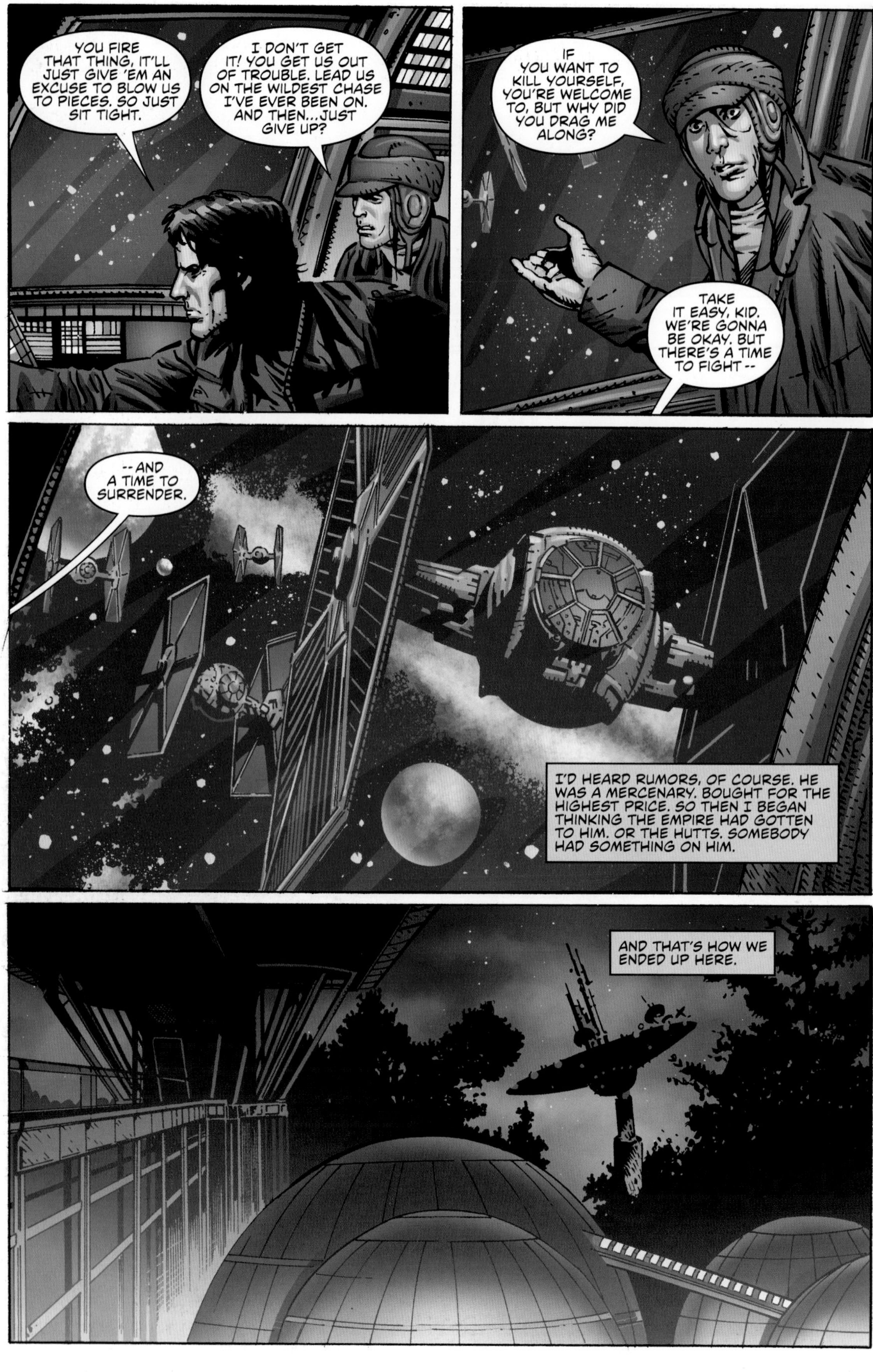
YOU FIRE THAT THING, IT'LL JUST GIVE 'EM AN EXCUSE TO BLOW US TO PIECES. SO JUST SIT TIGHT.
I DON'T GET IT! YOU GET US OUT OF TROUBLE. LEAD US ON THE WILDEST CHASE I'VE EVER BEEN ON. AND THEN...JUST GIVE UP?
IF YOU WANT TO KILL YOURSELF, YOU'RE WELCOME TO, BUT WHY DID YOU DRAG ME ALONG?
TAKE IT EASY, KID. WE'RE GONNA BE OKAY. BUT THERE'S A TIME TO FIGHT --
--AND A TIME TO SURRENDER.
I'D HEARD RUMORS, OF COURSE. HE WAS A MERCENARY. BOUGHT FOR THE HIGHEST PRICE. SO THEN I BEGAN THINKING THE EMPIRE HAD GOTTEN TO HIM. OR THE HUTTS. SOMEBODY HAD SOMETHING ON HIM.
AND THAT'S HOW WE ENDED UP HERE.

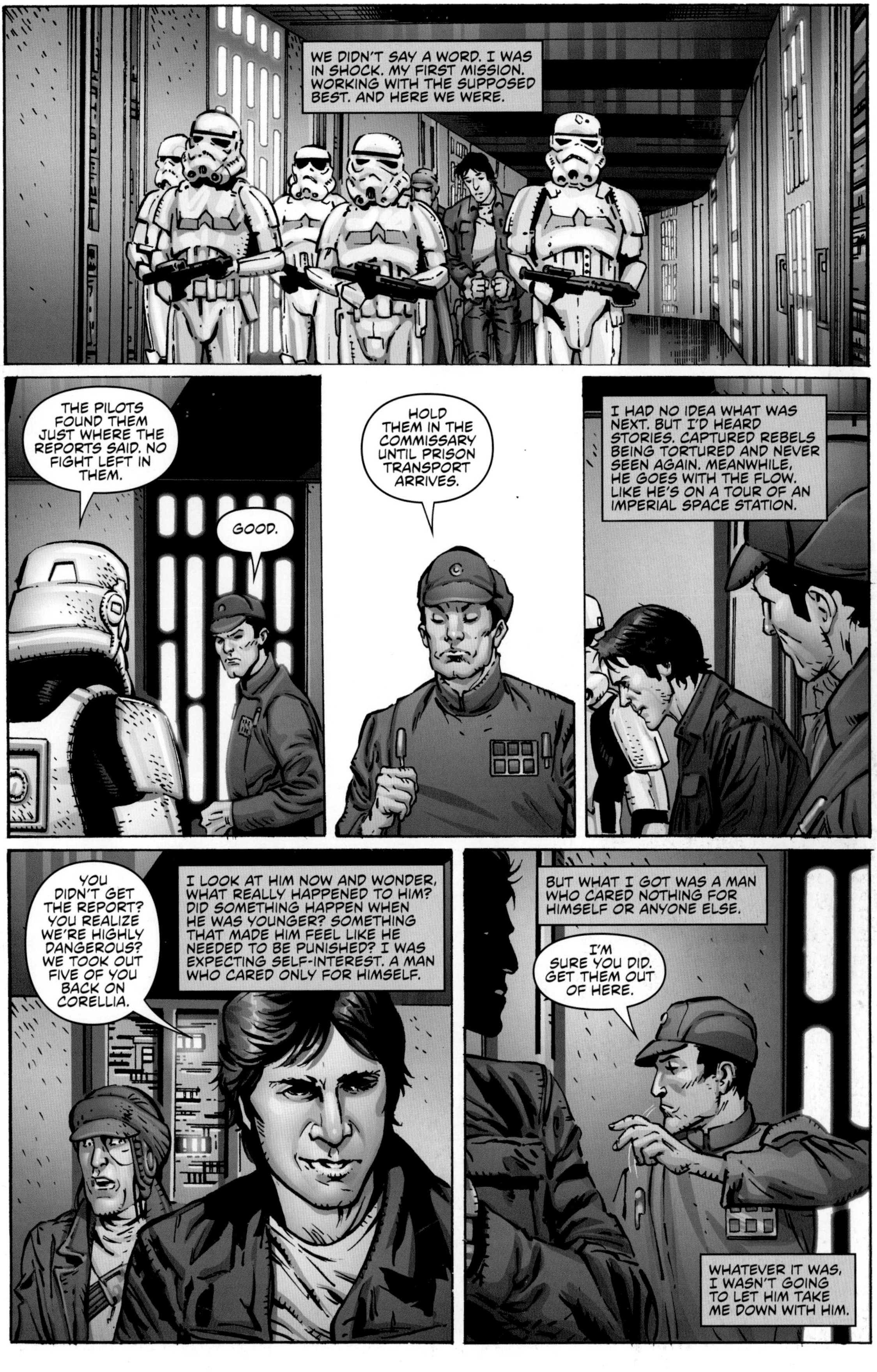

WE DIDN'T SAY A WORD. I WAS IN SHOCK. MY FIRST MISSION. WORKING WITH THE SUPPOSED BEST. AND HERE WE WERE.
THE PILOTS FOUND THEM JUST WHERE THE REPORTS SAID. NO FIGHT LEFT IN THEM.
GOOD.
HOLD THEM IN THE COMMISSARY UNTIL PRISON TRANSPORT ARRIVES.
I HAD NO IDEA WHAT WAS NEXT. BUT I'D HEARD STORIES. CAPTURED REBELS BEING TORTURED AND NEVER SEEN AGAIN. MEANWHILE, HE GOES WITH THE FLOW. LIKE HE'S ON A TOUR OF AN IMPERIAL SPACE STATION.
YOU DIDN'T GET THE REPORT? YOU REALIZE WE'RE HIGHLY DANGEROUS? WE TOOK OUT FIVE OF YOU BACK ON CORELLIA.
I LOOK AT HIM NOW AND WONDER, WHAT REALLY HAPPENED TO HIM? DID SOMETHING HAPPEN WHEN HE WAS YOUNGER? SOMETHING THAT MADE HIM FEEL LIKE HE NEEDED TO BE PUNISHED? I WAS EXPECTING SELF-INTEREST. A MAN WHO CARED ONLY FOR HIMSELF.
BUT WHAT I GOT WAS A MAN WHO CARED NOTHING FOR HIMSELF OR ANYONE ELSE.
I'M SURE YOU DID. GET THEM OUT OF HERE.
WHATEVER IT WAS, I WASN'T GOING TO LET HIM TAKE ME DOWN WITH HIM.

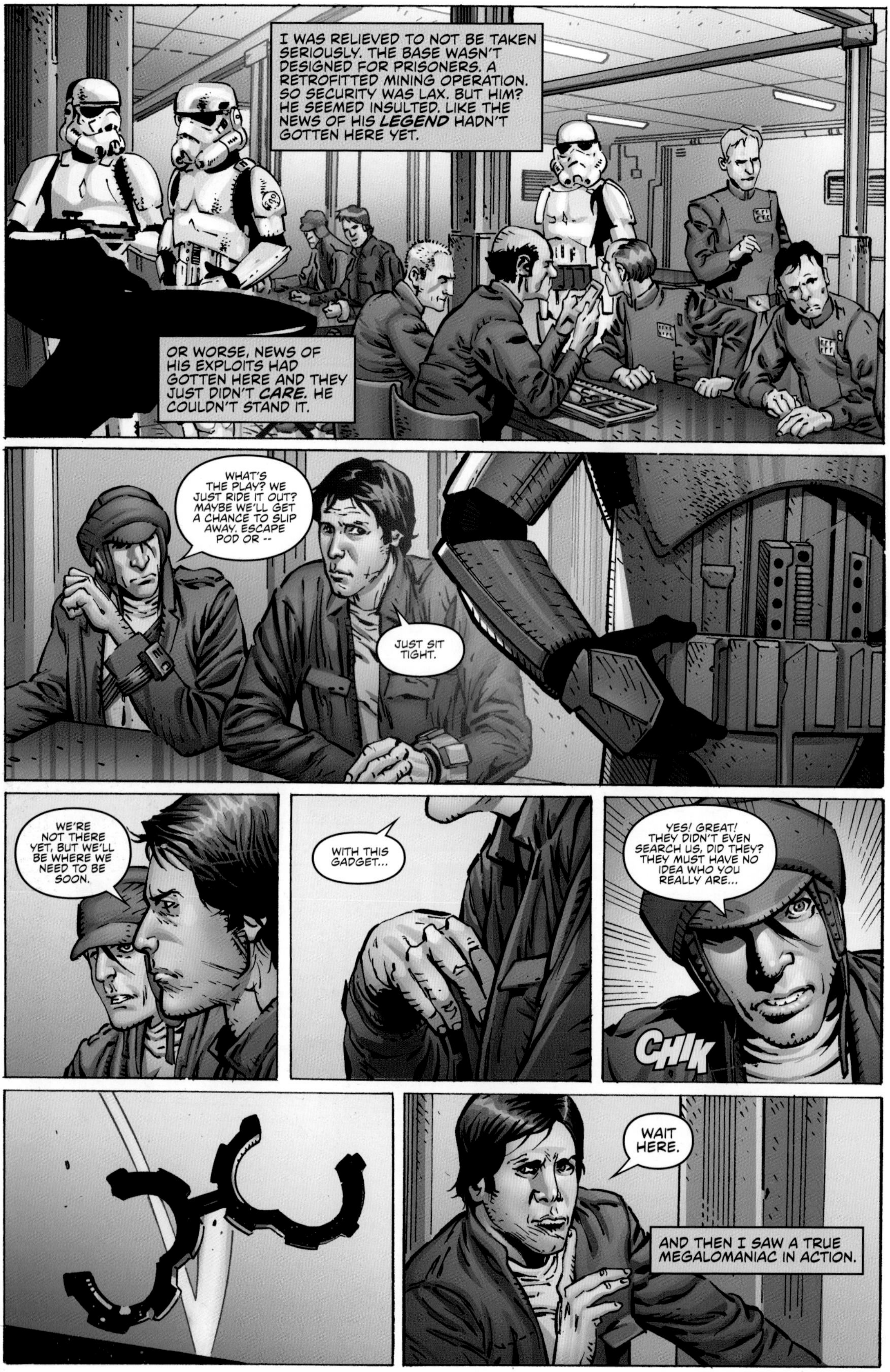

I WAS RELIEVED TO NOT BE TAKEN SERIOUSLY. THE BASE WASN'T DESIGNED FOR PRISONERS. A RETROFITTED MINING OPERATION. SO SECURITY WAS LAX. BUT HIM? HE SEEMED INSULTED. LIKE THE NEWS OF HIS LEGEND HADN'T GOTTEN HERE YET.
OR WORSE, NEWS OF HIS EXPLOITS HAD GOTTEN HERE AND THEY JUST DIDN'T CARE. HE COULDN'T STAND IT.
WHAT'S THE PLAY? WE JUST RIDE IT OUT? MAYBE WE'LL GET A CHANCE TO SLIP AWAY. ESCAPE POD OR --
JUST SIT TIGHT.
WE'RE NOT THERE YET, BUT WE'LL BE WHERE WE NEED TO BE SOON.
WITH THIS GADGET...
YES! GREAT! THEY DIDN'T EVEN SEARCH US, DID THEY? THEY MUST HAVE NO IDEA WHO YOU REALLY ARE...
CHIK
WAIT HERE.
AND THEN I SAW A TRUE MEGALOMANIAC IN ACTION.

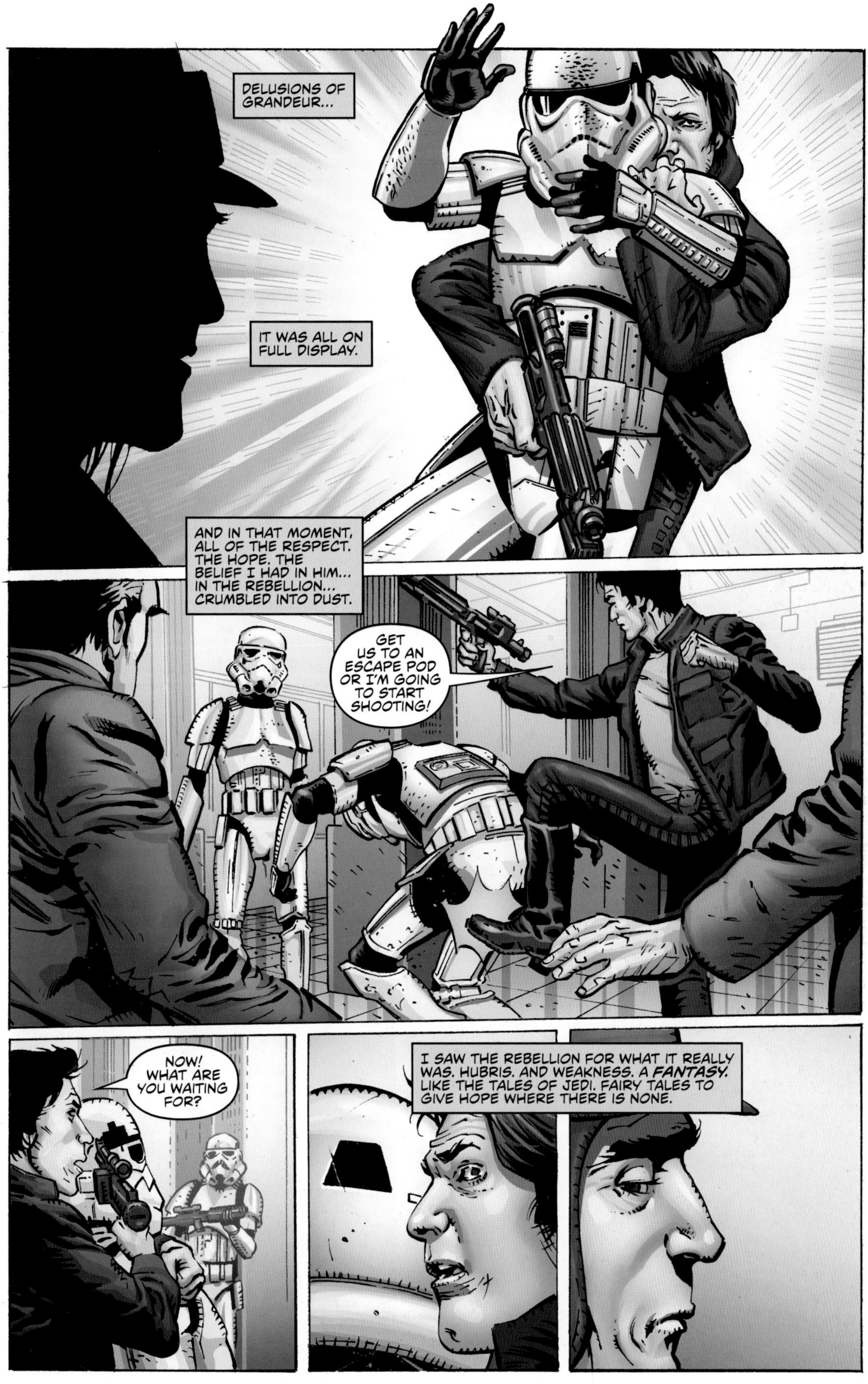
DELUSIONS OF GRANDEUR...
IT WAS ALL ON FULL DISPLAY.
AND IN THAT MOMENT, ALL OF THE RESPECT. THE HOPE. THE BELIEF I HAD IN HIM... IN THE REBELLION... CRUMBLED INTO DUST.
GET US TO AN ESCAPE POD OR I'M GOING TO START SHOOTING!
NOW! WHAT ARE YOU WAITING FOR?
I SAW THE REBELLION FOR WHAT IT REALLY WAS. HUBRIS. AND WEAKNESS. A *FANTASY.* LIKE THE TALES OF JEDI. FAIRY TALES TO GIVE HOPE WHERE THERE IS NONE.

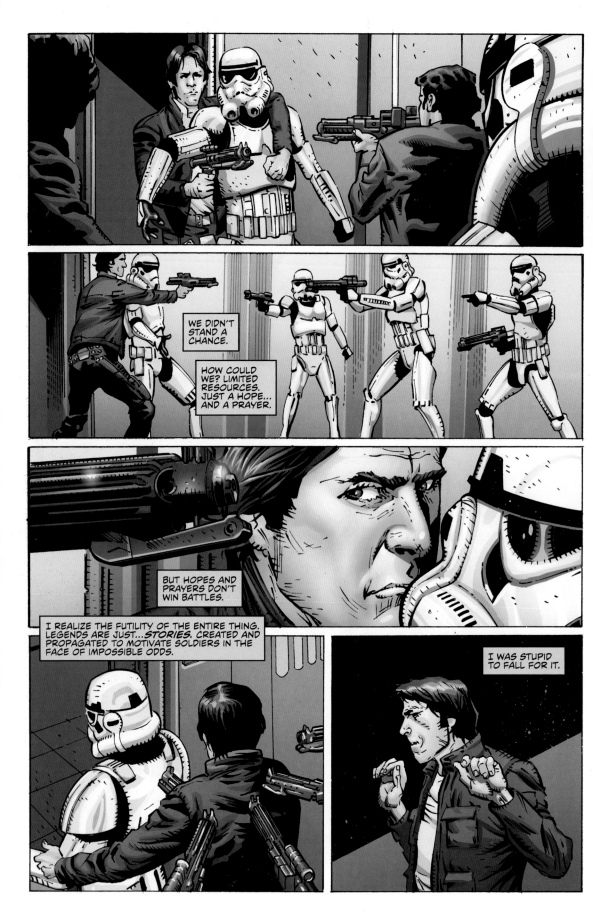

WE DIDN'T STAND A CHANCE.

HOW COULD WE? LIMITED RESOURCES. JUST A HOPE... AND A PRAYER.

BUT HOPES AND PRAYERS DON'T WIN BATTLES.

I REALIZE THE FUTILITY OF THE ENTIRE THING. LEGENDS ARE JUST...*STORIES*. CREATED AND PROPAGATED TO MOTIVATE SOLDIERS IN THE FACE OF IMPOSSIBLE ODDS.

I WAS STUPID TO FALL FOR IT.

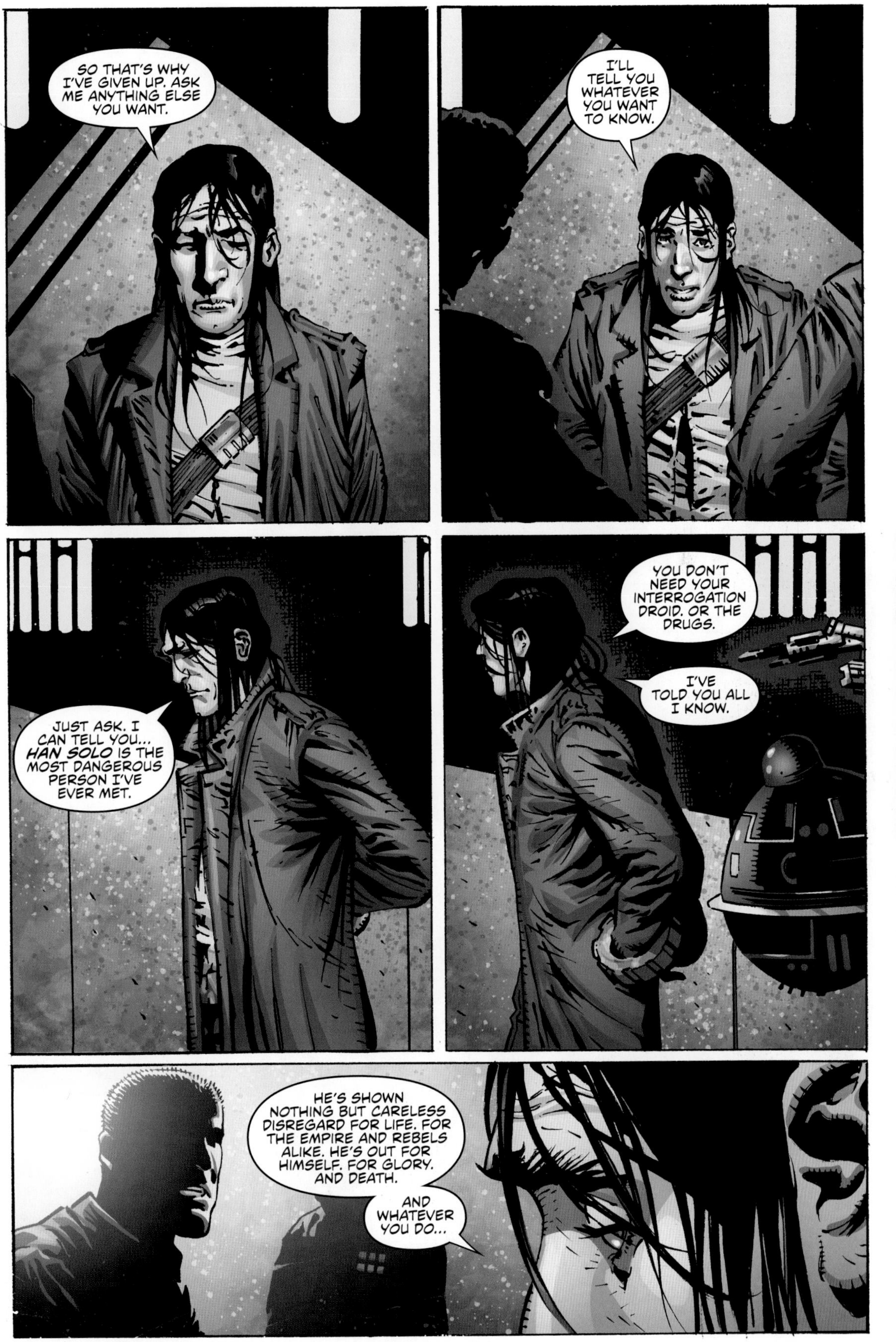

SO THAT'S WHY I'VE GIVEN UP. ASK ME ANYTHING ELSE YOU WANT.
I'LL TELL YOU WHATEVER YOU WANT TO KNOW.
JUST ASK. I CAN TELL YOU... HAN SOLO IS THE MOST DANGEROUS PERSON I'VE EVER MET.
YOU DON'T NEED YOUR INTERROGATION DROID. OR THE DRUGS.
I'VE TOLD YOU ALL I KNOW.
HE'S SHOWN NOTHING BUT CARELESS DISREGARD FOR LIFE. FOR THE EMPIRE AND REBELS ALIKE. HE'S OUT FOR HIMSELF. FOR GLORY. AND DEATH.
AND WHATEVER YOU DO...

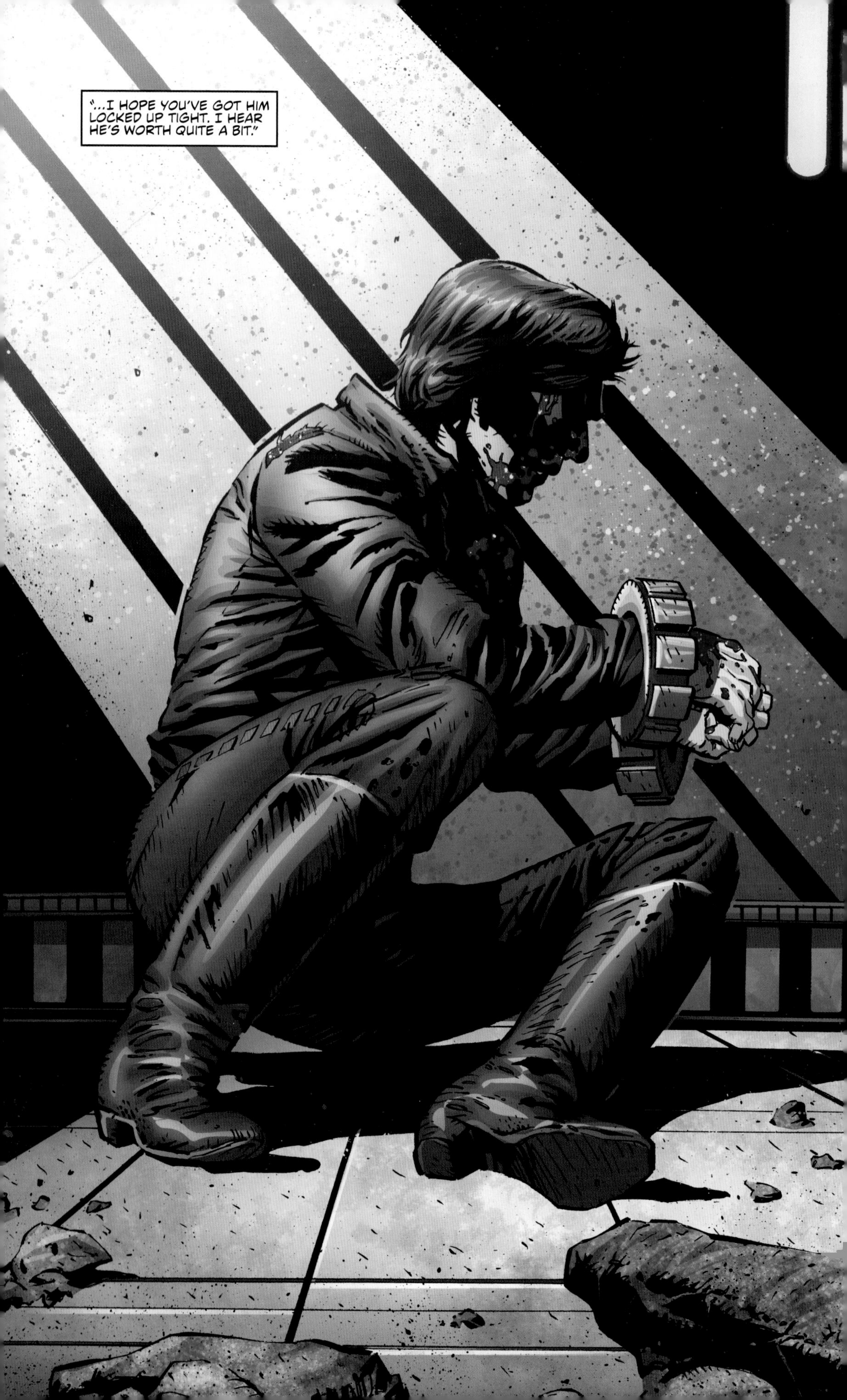
"...I HOPE YOU'VE GOT HIM LOCKED UP TIGHT. I HEAR HE'S WORTH QUITE A BIT."

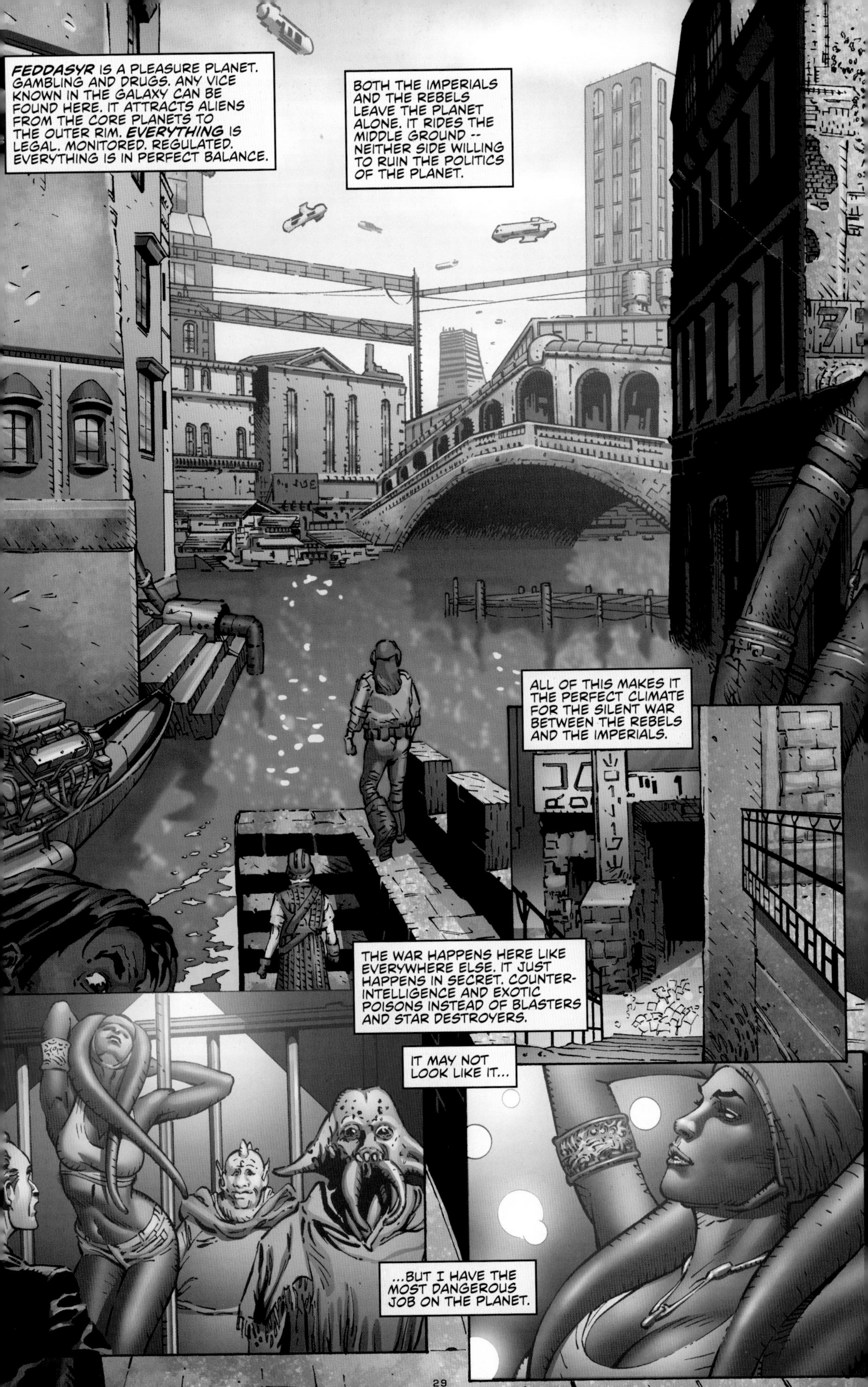
FEDDASYR IS A PLEASURE PLANET. GAMBLING AND DRUGS. ANY VICE KNOWN IN THE GALAXY CAN BE FOUND HERE. IT ATTRACTS ALIENS FROM THE CORE PLANETS TO THE OUTER RIM. EVERYTHING IS LEGAL. MONITORED. REGULATED. EVERYTHING IS IN PERFECT BALANCE.
BOTH THE IMPERIALS AND THE REBELS LEAVE THE PLANET ALONE. IT RIDES THE MIDDLE GROUND -- NEITHER SIDE WILLING TO RUIN THE POLITICS OF THE PLANET.
ALL OF THIS MAKES IT THE PERFECT CLIMATE FOR THE SILENT WAR BETWEEN THE REBELS AND THE IMPERIALS.
THE WAR HAPPENS HERE LIKE EVERYWHERE ELSE. IT JUST HAPPENS IN SECRET. COUNTER-INTELLIGENCE AND EXOTIC POISONS INSTEAD OF BLASTERS AND STAR DESTROYERS.
IT MAY NOT LOOK LIKE IT...
...BUT I HAVE THE MOST DANGEROUS JOB ON THE PLANET.

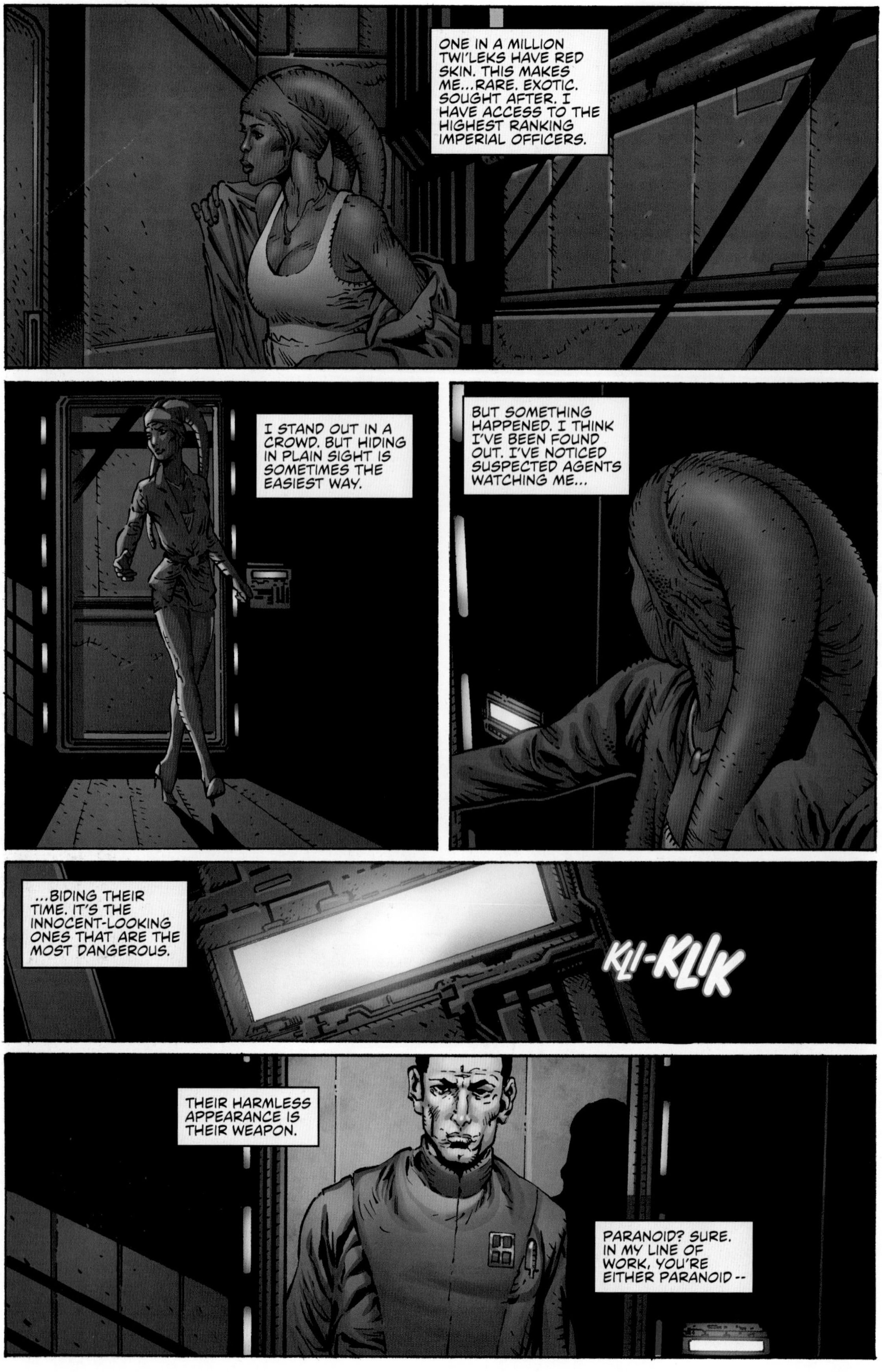
ONE IN A MILLION TWI'LEKS HAVE RED SKIN. THIS MAKES ME...RARE. EXOTIC. SOUGHT AFTER. I HAVE ACCESS TO THE HIGHEST RANKING IMPERIAL OFFICERS.
I STAND OUT IN A CROWD. BUT HIDING IN PLAIN SIGHT IS SOMETIMES THE EASIEST WAY.
BUT SOMETHING HAPPENED. I THINK I'VE BEEN FOUND OUT. I'VE NOTICED SUSPECTED AGENTS WATCHING ME...
...BIDING THEIR TIME. IT'S THE INNOCENT-LOOKING ONES THAT ARE THE MOST DANGEROUS.
KLI-KLIK
THEIR HARMLESS APPEARANCE IS THEIR WEAPON.
PARANOID? SURE. IN MY LINE OF WORK, YOU'RE EITHER PARANOID --

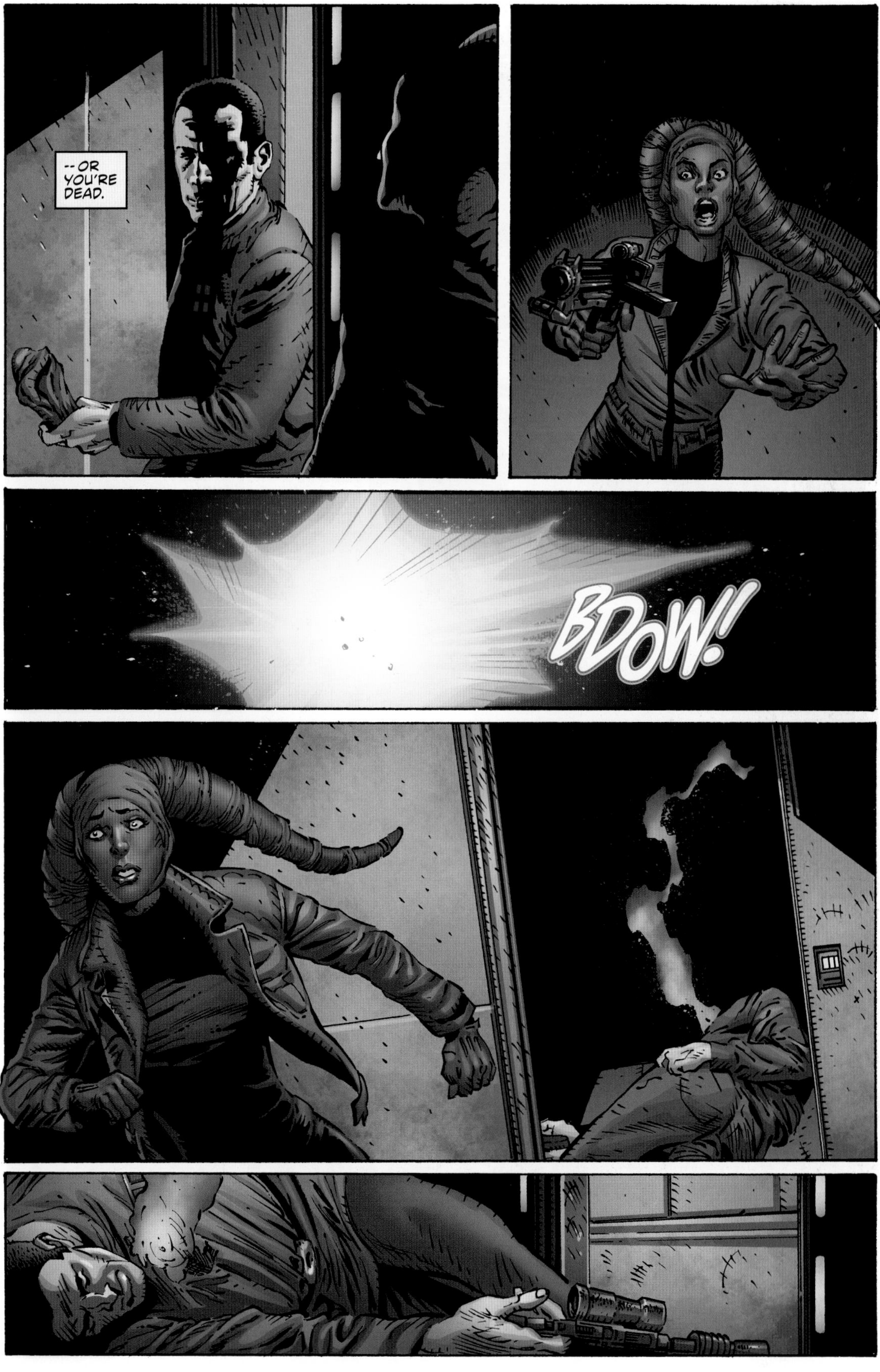
--OR YOU'RE DEAD.
BDOW!!

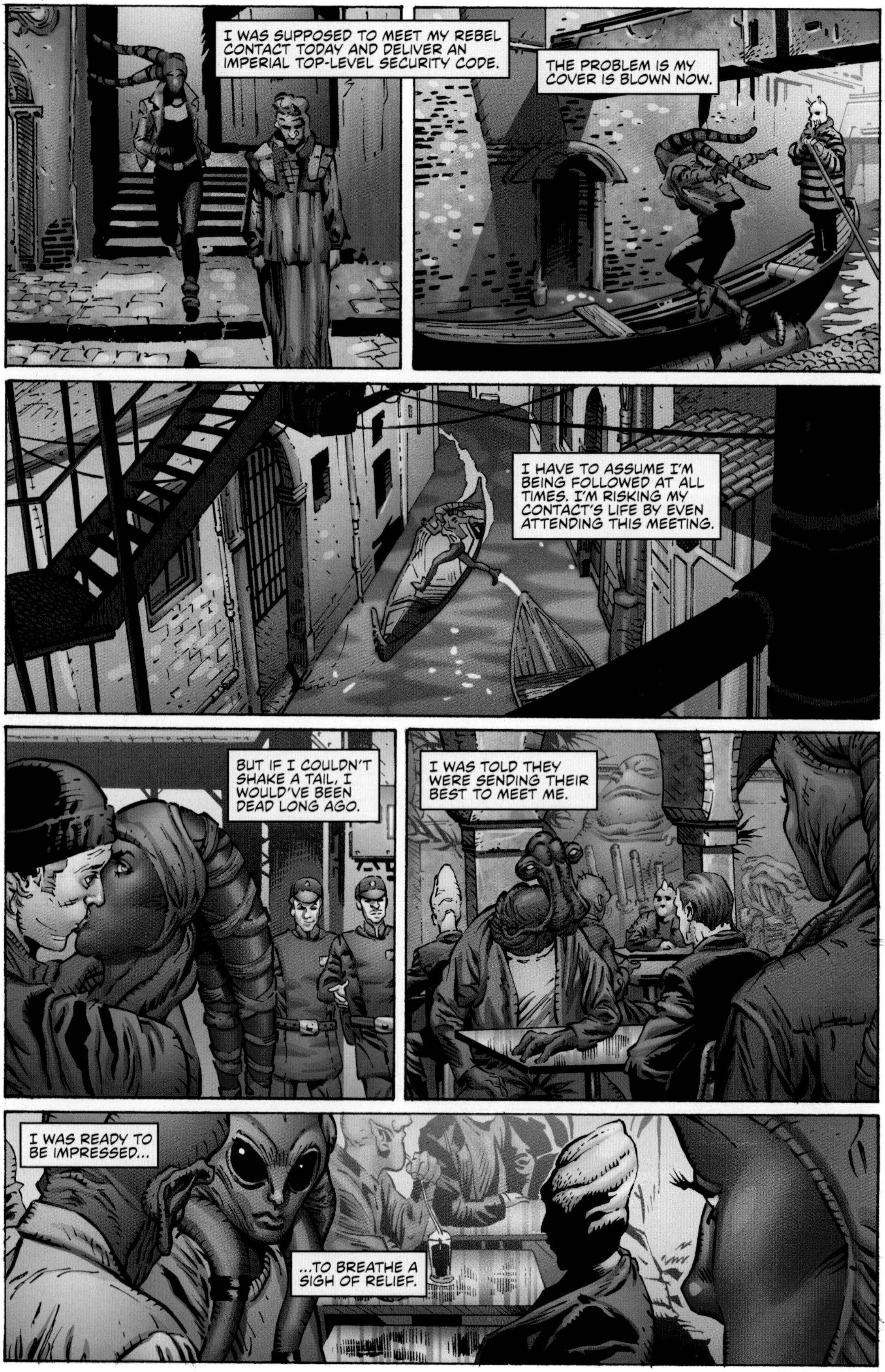
I WAS SUPPOSED TO MEET MY REBEL CONTACT TODAY AND DELIVER AN IMPERIAL TOP-LEVEL SECURITY CODE.
THE PROBLEM IS MY COVER IS BLOWN NOW.
I HAVE TO ASSUME I'M BEING FOLLOWED AT ALL TIMES. I'M RISKING MY CONTACT'S LIFE BY EVEN ATTENDING THIS MEETING.
BUT IF I COULDN'T SHAKE A TAIL, I WOULD'VE BEEN DEAD LONG AGO.
I WAS TOLD THEY WERE SENDING THEIR BEST TO MEET ME.
I WAS READY TO BE IMPRESSED...
...TO BREATHE A SIGH OF RELIEF.

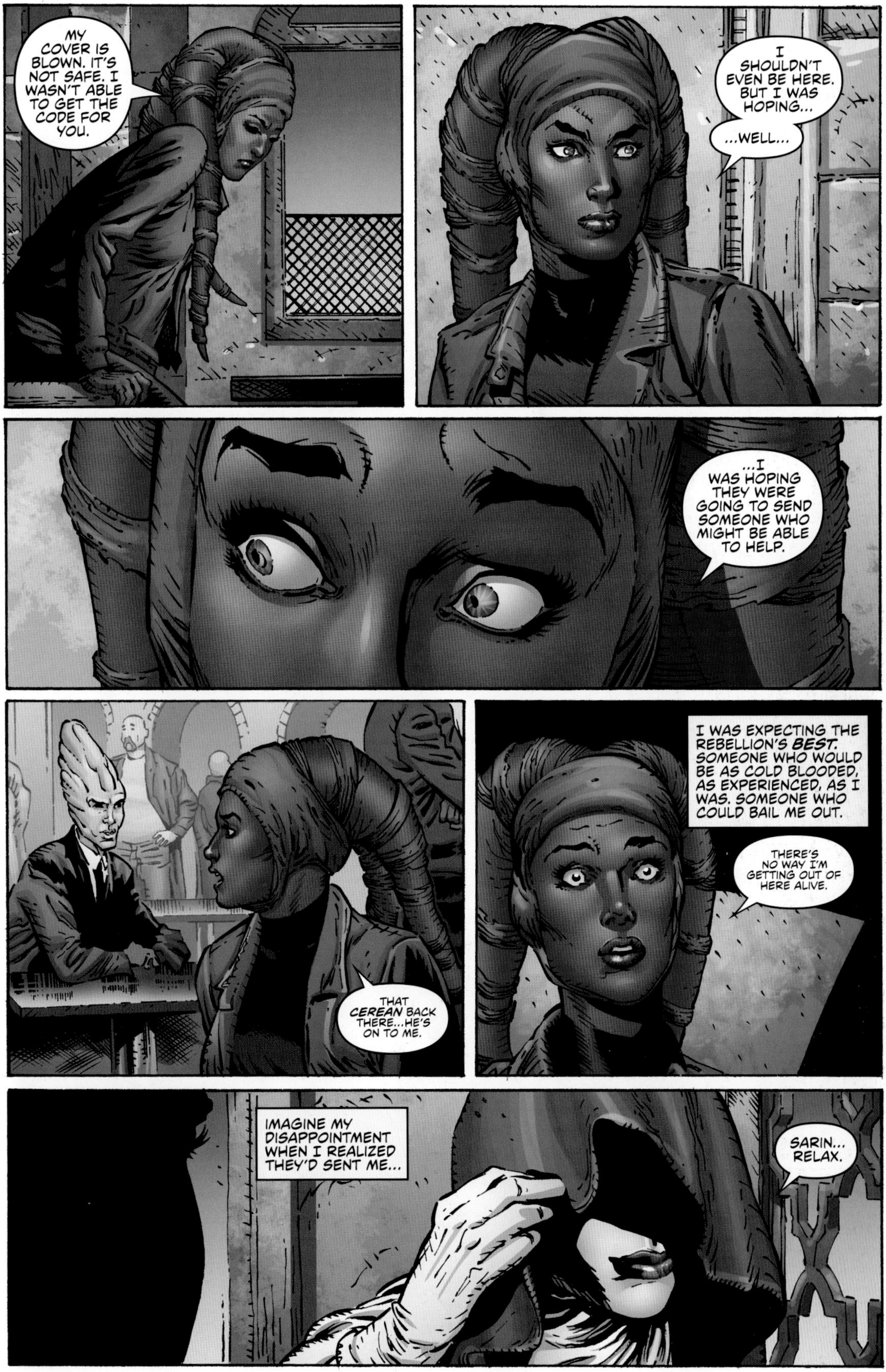
MY COVER IS BLOWN. IT'S NOT SAFE. I WASN'T ABLE TO GET THE CODE FOR YOU.
I SHOULDN'T EVEN BE HERE. BUT I WAS HOPING...
...WELL...
...I WAS HOPING THEY WERE GOING TO SEND SOMEONE WHO MIGHT BE ABLE TO HELP.
THAT CEREAN BACK THERE...HE'S ON TO ME.
I WAS EXPECTING THE REBELLION'S BEST. SOMEONE WHO WOULD BE AS COLD BLOODED, AS EXPERIENCED, AS I WAS. SOMEONE WHO COULD BAIL ME OUT.
THERE'S NO WAY I'M GETTING OUT OF HERE ALIVE.
IMAGINE MY DISAPPOINTMENT WHEN I REALIZED THEY'D SENT ME...
SARIN... RELAX.

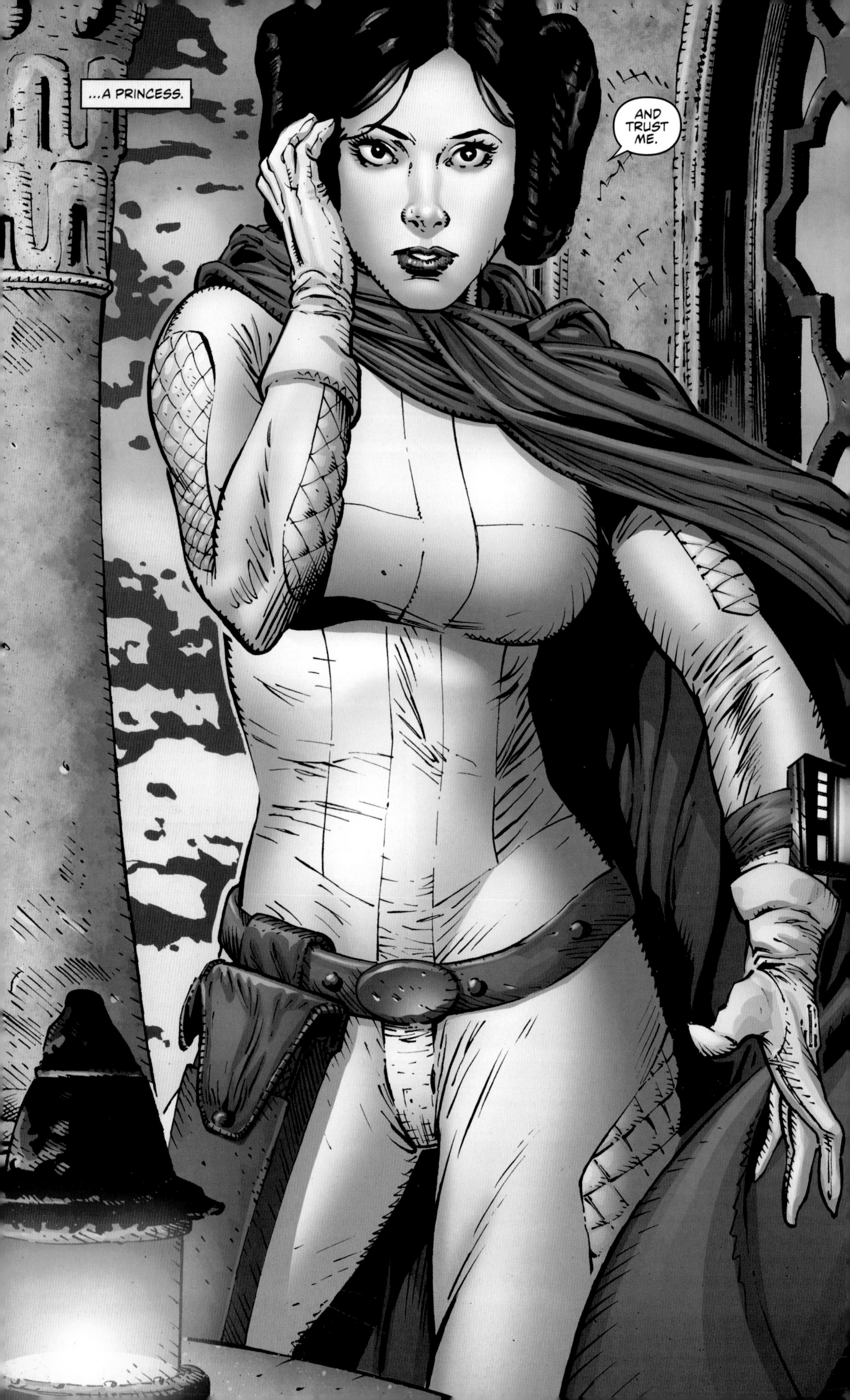
...A PRINCESS.
AND TRUST ME.

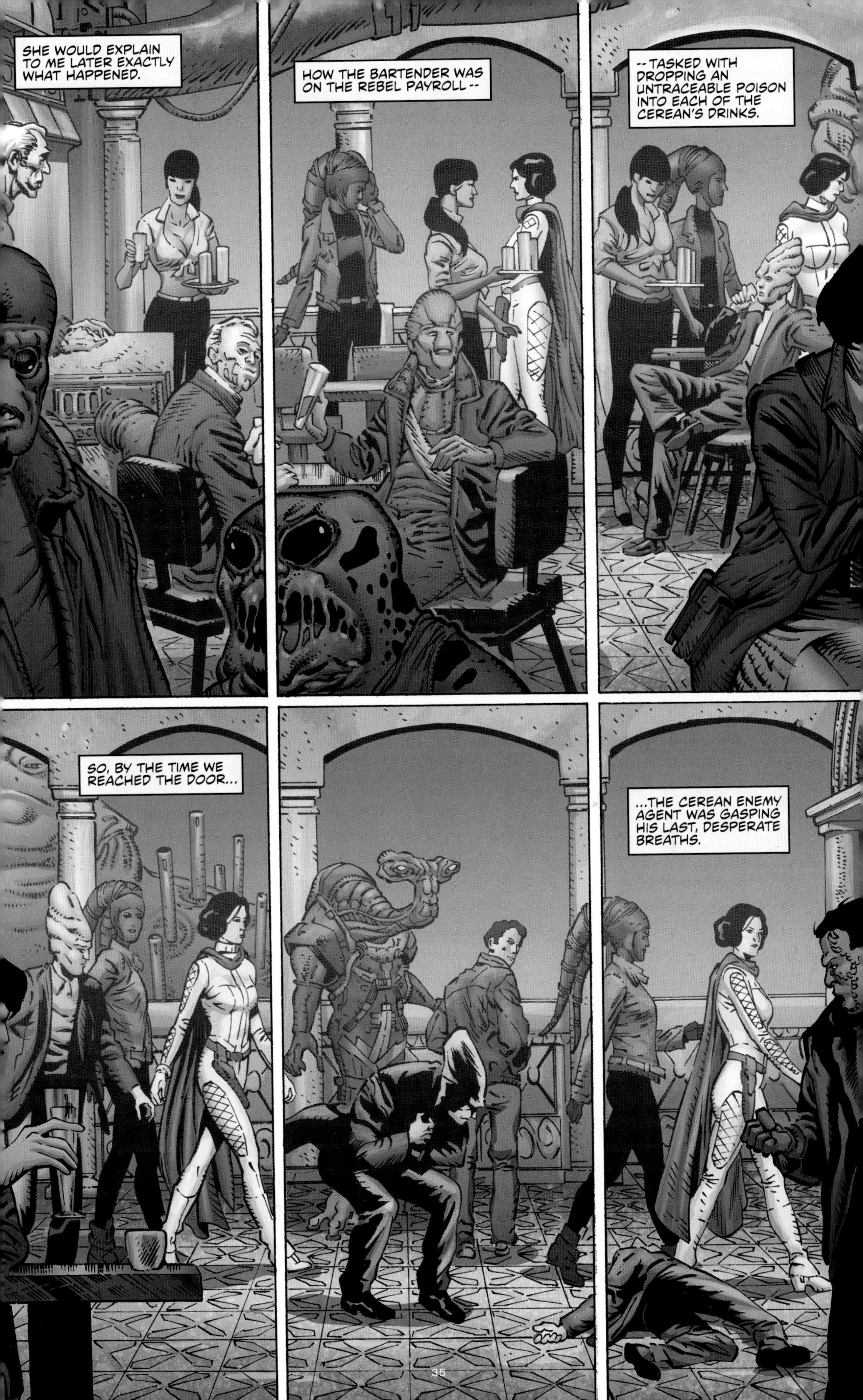
SHE WOULD EXPLAIN TO ME LATER EXACTLY WHAT HAPPENED.
HOW THE BARTENDER WAS ON THE REBEL PAYROLL --
-- TASKED WITH DROPPING AN UNTRACEABLE POISON INTO EACH OF THE CEREAN'S DRINKS.
SO, BY THE TIME WE REACHED THE DOOR...
...THE CEREAN ENEMY AGENT WAS GASPING HIS LAST, DESPERATE BREATHS.

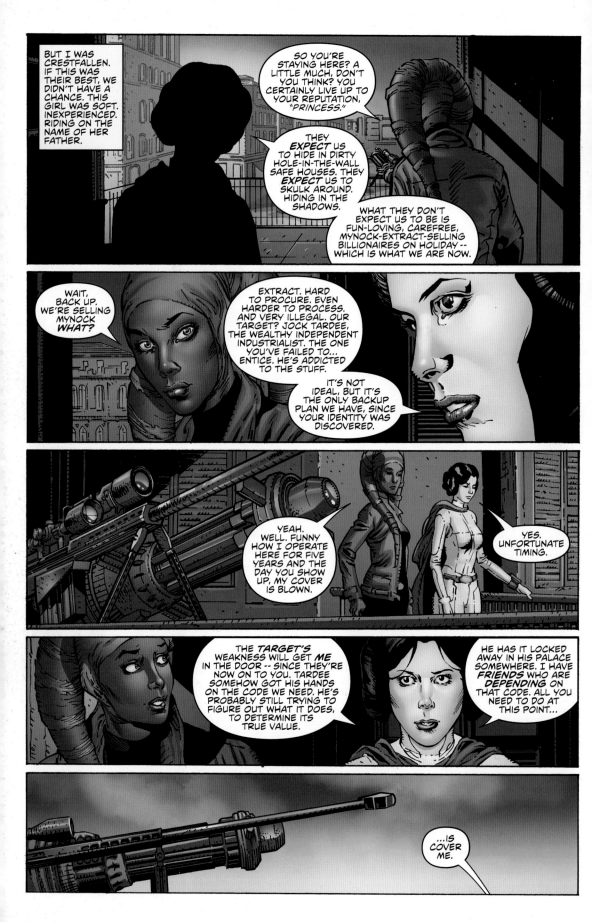

BUT I WAS CRESTFALLEN. IF THIS WAS THEIR BEST, WE DIDN'T HAVE A CHANCE. THIS GIRL WAS SOFT. INEXPERIENCED. RIDING ON THE NAME OF HER FATHER.

SO YOU'RE STAYING HERE? A LITTLE MUCH, DON'T YOU THINK? YOU CERTAINLY LIVE UP TO YOUR REPUTATION, "PRINCESS."

THEY *EXPECT* US TO HIDE IN DIRTY HOLE-IN-THE-WALL SAFE HOUSES. THEY *EXPECT* US TO SKULK AROUND. HIDING IN THE SHADOWS.

WHAT THEY DON'T EXPECT US TO BE IS FUN-LOVING, CAREFREE, MYNOCK-EXTRACT-SELLING BILLIONAIRES ON HOLIDAY -- WHICH IS WHAT WE ARE NOW.

WAIT, BACK UP. WE'RE SELLING MYNOCK *WHAT?*

EXTRACT. HARD TO PROCURE. EVEN HARDER TO PROCESS. AND VERY ILLEGAL. OUR TARGET? JOCK TARDEE, THE WEALTHY INDEPENDENT INDUSTRIALIST. THE ONE YOU'VE FAILED TO... ENTICE. HE'S ADDICTED TO THE STUFF.

IT'S NOT IDEAL, BUT IT'S THE ONLY BACKUP PLAN WE HAVE, SINCE YOUR IDENTITY WAS DISCOVERED.

YEAH. WELL. FUNNY HOW I OPERATE HERE FOR FIVE YEARS AND THE DAY YOU SHOW UP, MY COVER IS BLOWN.

YES. UNFORTUNATE TIMING.

THE *TARGET'S* WEAKNESS WILL GET *ME* IN THE DOOR -- SINCE THEY'RE NOW ON TO YOU. TARDEE SOMEHOW GOT HIS HANDS ON THE CODE WE NEED. HE'S PROBABLY STILL TRYING TO FIGURE OUT WHAT IT DOES, TO DETERMINE ITS TRUE VALUE.

HE HAS IT LOCKED AWAY IN HIS PALACE SOMEWHERE. I HAVE *FRIENDS* WHO ARE *DEPENDING* ON THAT CODE. ALL YOU NEED TO DO AT THIS POINT...

...IS COVER ME.

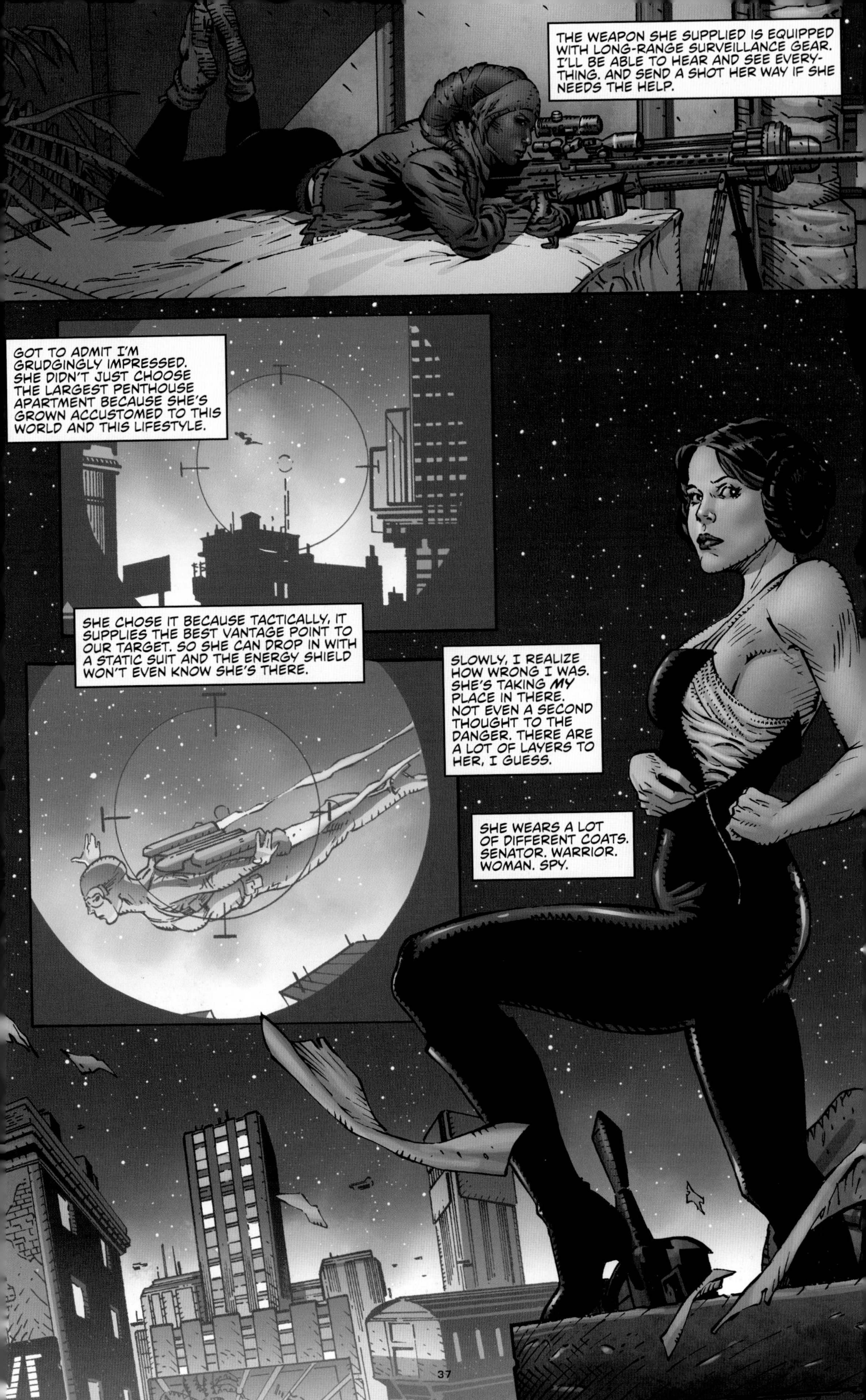
THE WEAPON SHE SUPPLIED IS EQUIPPED WITH LONG-RANGE SURVEILLANCE GEAR. I'LL BE ABLE TO HEAR AND SEE EVERY-THING, AND SEND A SHOT HER WAY IF SHE NEEDS THE HELP.
GOT TO ADMIT I'M GRUDGINGLY IMPRESSED. SHE DIDN'T JUST CHOOSE THE LARGEST PENTHOUSE APARTMENT BECAUSE SHE'S GROWN ACCUSTOMED TO THIS WORLD AND THIS LIFESTYLE.
SHE CHOSE IT BECAUSE TACTICALLY, IT SUPPLIES THE BEST VANTAGE POINT TO OUR TARGET. SO SHE CAN DROP IN WITH A STATIC SUIT AND THE ENERGY SHIELD WON'T EVEN KNOW SHE'S THERE.
SLOWLY, I REALIZE HOW WRONG I WAS. SHE'S TAKING *MY* PLACE IN THERE. NOT EVEN A SECOND THOUGHT TO THE DANGER. THERE ARE A LOT OF LAYERS TO HER, I GUESS.
SHE WEARS A LOT OF DIFFERENT COATS. SENATOR. WARRIOR. WOMAN. SPY.

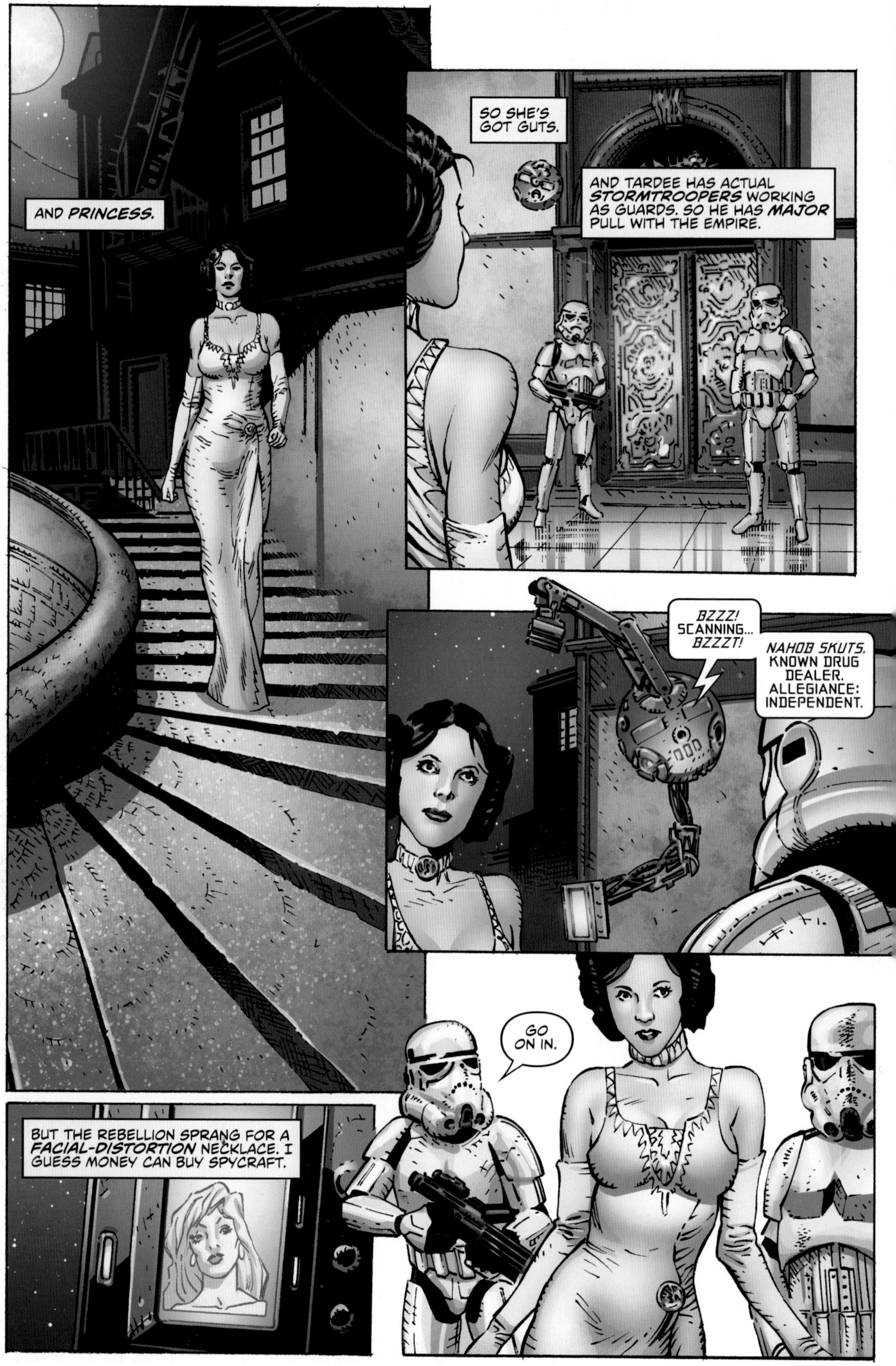
AND PRINCESS.
SO SHE'S GOT GUTS.
AND TARDEE HAS ACTUAL STORMTROOPERS WORKING AS GUARDS. SO HE HAS MAJOR PULL WITH THE EMPIRE.
BZZZ! SCANNING... BZZZT!
NAHOB SKUTS. KNOWN DRUG DEALER. ALLEGIANCE: INDEPENDENT.
BUT THE REBELLION SPRANG FOR A FACIAL-DISTORTION NECKLACE. I GUESS MONEY CAN BUY SPYCRAFT.
GO ON IN.

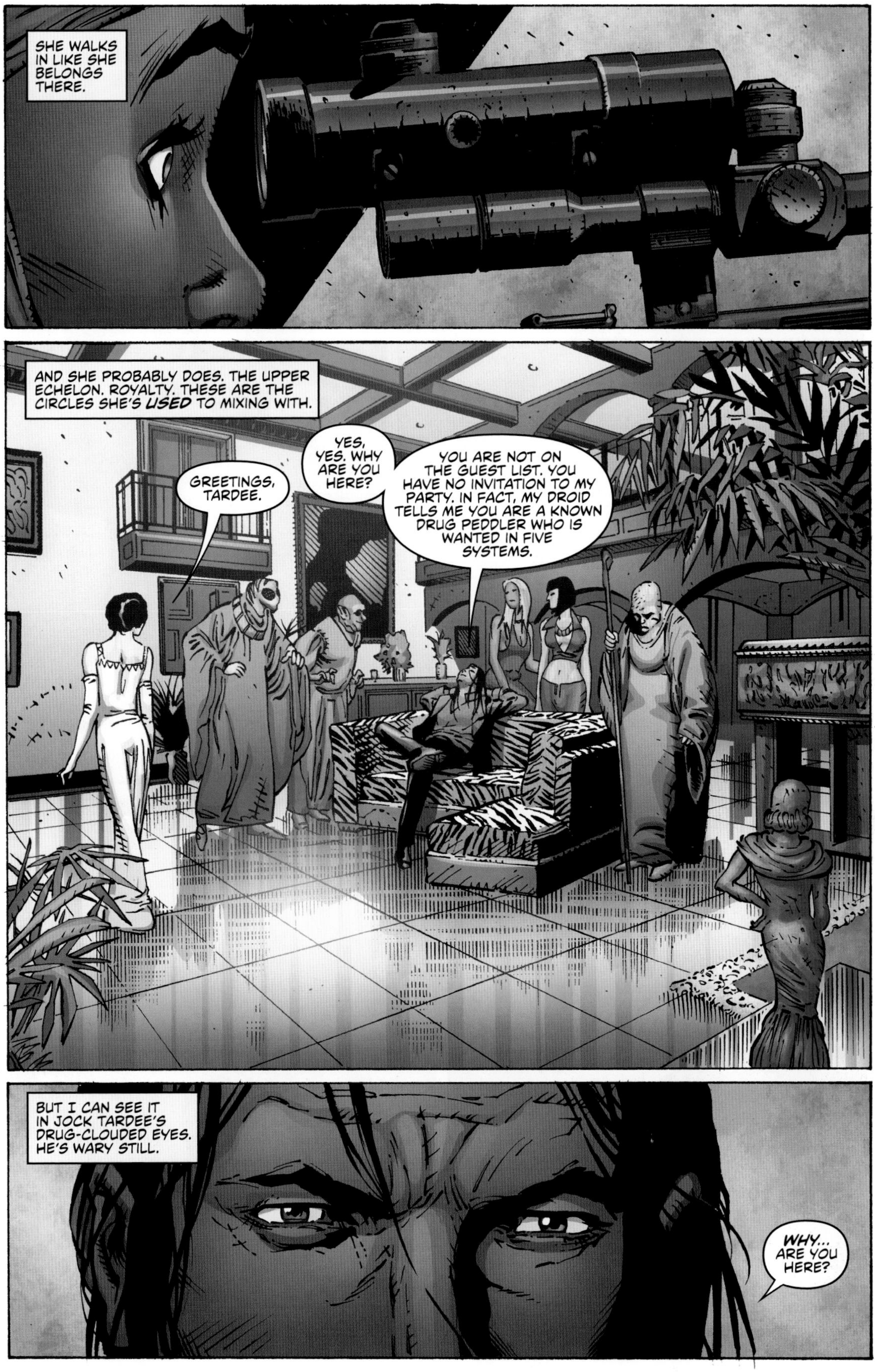
SHE WALKS IN LIKE SHE BELONGS THERE.
AND SHE PROBABLY DOES. THE UPPER ECHELON. ROYALTY. THESE ARE THE CIRCLES SHE'S *USED* TO MIXING WITH.
GREETINGS, TARDEE.
YES, YES. WHY ARE YOU HERE?
YOU ARE NOT ON THE GUEST LIST. YOU HAVE NO INVITATION TO MY PARTY. IN FACT, MY DROID TELLS ME YOU ARE A KNOWN DRUG PEDDLER WHO IS WANTED IN FIVE SYSTEMS.
BUT I CAN SEE IT IN JOCK TARDEE'S DRUG-CLOUDED EYES. HE'S WARY STILL.
WHY... ARE YOU HERE?

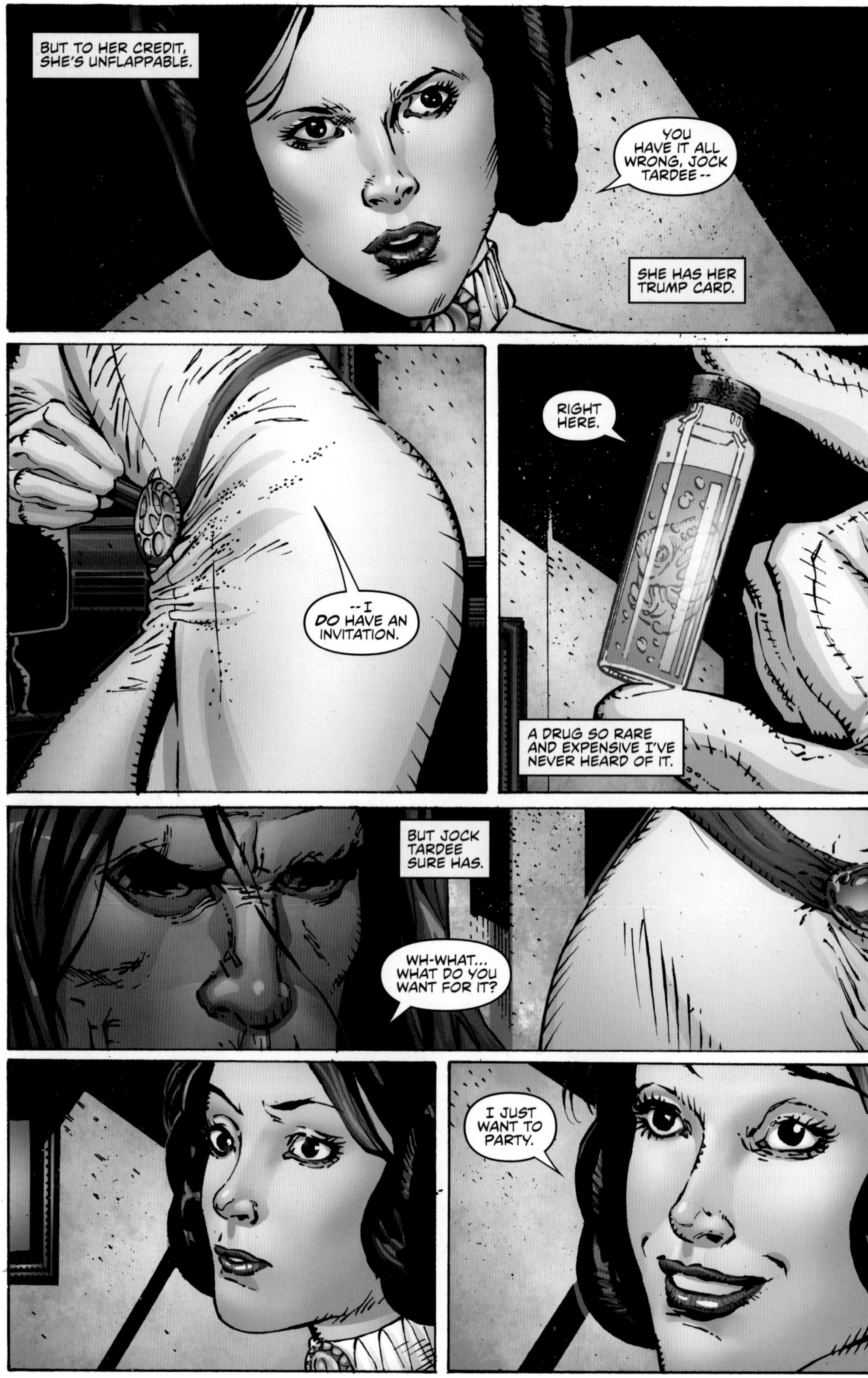
BUT TO HER CREDIT, SHE'S UNFLAPPABLE.
YOU HAVE IT ALL WRONG, JOCK TARDEE --
SHE HAS HER TRUMP CARD.
-- I DO HAVE AN INVITATION.
RIGHT HERE.
A DRUG SO RARE AND EXPENSIVE I'VE NEVER HEARD OF IT.
BUT JOCK TARDEE SURE HAS.
WH-WHAT... WHAT DO YOU WANT FOR IT?
I JUST WANT TO PARTY.

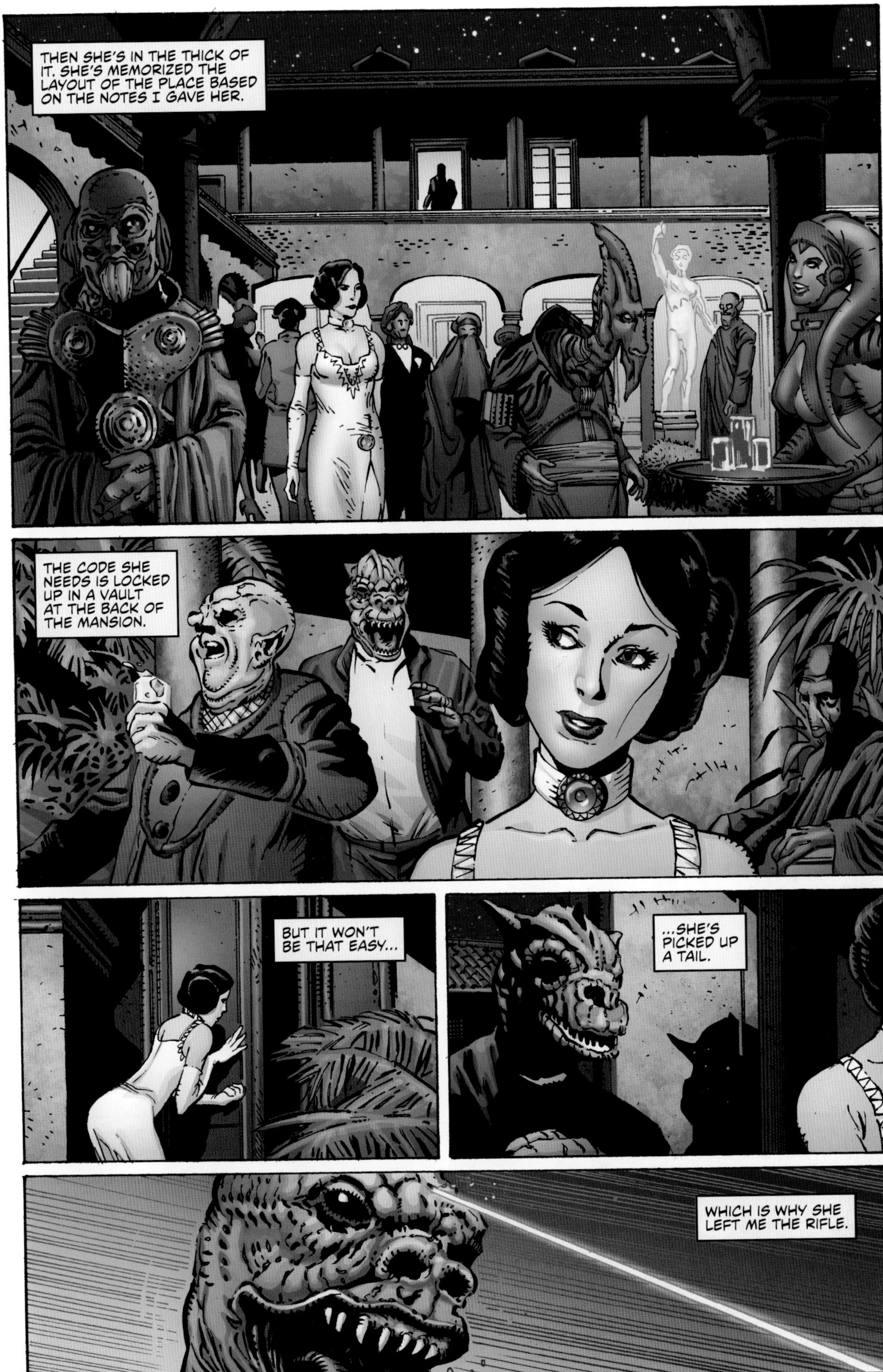
THEN SHE'S IN THE THICK OF IT. SHE'S MEMORIZED THE LAYOUT OF THE PLACE BASED ON THE NOTES I GAVE HER.
THE CODE SHE NEEDS IS LOCKED UP IN A VAULT AT THE BACK OF THE MANSION.
BUT IT WON'T BE THAT EASY...
...SHE'S PICKED UP A TAIL.
WHICH IS WHY SHE LEFT ME THE RIFLE.

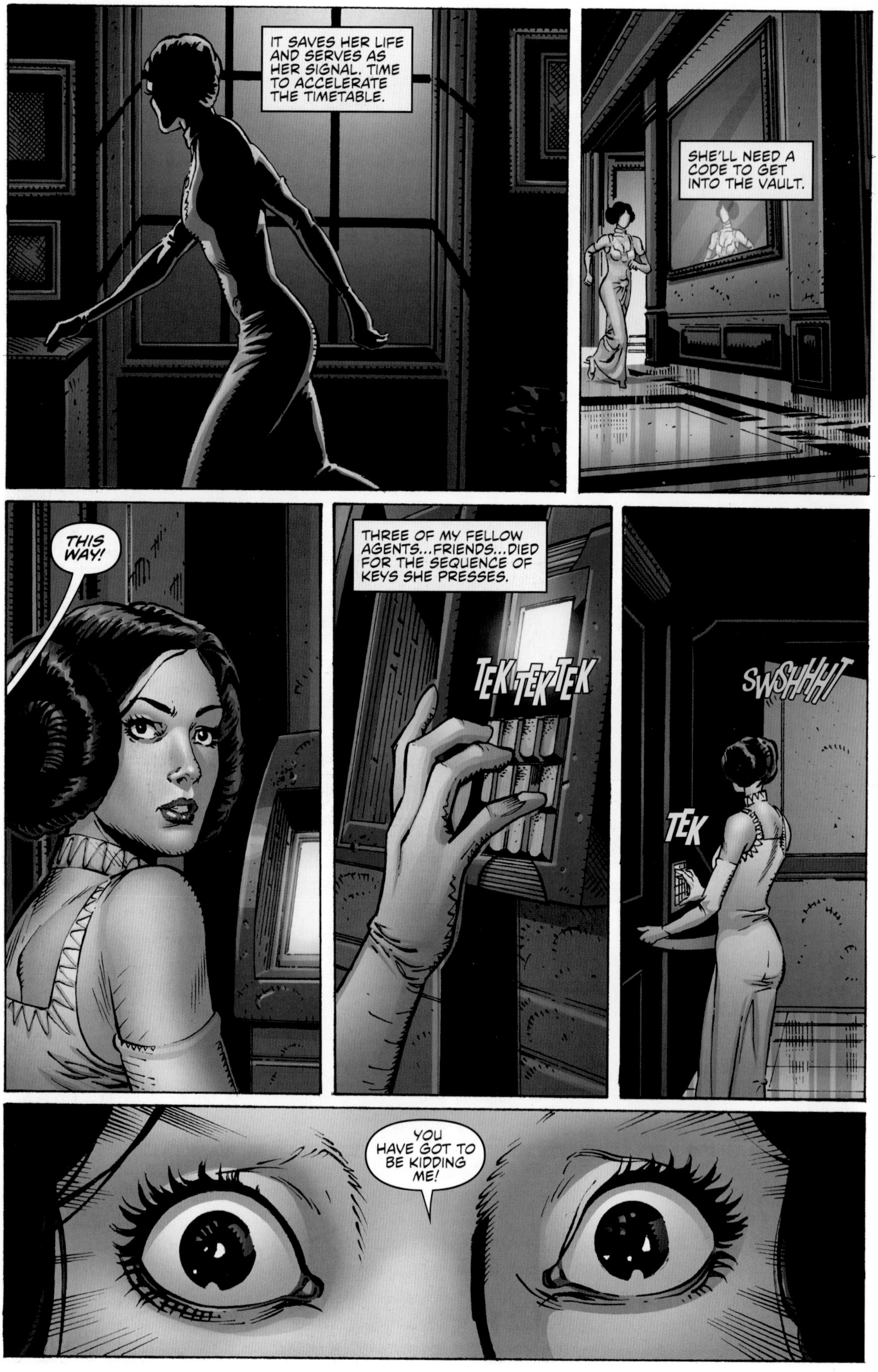

IT SAVES HER LIFE AND SERVES AS HER SIGNAL. TIME TO ACCELERATE THE TIMETABLE.
SHE'LL NEED A CODE TO GET INTO THE VAULT.
THIS WAY!
THREE OF MY FELLOW AGENTS...FRIENDS...DIED FOR THE SEQUENCE OF KEYS SHE PRESSES.
TEK TEK TEK
SWSHHHT
TEK
YOU HAVE GOT TO BE KIDDING ME!

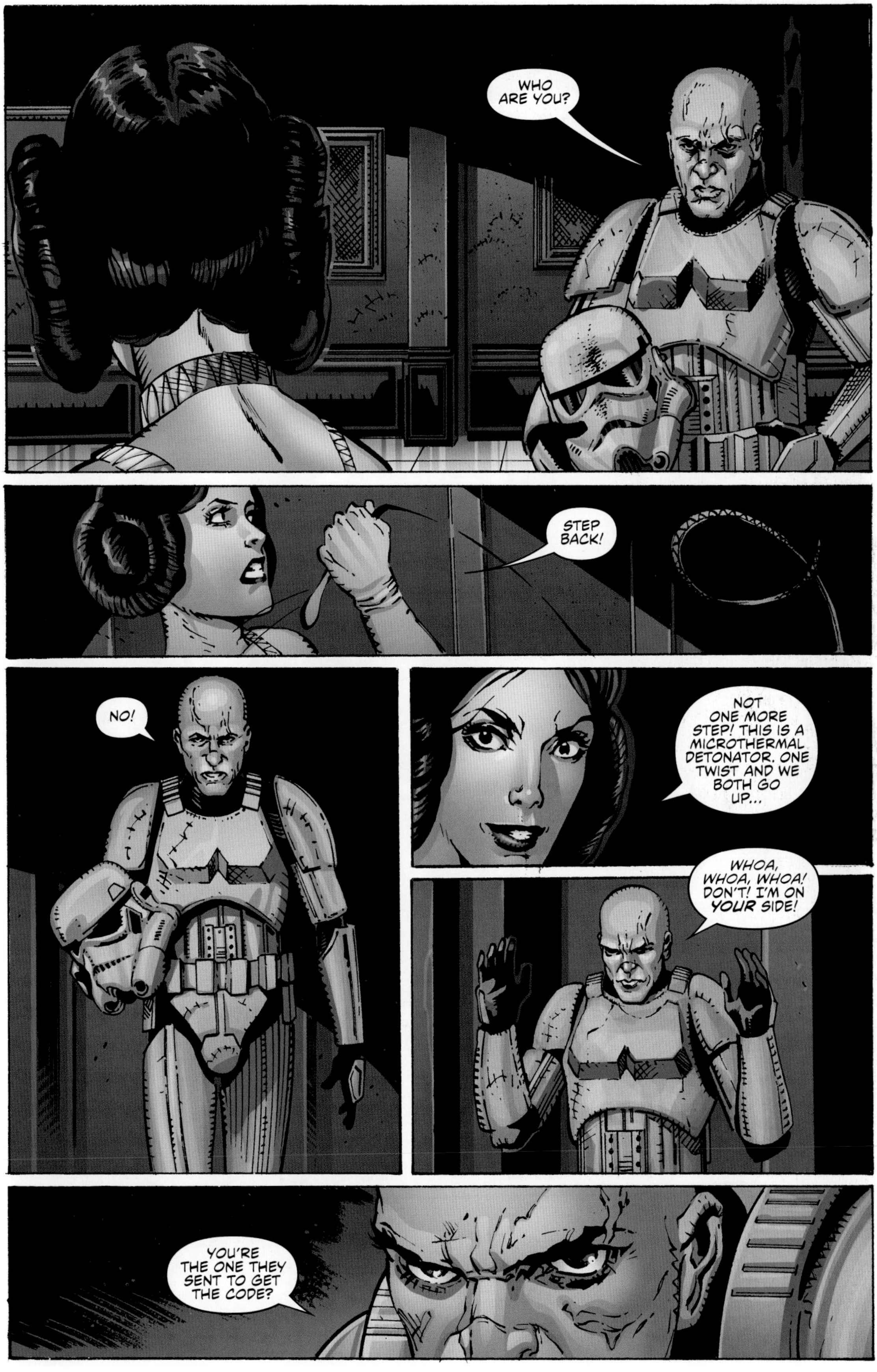
WHO ARE YOU?
STEP BACK!
NO!
NOT ONE MORE STEP! THIS IS A MICROTHERMAL DETONATOR. ONE TWIST AND WE BOTH GO UP...
WHOA, WHOA, WHOA! DON'T! I'M ON YOUR SIDE!
YOU'RE THE ONE THEY SENT TO GET THE CODE?

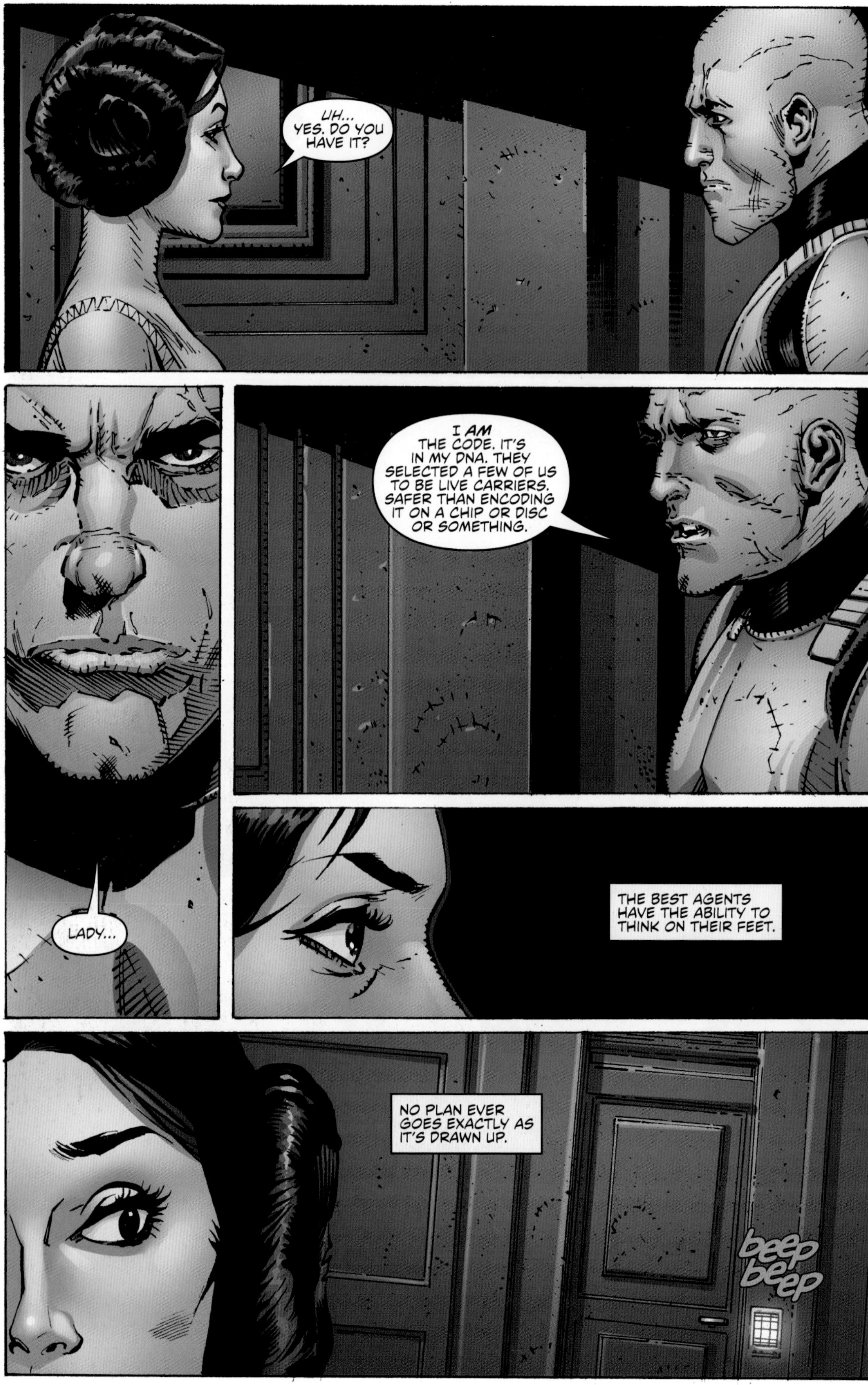
UH... YES. DO YOU HAVE IT?
I AM THE CODE. IT'S IN MY DNA. THEY SELECTED A FEW OF US TO BE LIVE CARRIERS. SAFER THAN ENCODING IT ON A CHIP OR DISC OR SOMETHING.
LADY...
THE BEST AGENTS HAVE THE ABILITY TO THINK ON THEIR FEET.
NO PLAN EVER GOES EXACTLY AS IT'S DRAWN UP.
beep beep

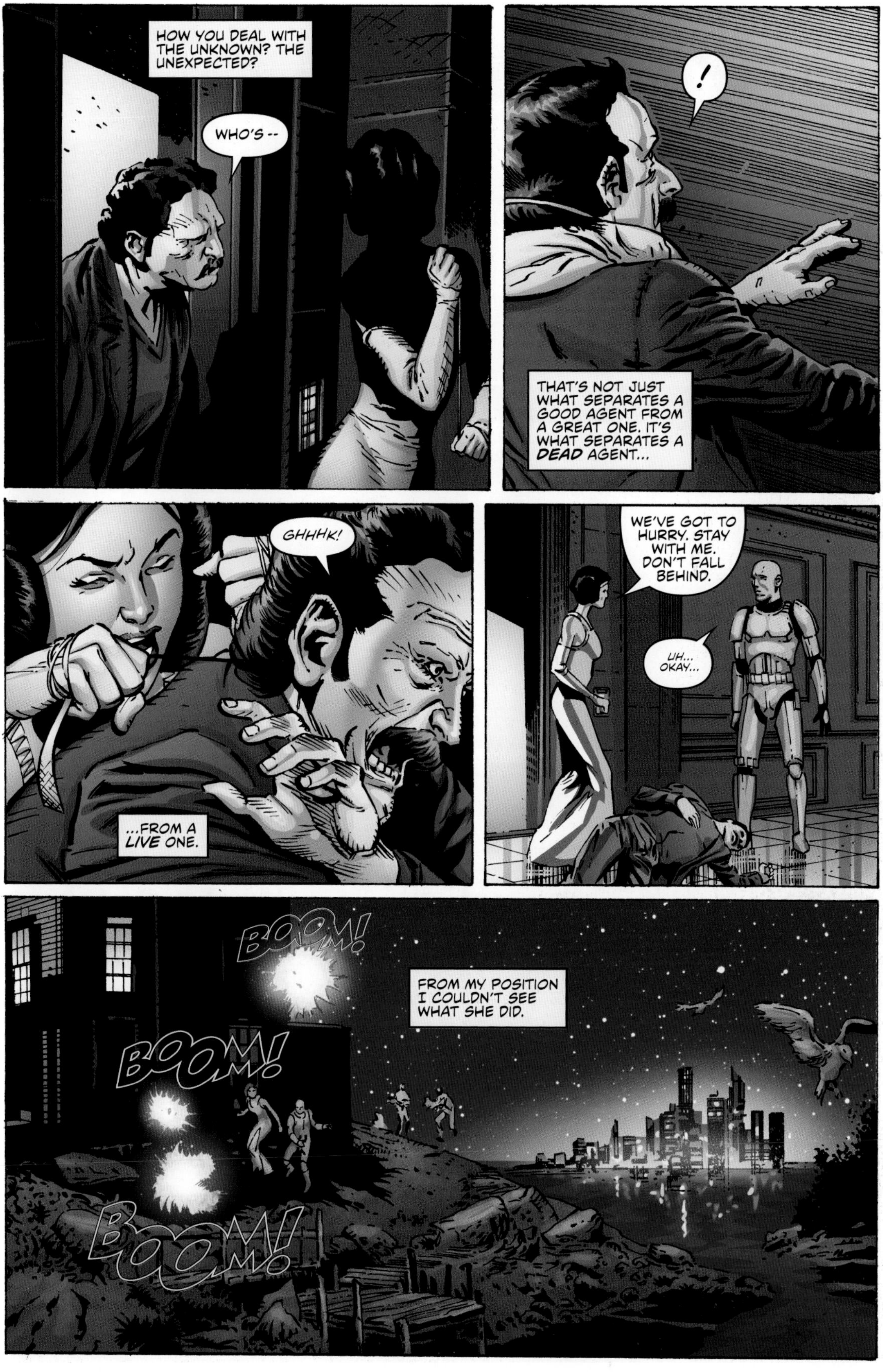

HOW YOU DEAL WITH THE UNKNOWN? THE UNEXPECTED?
WHO'S --
!
THAT'S NOT JUST WHAT SEPARATES A GOOD AGENT FROM A GREAT ONE. IT'S WHAT SEPARATES A DEAD AGENT...
GHHHK!
...FROM A LIVE ONE.
WE'VE GOT TO HURRY. STAY WITH ME. DON'T FALL BEHIND.
UH... OKAY...
BOOM!
FROM MY POSITION I COULDN'T SEE WHAT SHE DID.
BOOM!
BOOM!

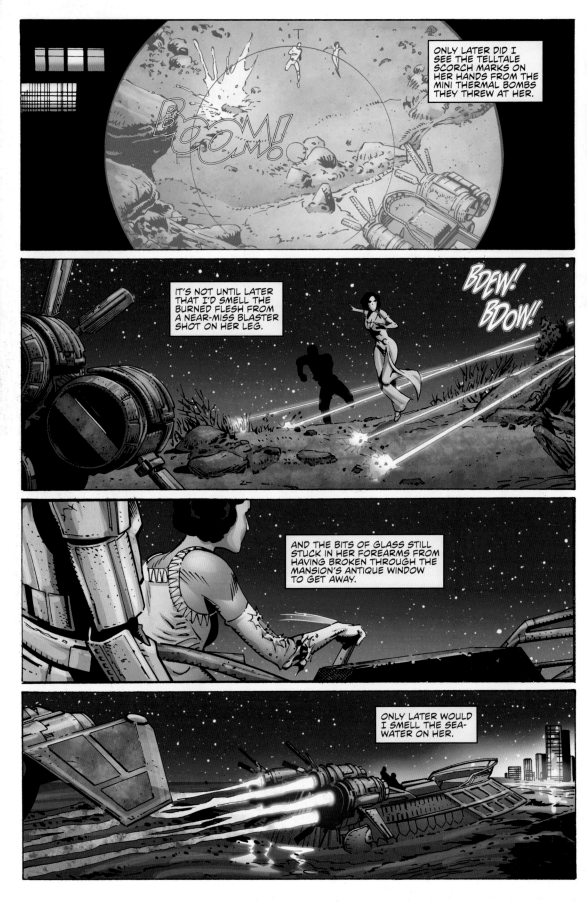

ONLY LATER DID I SEE THE TELLTALE SCORCH MARKS ON HER HANDS FROM THE MINI THERMAL BOMBS THEY THREW AT HER.

BOOM!

IT'S NOT UNTIL LATER THAT I'D SMELL THE BURNED FLESH FROM A NEAR-MISS BLASTER SHOT ON HER LEG.

BDEW!
BDOW!

AND THE BITS OF GLASS STILL STUCK IN HER FOREARMS FROM HAVING BROKEN THROUGH THE MANSION'S ANTIQUE WINDOW TO GET AWAY.

ONLY LATER WOULD I SMELL THE SEA-WATER ON HER.

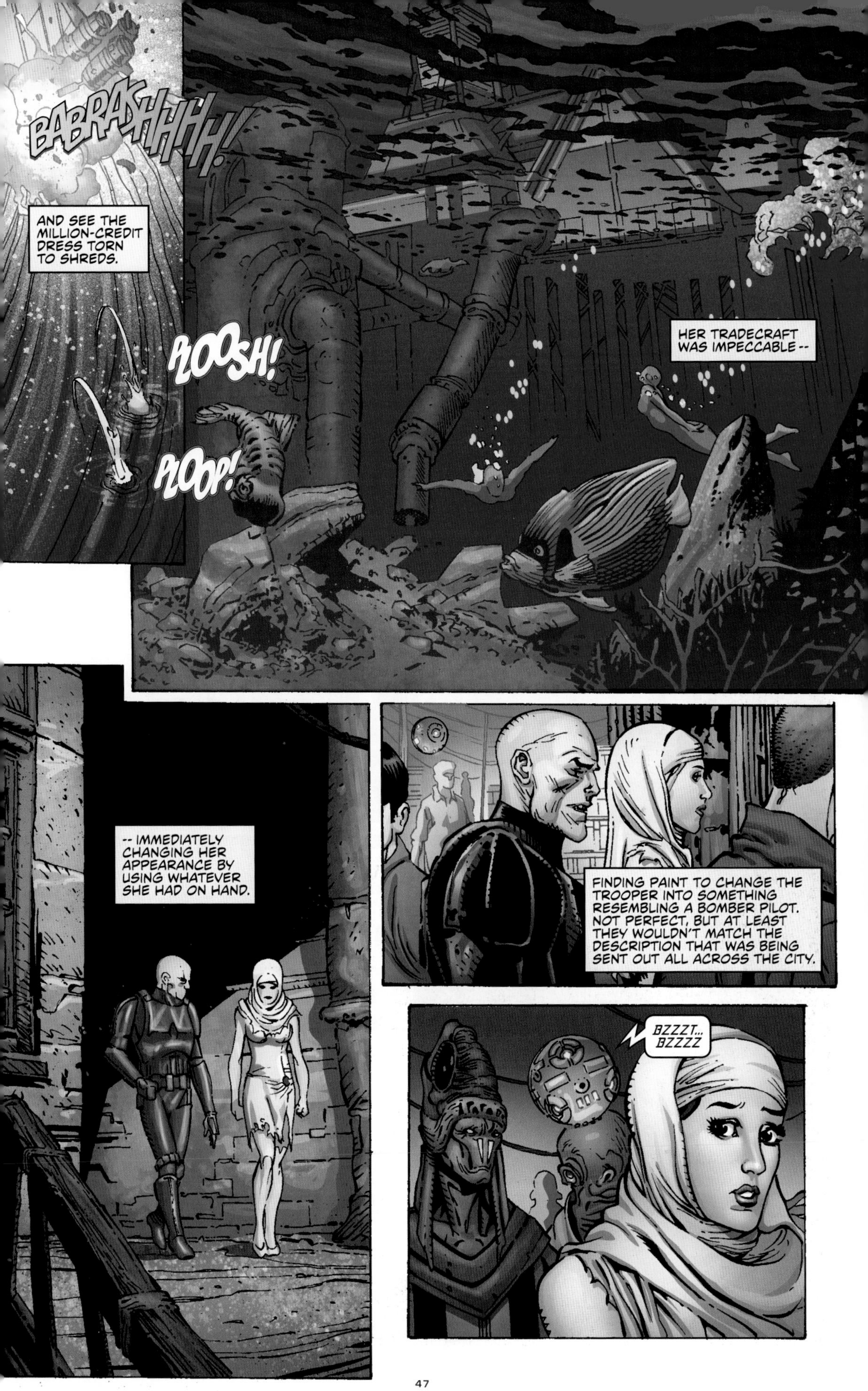
BABRASHHHH!
AND SEE THE MILLION-CREDIT DRESS TORN TO SHREDS.
PLOOSH!
PLOOP!
HER TRADECRAFT WAS IMPECCABLE --
-- IMMEDIATELY CHANGING HER APPEARANCE BY USING WHATEVER SHE HAD ON HAND.
FINDING PAINT TO CHANGE THE TROOPER INTO SOMETHING RESEMBLING A BOMBER PILOT. NOT PERFECT, BUT AT LEAST THEY WOULDN'T MATCH THE DESCRIPTION THAT WAS BEING SENT OUT ALL ACROSS THE CITY.
BZZZT... BZZZZ

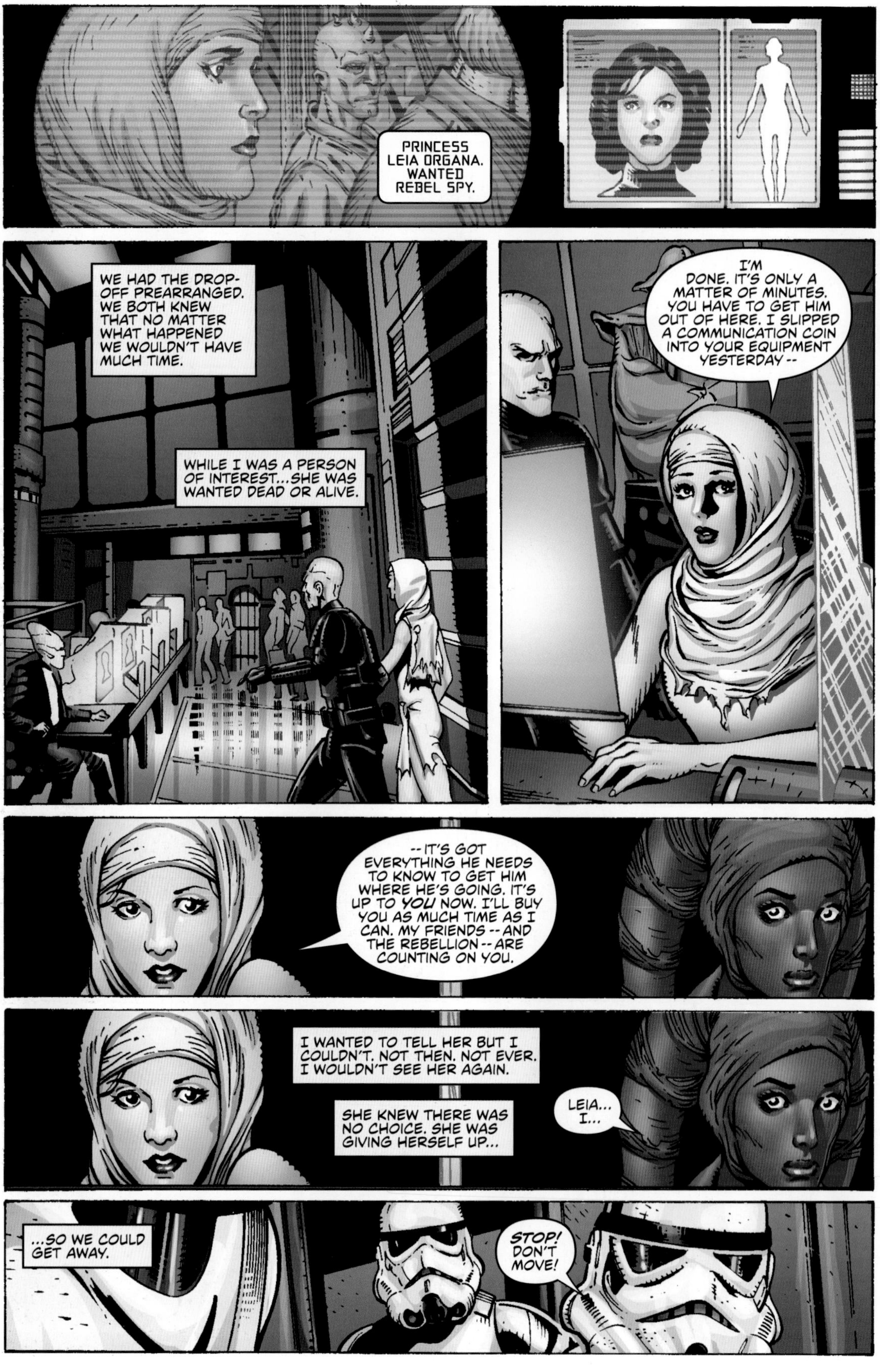
PRINCESS LEIA ORGANA. WANTED REBEL SPY.
WE HAD THE DROP-OFF PREARRANGED. WE BOTH KNEW THAT NO MATTER WHAT HAPPENED WE WOULDN'T HAVE MUCH TIME.
WHILE I WAS A PERSON OF INTEREST...SHE WAS WANTED DEAD OR ALIVE.
I'M DONE. IT'S ONLY A MATTER OF MINUTES. YOU HAVE TO GET HIM OUT OF HERE. I SLIPPED A COMMUNICATION COIN INTO YOUR EQUIPMENT YESTERDAY --
-- IT'S GOT EVERYTHING HE NEEDS TO KNOW TO GET HIM WHERE HE'S GOING. IT'S UP TO YOU NOW. I'LL BUY YOU AS MUCH TIME AS I CAN. MY FRIENDS -- AND THE REBELLION -- ARE COUNTING ON YOU.
I WANTED TO TELL HER BUT I COULDN'T. NOT THEN. NOT EVER. I WOULDN'T SEE HER AGAIN.
SHE KNEW THERE WAS NO CHOICE. SHE WAS GIVING HERSELF UP...
LEIA... I...
...SO WE COULD GET AWAY.
STOP! DON'T MOVE!

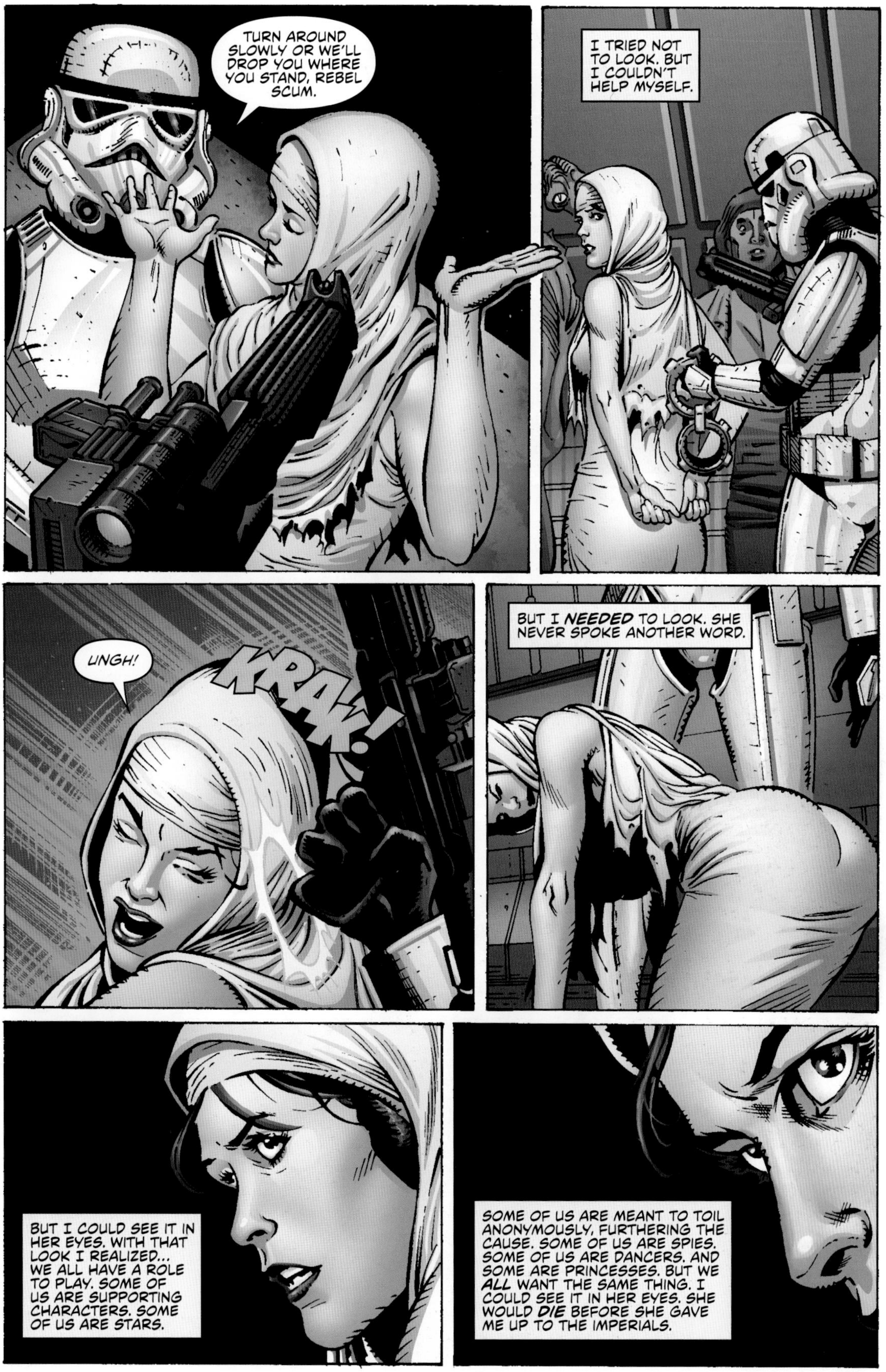
TURN AROUND SLOWLY OR WE'LL DROP YOU WHERE YOU STAND, REBEL SCUM.
I TRIED NOT TO LOOK. BUT I COULDN'T HELP MYSELF.
UNGH!
KRAK!
BUT I NEEDED TO LOOK. SHE NEVER SPOKE ANOTHER WORD.
BUT I COULD SEE IT IN HER EYES. WITH THAT LOOK I REALIZED... WE ALL HAVE A ROLE TO PLAY. SOME OF US ARE SUPPORTING CHARACTERS. SOME OF US ARE STARS.
SOME OF US ARE MEANT TO TOIL ANONYMOUSLY, FURTHERING THE CAUSE. SOME OF US ARE SPIES. SOME OF US ARE DANCERS. AND SOME ARE PRINCESSES. BUT WE ALL WANT THE SAME THING. I COULD SEE IT IN HER EYES. SHE WOULD DIE BEFORE SHE GAVE ME UP TO THE IMPERIALS.

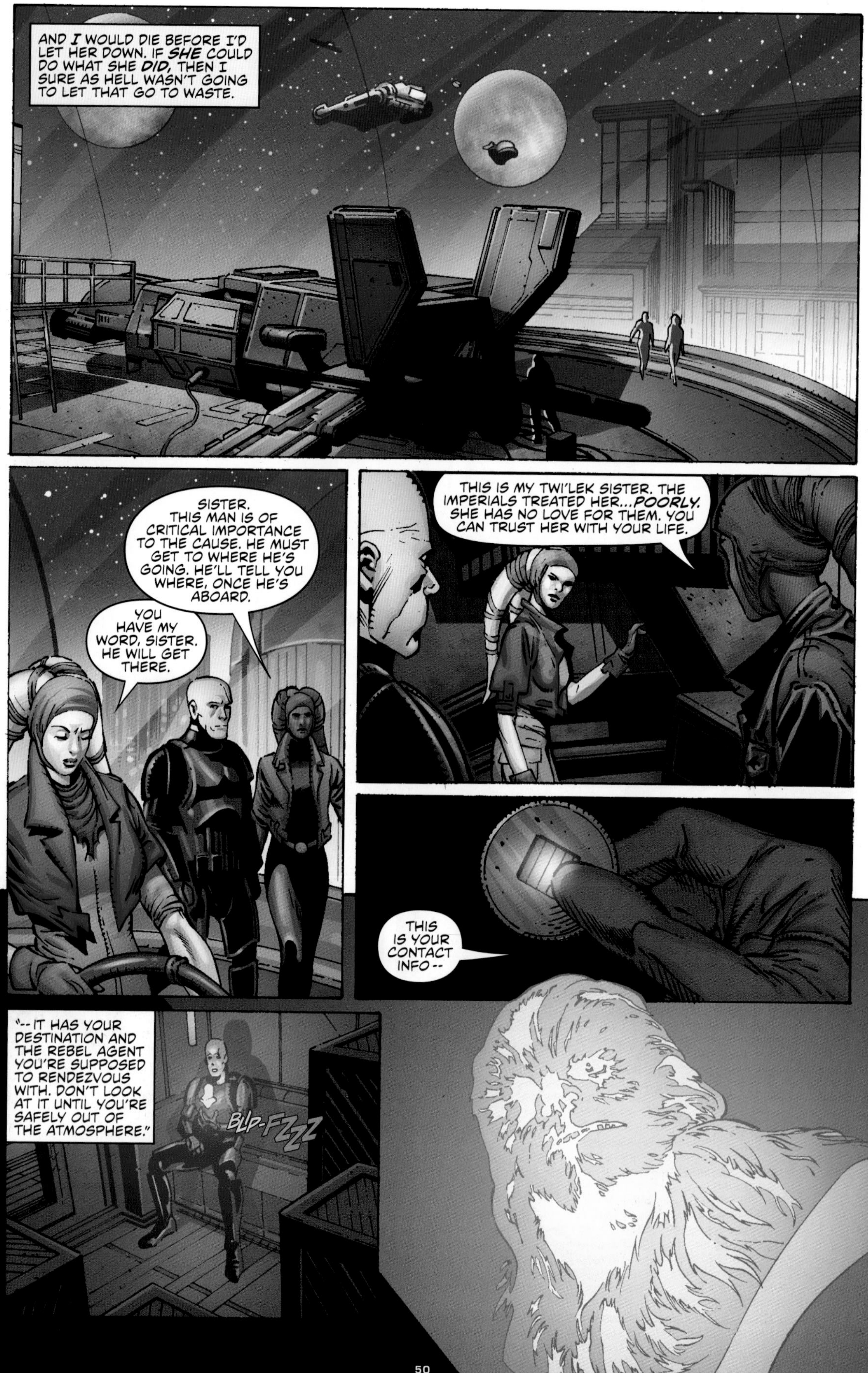

AND I WOULD DIE BEFORE I'D LET HER DOWN. IF SHE COULD DO WHAT SHE DID, THEN I SURE AS HELL WASN'T GOING TO LET THAT GO TO WASTE.
SISTER. THIS MAN IS OF CRITICAL IMPORTANCE TO THE CAUSE. HE MUST GET TO WHERE HE'S GOING. HE'LL TELL YOU WHERE, ONCE HE'S ABOARD.
YOU HAVE MY WORD, SISTER. HE WILL GET THERE.
THIS IS MY TWI'LEK SISTER. THE IMPERIALS TREATED HER...POORLY. SHE HAS NO LOVE FOR THEM. YOU CAN TRUST HER WITH YOUR LIFE.
THIS IS YOUR CONTACT INFO--
"--IT HAS YOUR DESTINATION AND THE REBEL AGENT YOU'RE SUPPOSED TO RENDEZVOUS WITH. DON'T LOOK AT IT UNTIL YOU'RE SAFELY OUT OF THE ATMOSPHERE."
BLIP-FZZZ

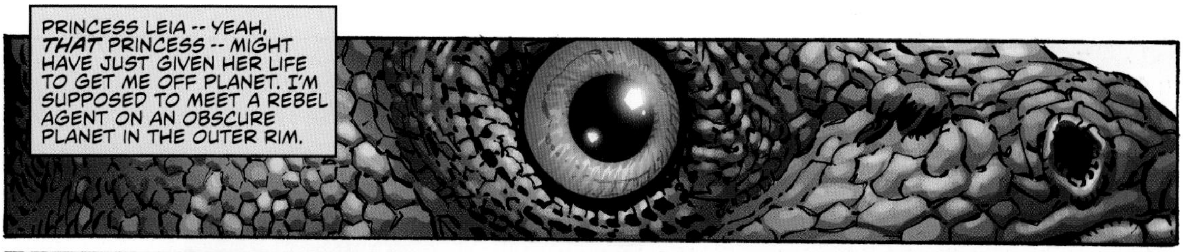
PRINCESS LEIA -- YEAH, THAT PRINCESS -- MIGHT HAVE JUST GIVEN HER LIFE TO GET ME OFF PLANET. I'M SUPPOSED TO MEET A REBEL AGENT ON AN OBSCURE PLANET IN THE OUTER RIM.

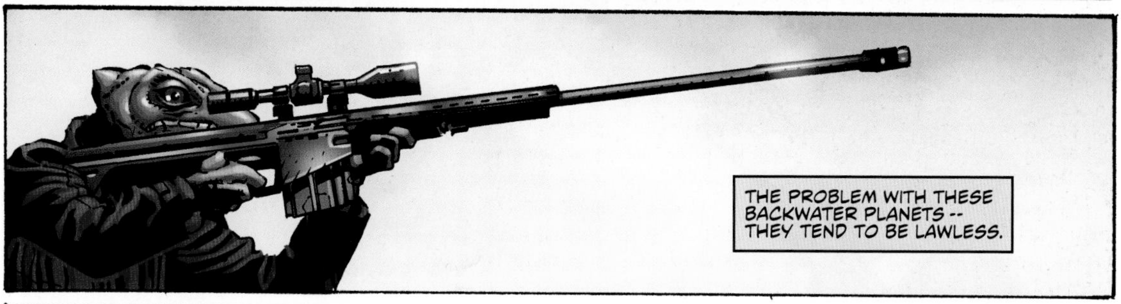
THE PROBLEM WITH THESE BACKWATER PLANETS -- THEY TEND TO BE LAWLESS.

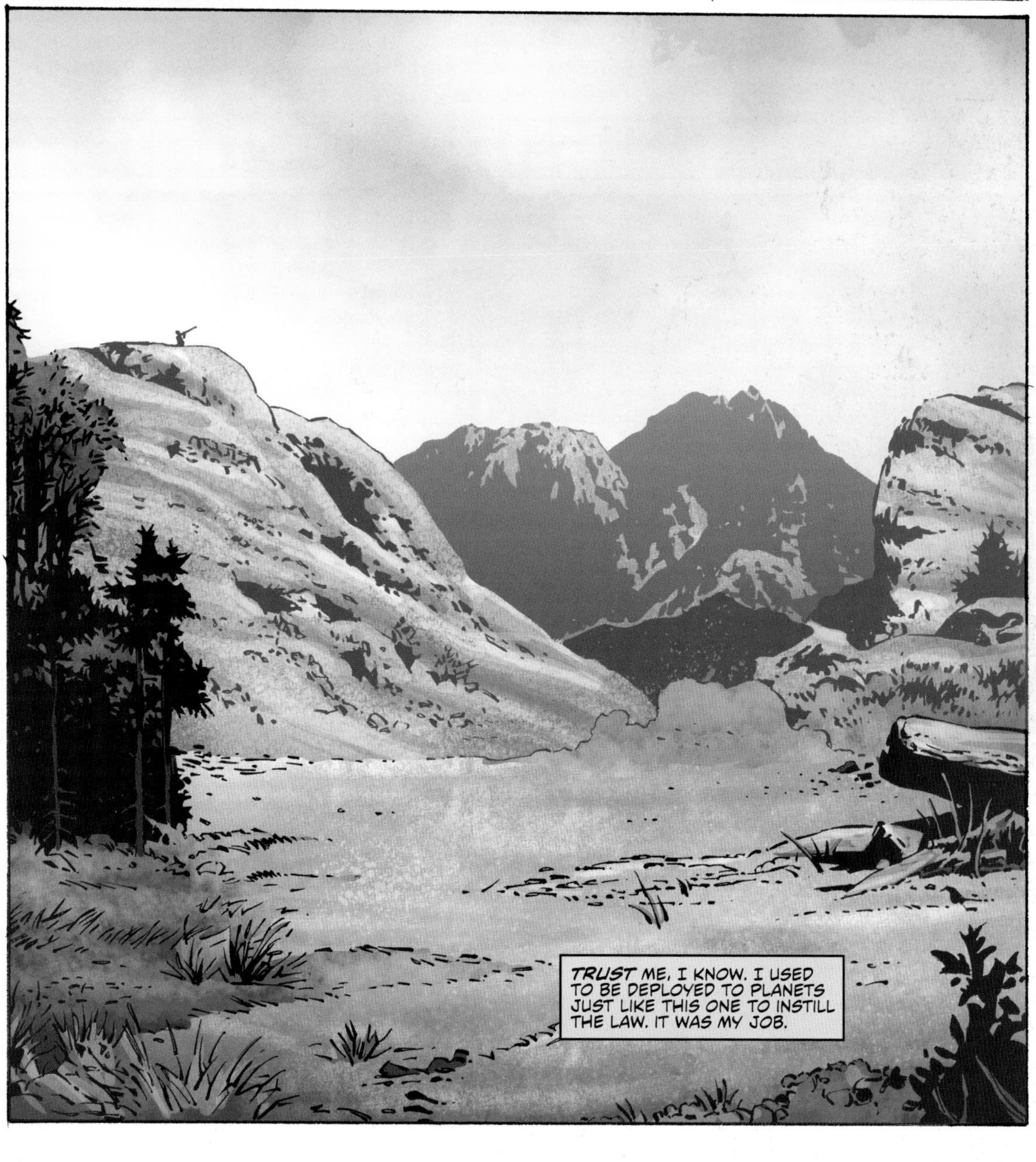
TRUST ME, I KNOW. I USED TO BE DEPLOYED TO PLANETS JUST LIKE THIS ONE TO INSTILL THE LAW. IT WAS MY JOB.

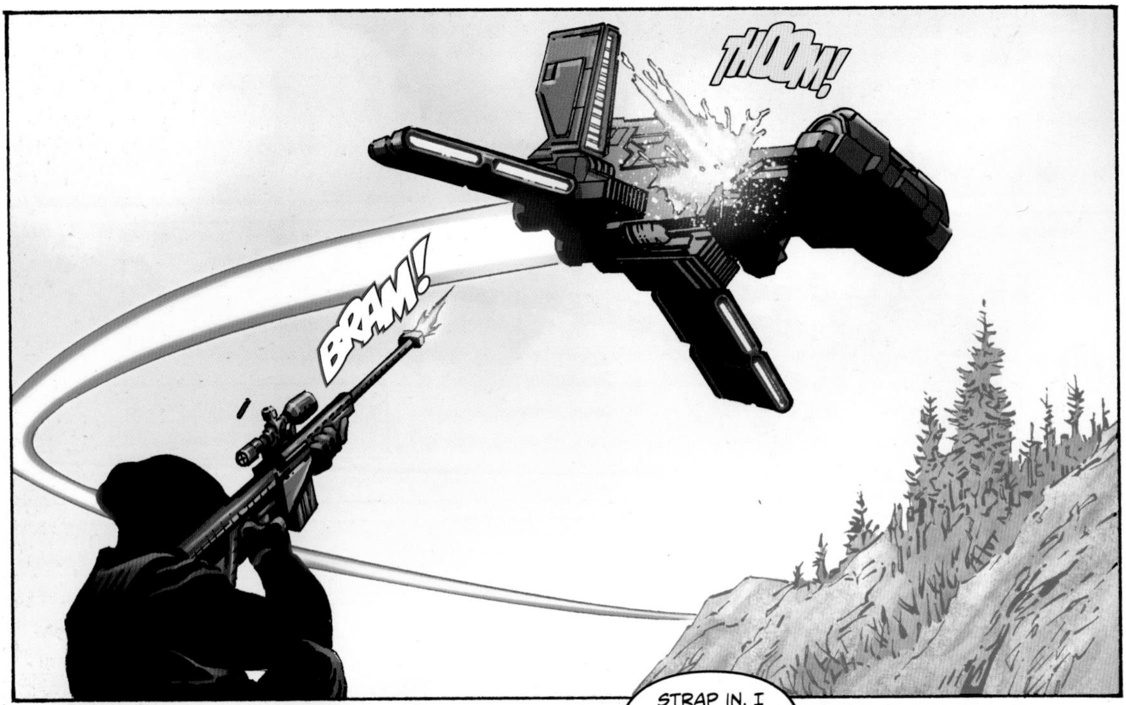
THOOM!
BRAM!

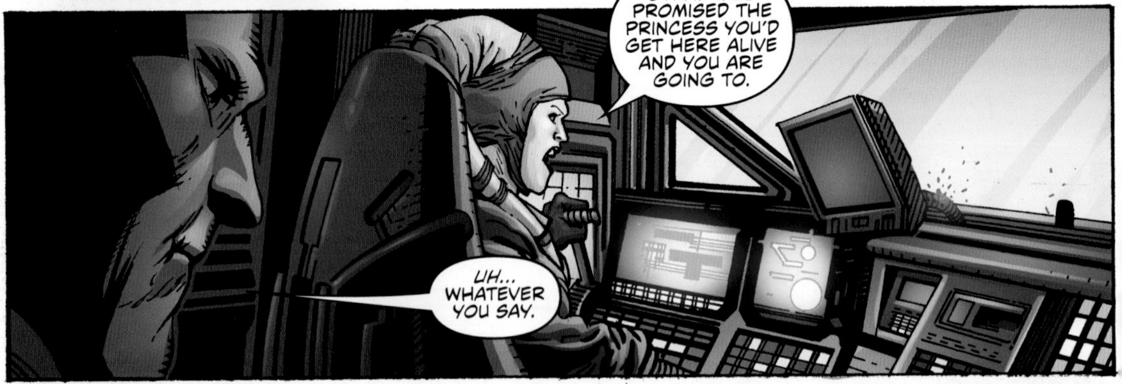
STRAP IN. I PROMISED THE PRINCESS YOU'D GET HERE ALIVE AND YOU ARE GOING TO.
UH... WHATEVER YOU SAY.

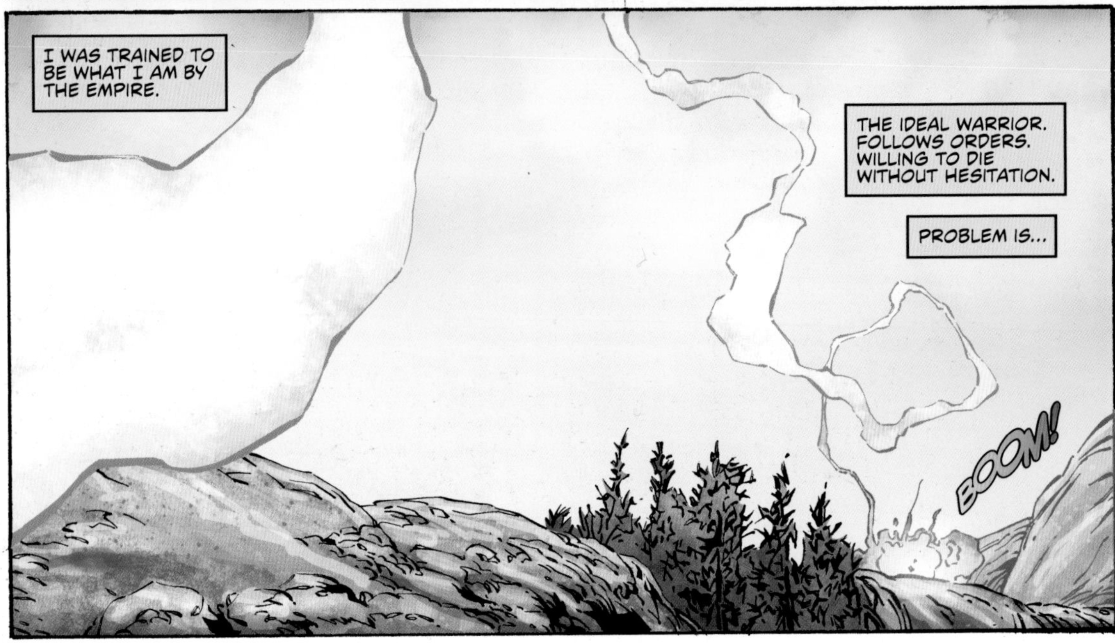
I WAS TRAINED TO BE WHAT I AM BY THE EMPIRE.
THE IDEAL WARRIOR. FOLLOWS ORDERS. WILLING TO DIE WITHOUT HESITATION.
PROBLEM IS...
BOOM!

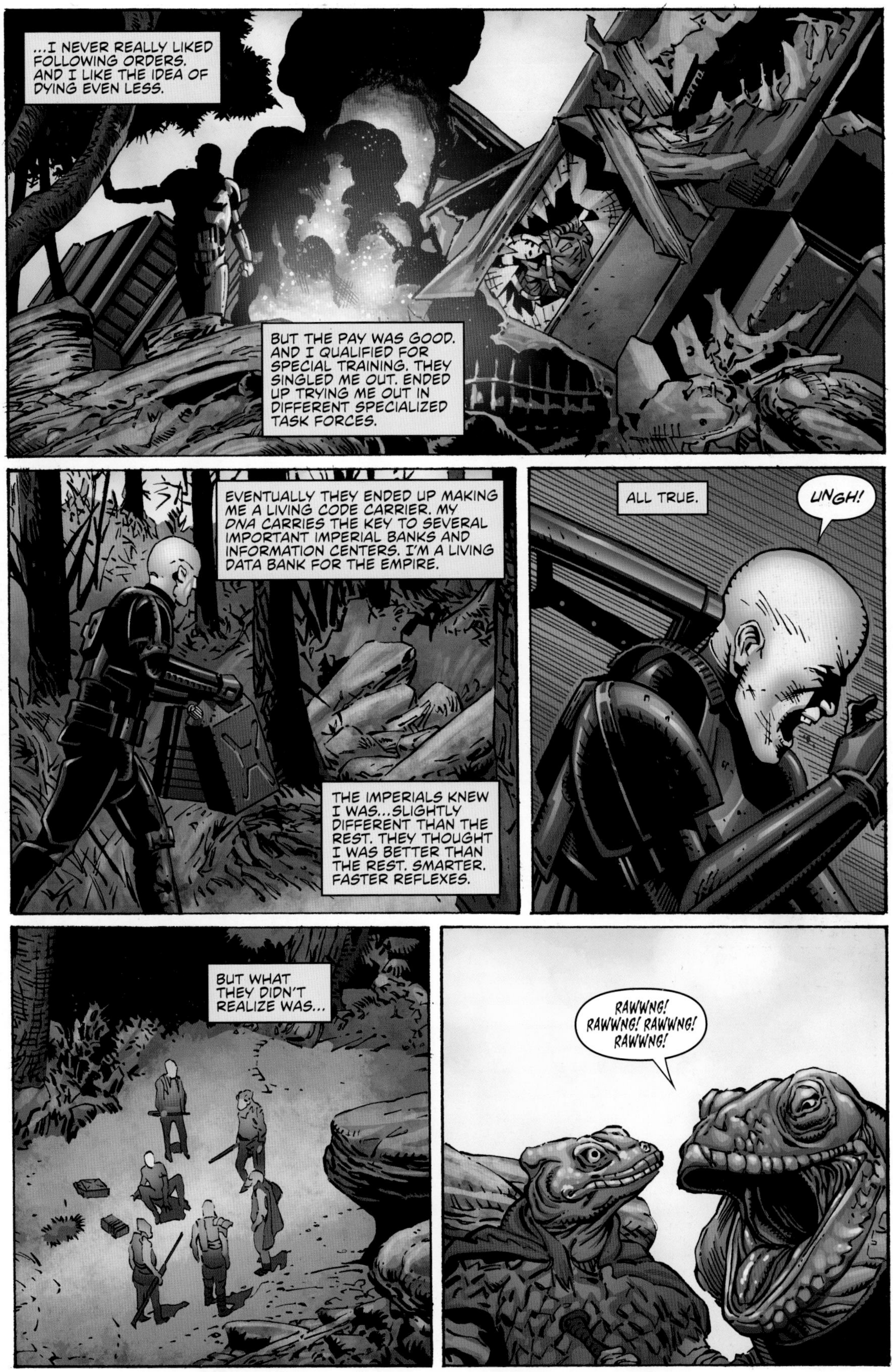
...I NEVER REALLY LIKED FOLLOWING ORDERS. AND I LIKE THE IDEA OF DYING EVEN LESS.
BUT THE PAY WAS GOOD. AND I QUALIFIED FOR SPECIAL TRAINING. THEY SINGLED ME OUT. ENDED UP TRYING ME OUT IN DIFFERENT SPECIALIZED TASK FORCES.
EVENTUALLY THEY ENDED UP MAKING ME A LIVING CODE CARRIER. MY DNA CARRIES THE KEY TO SEVERAL IMPORTANT IMPERIAL BANKS AND INFORMATION CENTERS. I'M A LIVING DATA BANK FOR THE EMPIRE.
THE IMPERIALS KNEW I WAS...SLIGHTLY DIFFERENT THAN THE REST. THEY THOUGHT I WAS BETTER THAN THE REST. SMARTER. FASTER REFLEXES.
ALL TRUE.
UNGH!
BUT WHAT THEY DIDN'T REALIZE WAS...
RAWWNG! RAWWNG! RAWWNG! RAWWNG!

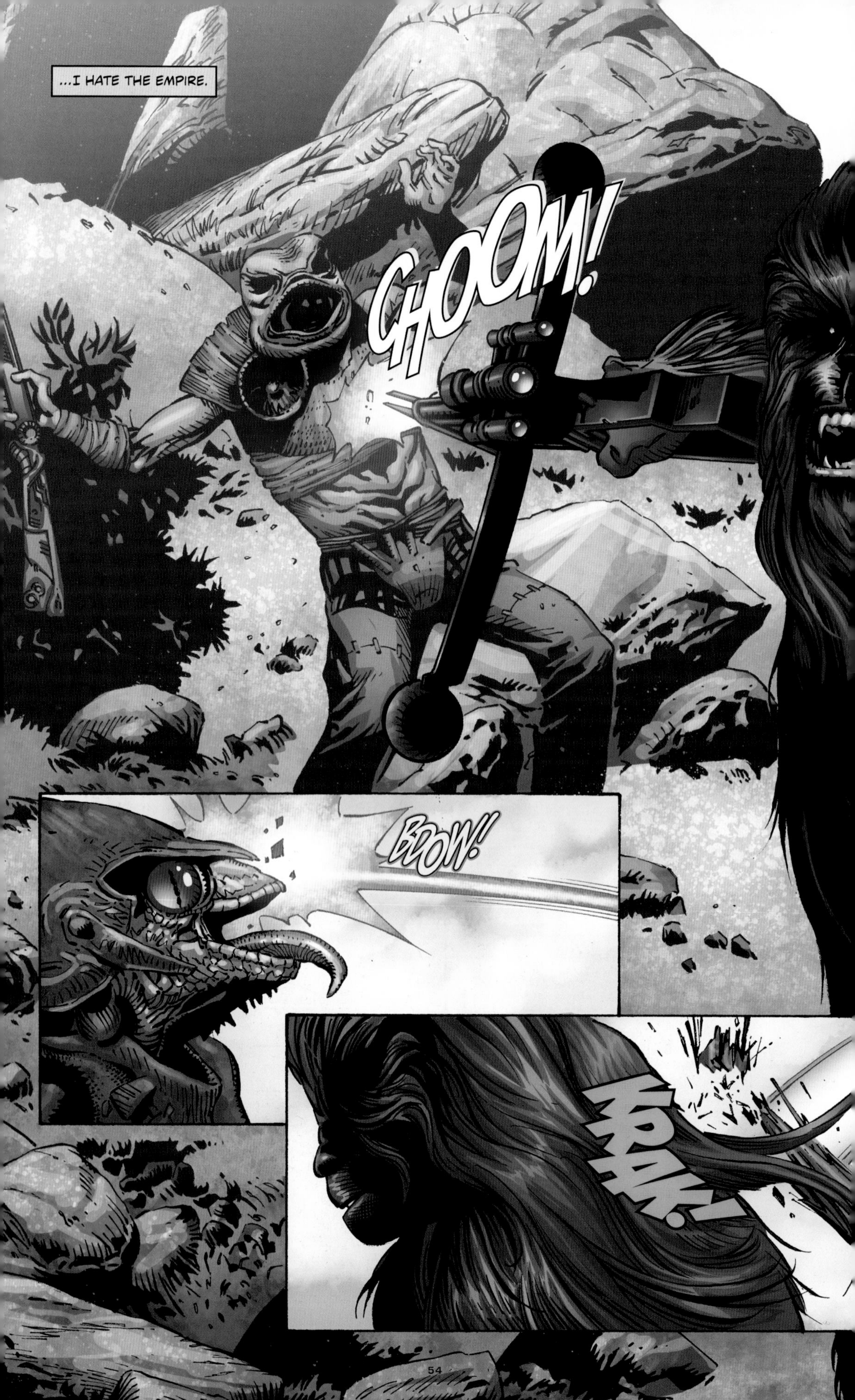
...I HATE THE EMPIRE.
CHOOM!
BOOW!
KRAK!

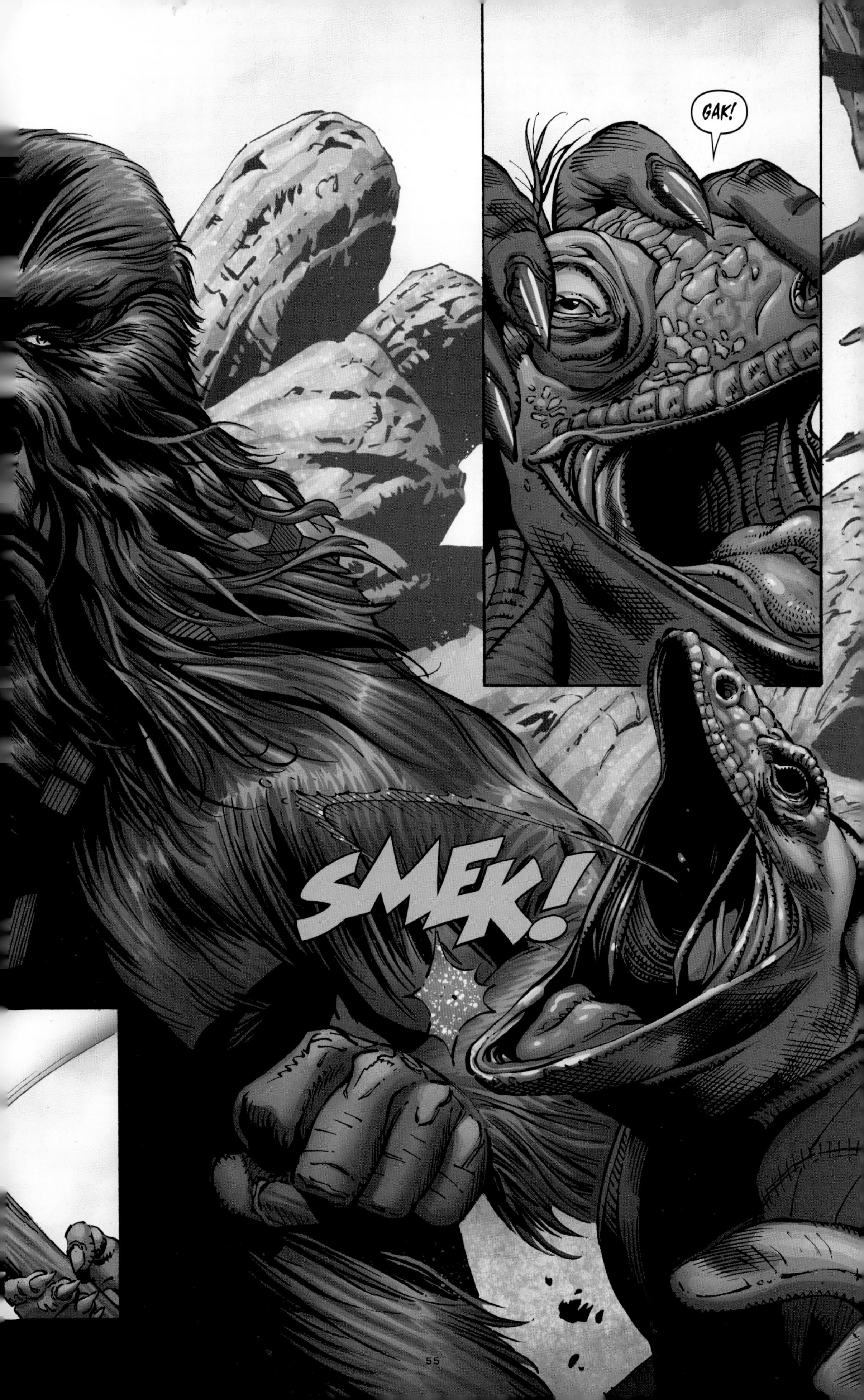
GAK!
SMEK!

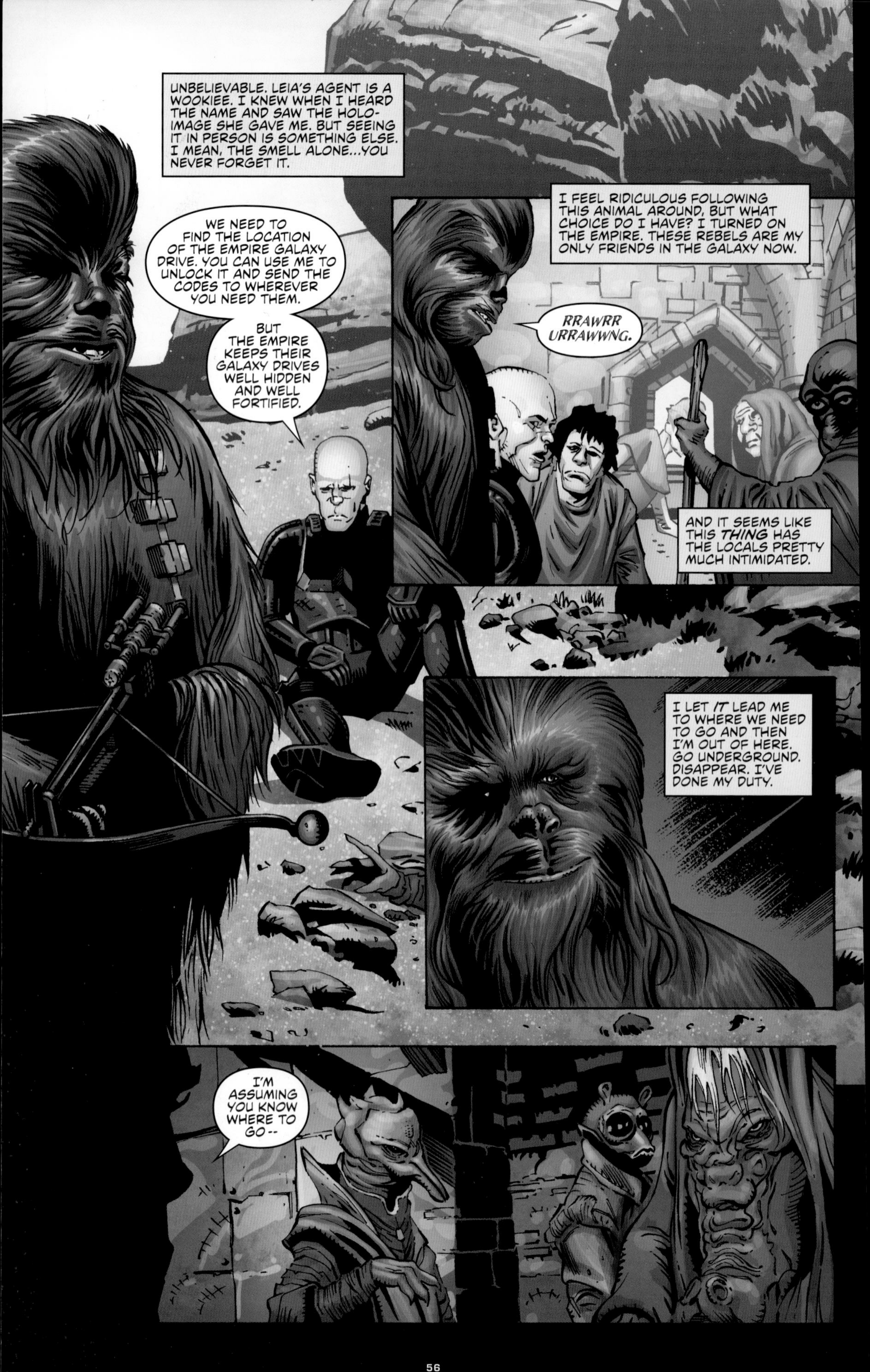
UNBELIEVABLE. LEIA'S AGENT IS A WOOKIEE. I KNEW WHEN I HEARD THE NAME AND SAW THE HOLO-IMAGE SHE GAVE ME. BUT SEEING IT IN PERSON IS SOMETHING ELSE. I MEAN, THE SMELL ALONE...YOU NEVER FORGET IT.
WE NEED TO FIND THE LOCATION OF THE EMPIRE GALAXY DRIVE. YOU CAN USE ME TO UNLOCK IT AND SEND THE CODES TO WHEREVER YOU NEED THEM.
BUT THE EMPIRE KEEPS THEIR GALAXY DRIVES WELL HIDDEN AND WELL FORTIFIED.
I FEEL RIDICULOUS FOLLOWING THIS ANIMAL AROUND, BUT WHAT CHOICE DO I HAVE? I TURNED ON THE EMPIRE. THESE REBELS ARE MY ONLY FRIENDS IN THE GALAXY NOW.
RRAWRR URRAWWNG.
AND IT SEEMS LIKE THIS THING HAS THE LOCALS PRETTY MUCH INTIMIDATED.
I LET IT LEAD ME TO WHERE WE NEED TO GO AND THEN I'M OUT OF HERE. GO UNDERGROUND. DISAPPEAR. I'VE DONE MY DUTY.
I'M ASSUMING YOU KNOW WHERE TO GO--

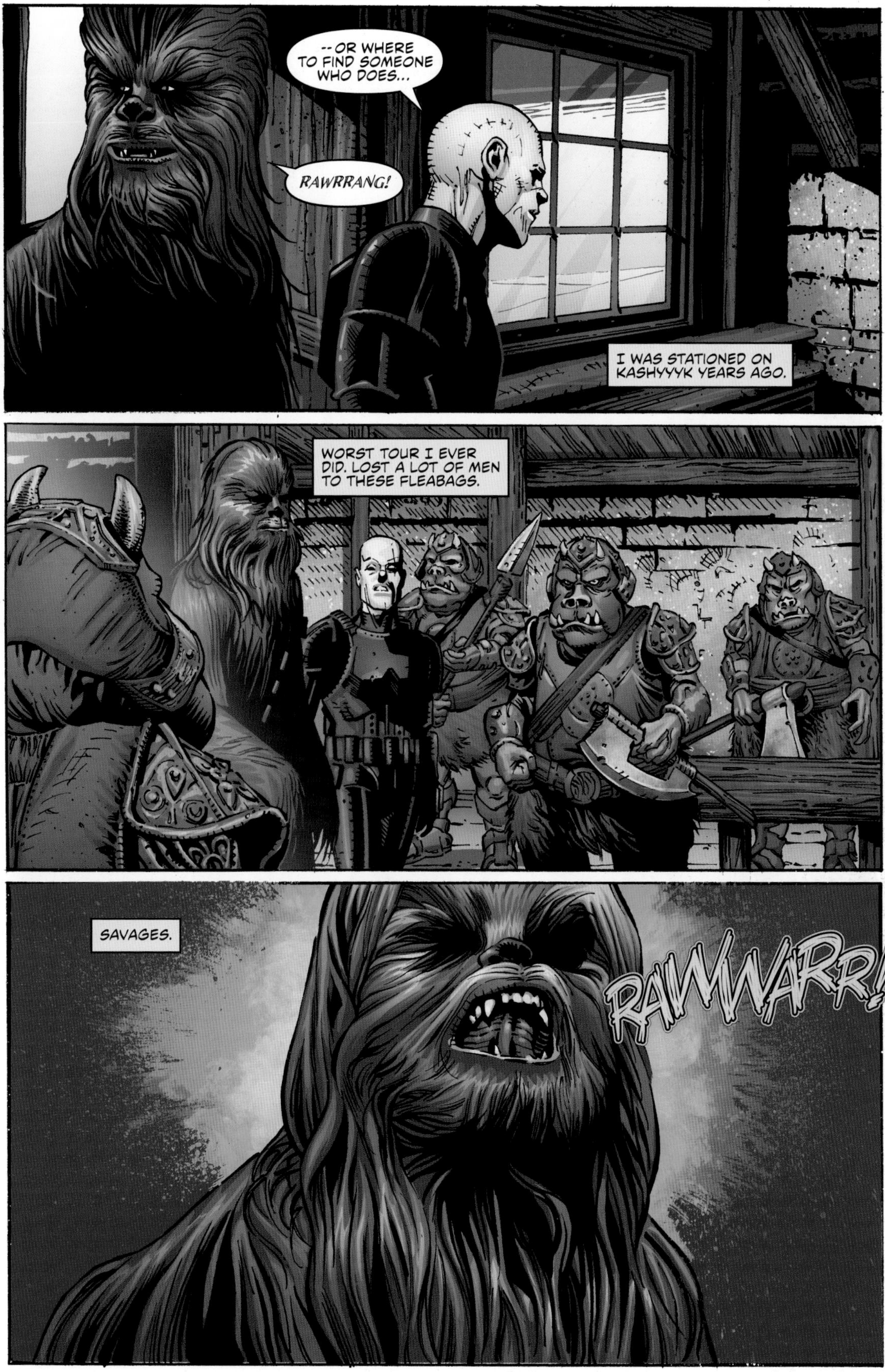
--OR WHERE TO FIND SOMEONE WHO DOES...
RAWRRANG!
I WAS STATIONED ON KASHYYYK YEARS AGO.
WORST TOUR I EVER DID. LOST A LOT OF MEN TO THESE FLEABAGS.
SAVAGES.
RAWWARR!

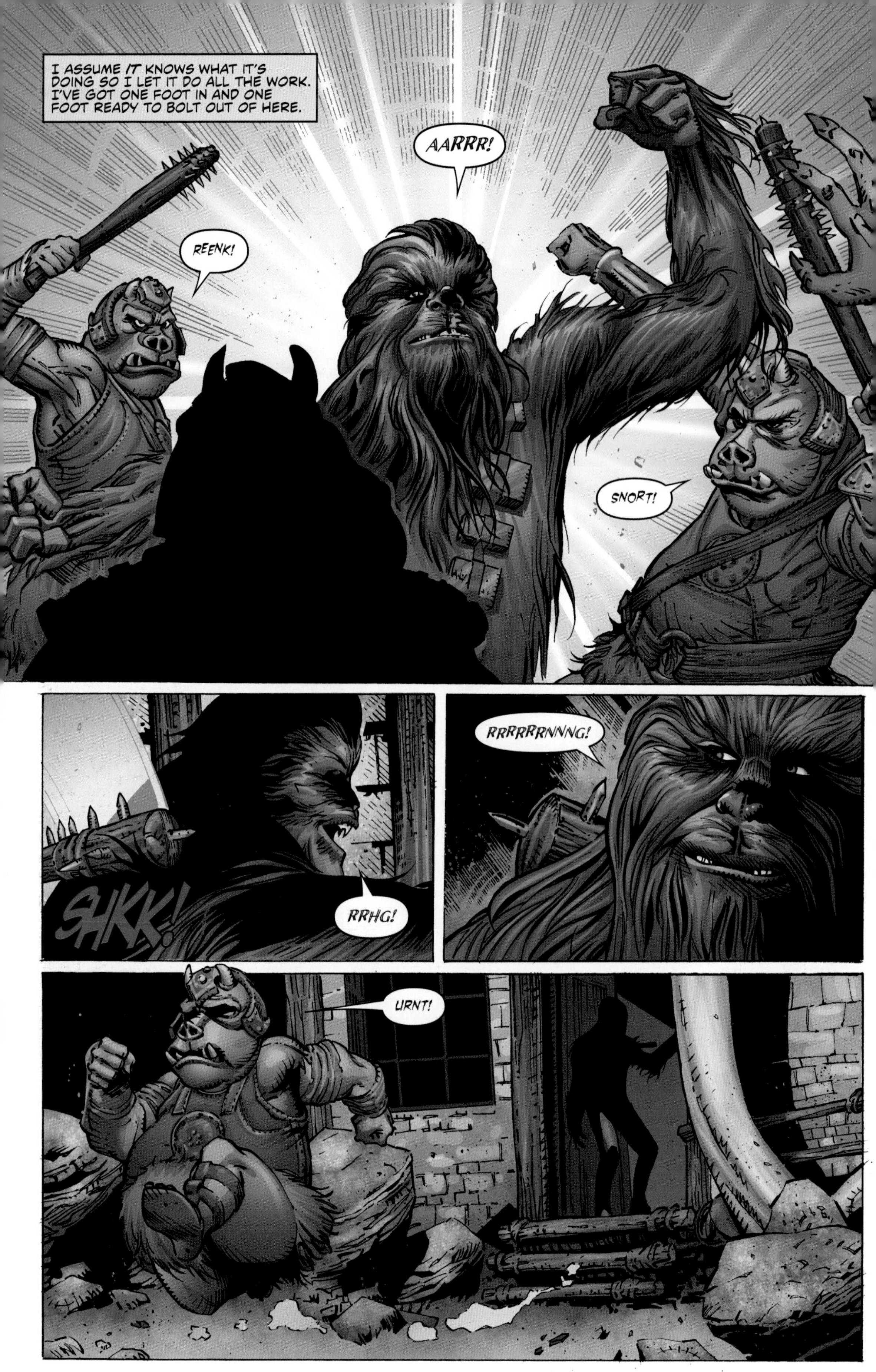
I ASSUME *IT* KNOWS WHAT IT'S DOING SO I LET IT DO ALL THE WORK. I'VE GOT ONE FOOT IN AND ONE FOOT READY TO BOLT OUT OF HERE.
AARRR!
REENK!
SNORT!
SHKK!
RRHG!
RRRRRRNNNG!
URNT!

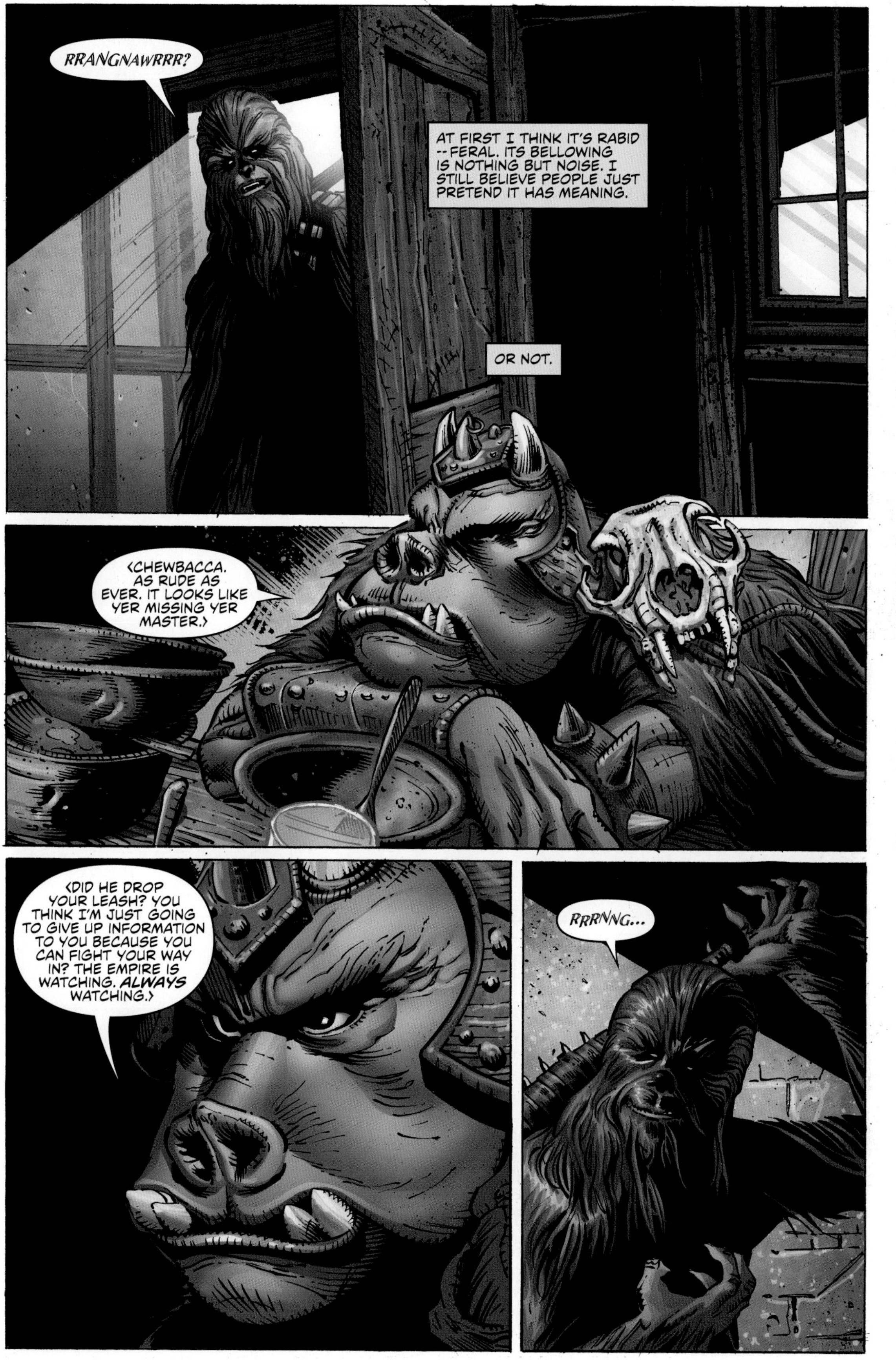
RRANGNAWRRR?
AT FIRST I THINK IT'S RABID --FERAL. ITS BELLOWING IS NOTHING BUT NOISE. I STILL BELIEVE PEOPLE JUST PRETEND IT HAS MEANING.
OR NOT.
‹CHEWBACCA. AS RUDE AS EVER. IT LOOKS LIKE YER MISSING YER MASTER.›
‹DID HE DROP YOUR LEASH? YOU THINK I'M JUST GOING TO GIVE UP INFORMATION TO YOU BECAUSE YOU CAN FIGHT YOUR WAY IN? THE EMPIRE IS WATCHING. ***ALWAYS*** WATCHING.›
RRRNNG...

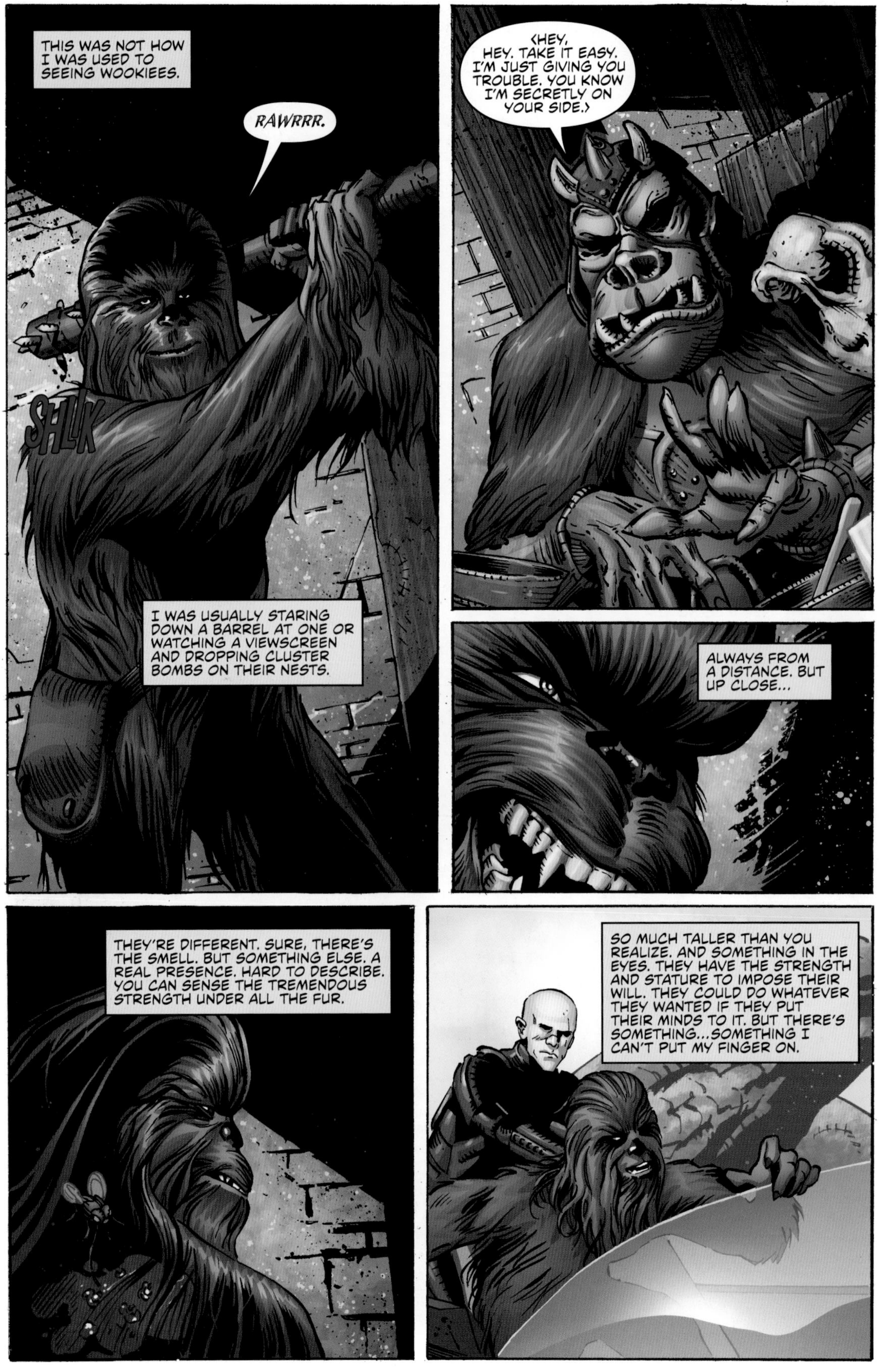
THIS WAS NOT HOW I WAS USED TO SEEING WOOKIEES.
RAWRRR.
SHLIK
I WAS USUALLY STARING DOWN A BARREL AT ONE OR WATCHING A VIEWSCREEN AND DROPPING CLUSTER BOMBS ON THEIR NESTS.
<HEY, HEY. TAKE IT EASY. I'M JUST GIVING YOU TROUBLE. YOU KNOW I'M SECRETLY ON YOUR SIDE.>
ALWAYS FROM A DISTANCE. BUT UP CLOSE...
THEY'RE DIFFERENT. SURE, THERE'S THE SMELL. BUT SOMETHING ELSE. A REAL PRESENCE. HARD TO DESCRIBE. YOU CAN SENSE THE TREMENDOUS STRENGTH UNDER ALL THE FUR.
SO MUCH TALLER THAN YOU REALIZE. AND SOMETHING IN THE EYES. THEY HAVE THE STRENGTH AND STATURE TO IMPOSE THEIR WILL. THEY COULD DO WHATEVER THEY WANTED IF THEY PUT THEIR MINDS TO IT. BUT THERE'S SOMETHING...SOMETHING I CAN'T PUT MY FINGER ON.

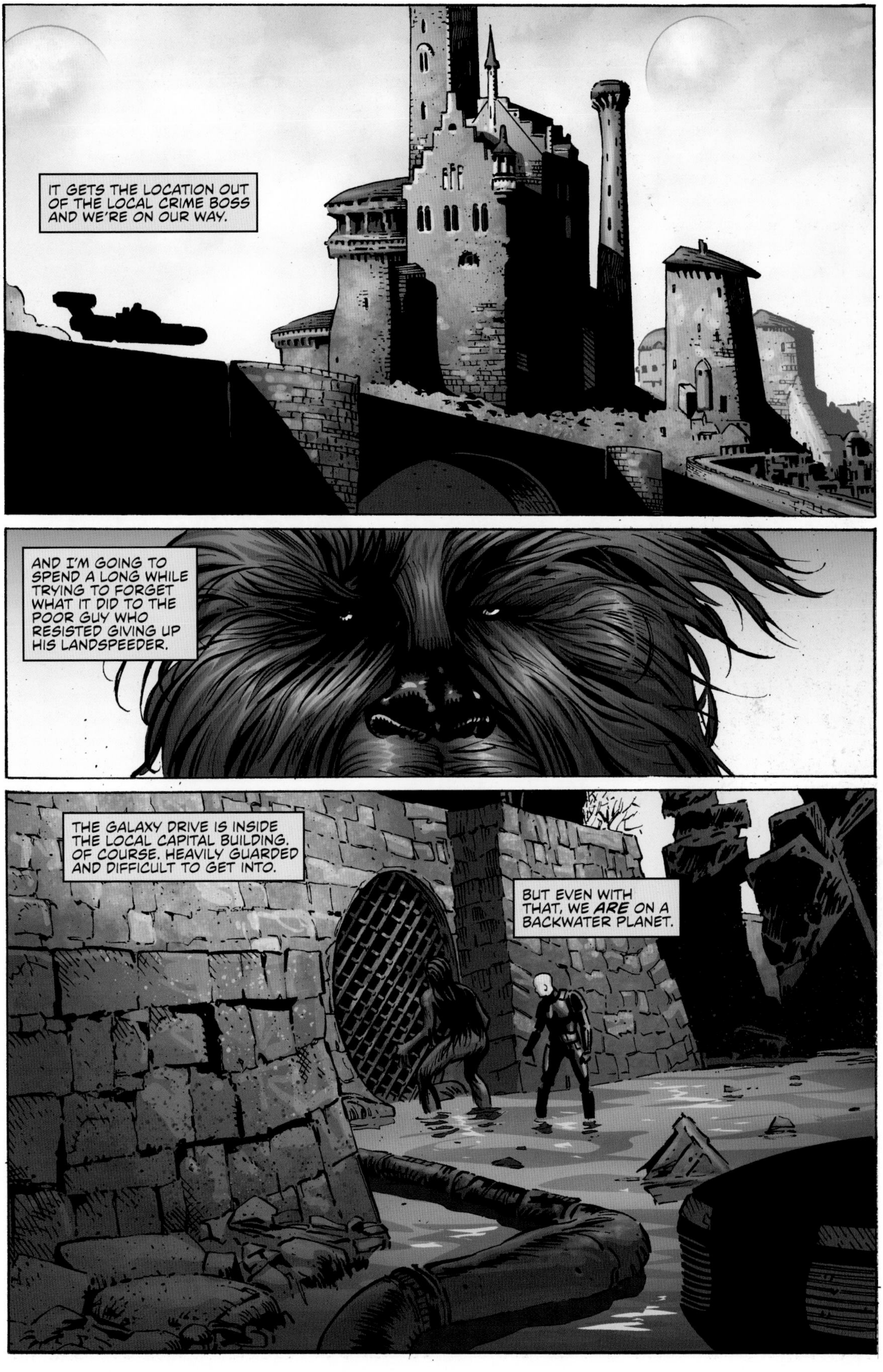
IT GETS THE LOCATION OUT OF THE LOCAL CRIME BOSS AND WE'RE ON OUR WAY.
AND I'M GOING TO SPEND A LONG WHILE TRYING TO FORGET WHAT IT DID TO THE POOR GUY WHO RESISTED GIVING UP HIS LANDSPEEDER.
THE GALAXY DRIVE IS INSIDE THE LOCAL CAPITAL BUILDING. OF COURSE. HEAVILY GUARDED AND DIFFICULT TO GET INTO.
BUT EVEN WITH THAT, WE ***ARE*** ON A BACKWATER PLANET.

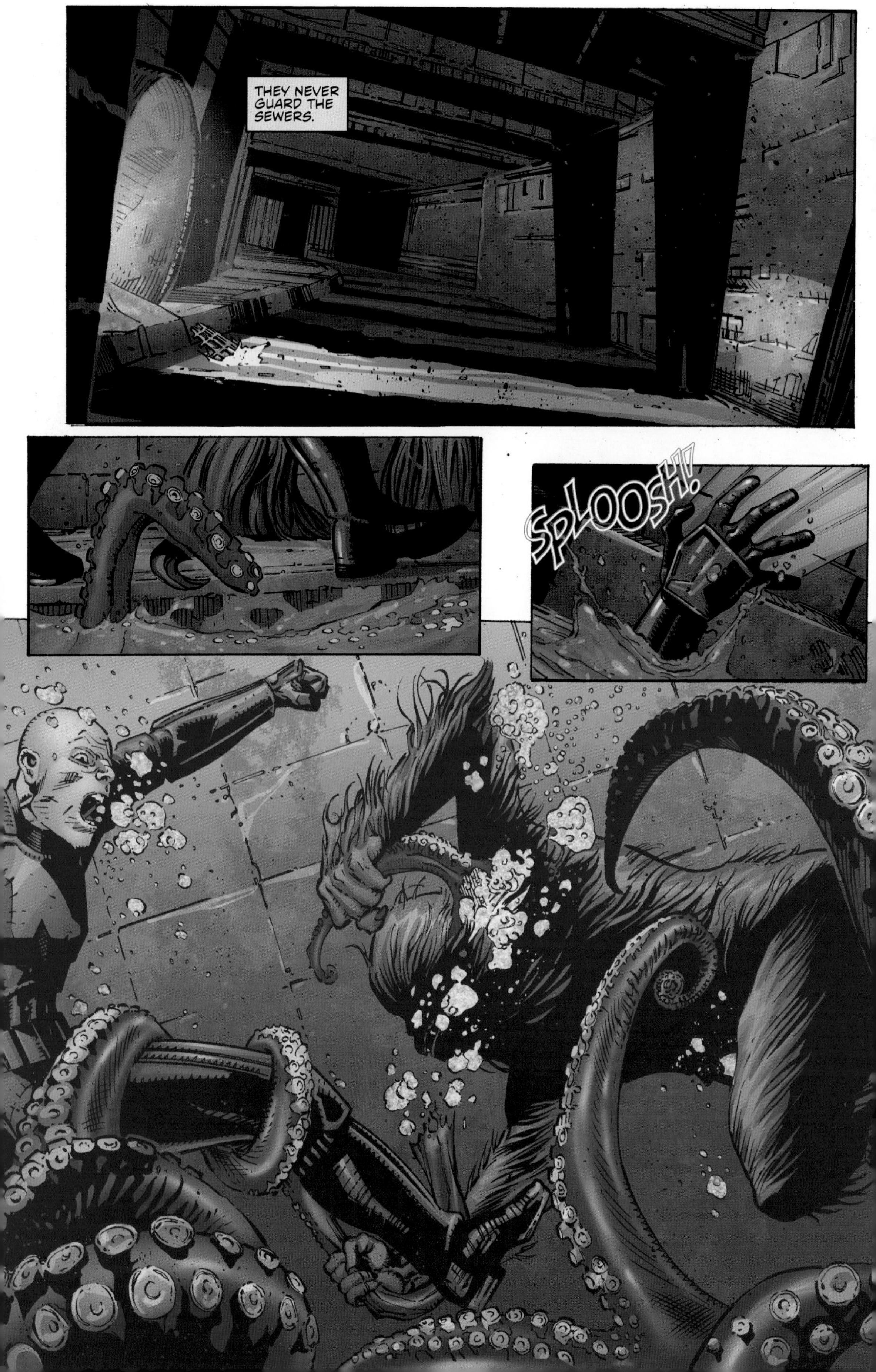
THEY NEVER GUARD THE SEWERS.
SPLOOSH!!

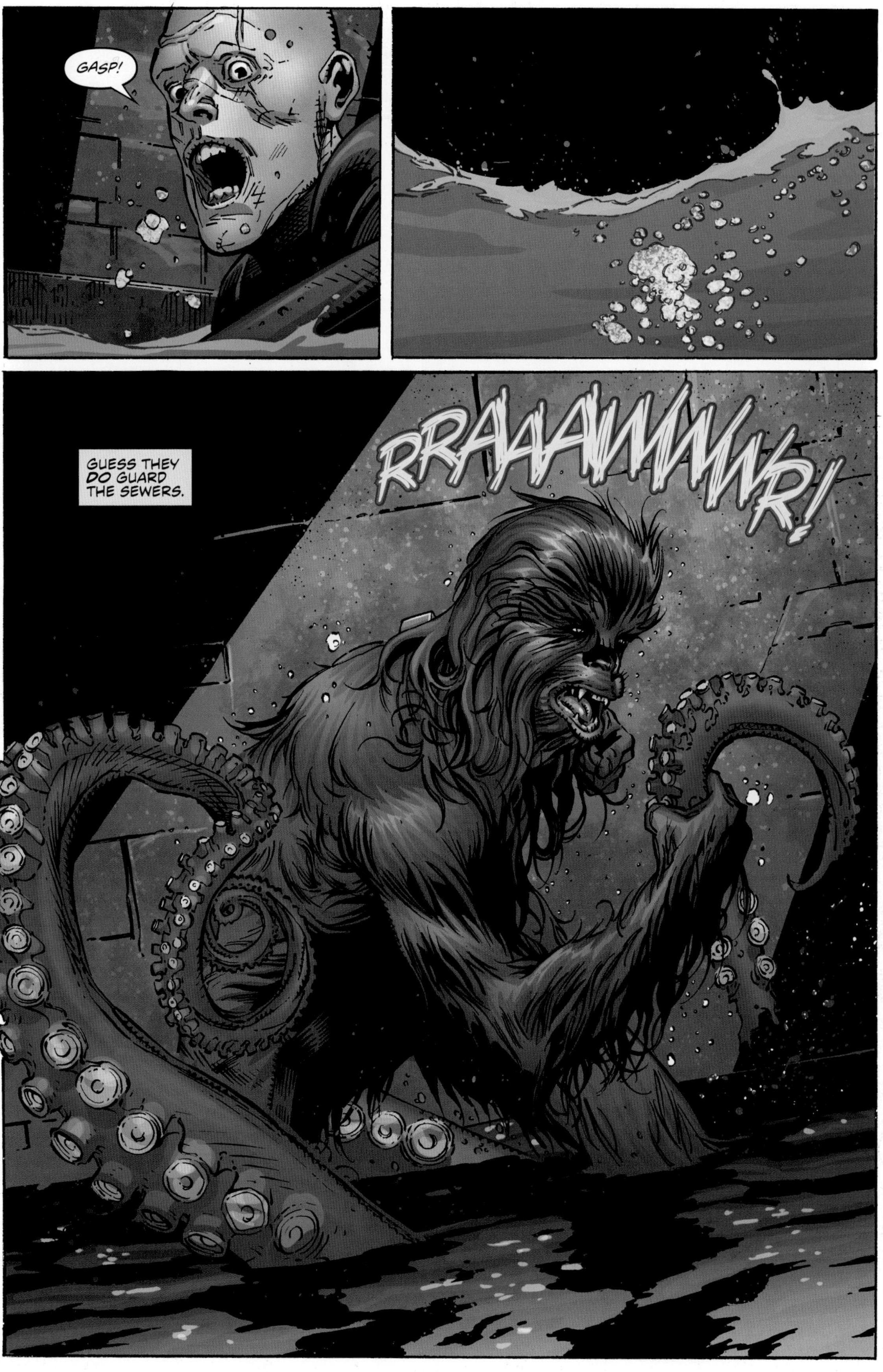
GASP!
GUESS THEY DO GUARD THE SEWERS.
RRAAAWWWR!

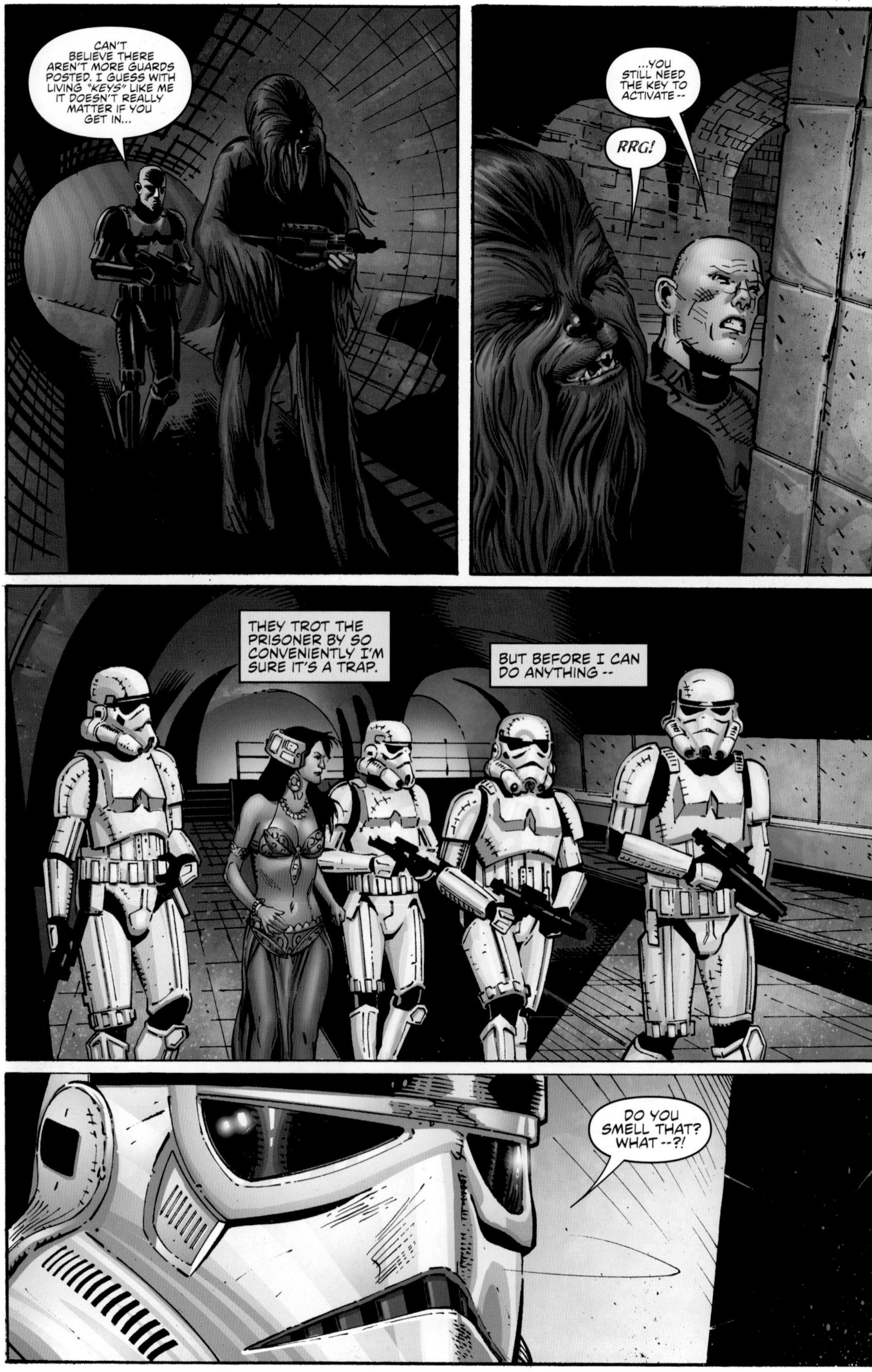
CAN'T BELIEVE THERE AREN'T MORE GUARDS POSTED. I GUESS WITH LIVING "KEYS" LIKE ME IT DOESN'T REALLY MATTER IF YOU GET IN...
...YOU STILL NEED THE KEY TO ACTIVATE --
RRG!
THEY TROT THE PRISONER BY SO CONVENIENTLY I'M SURE IT'S A TRAP.
BUT BEFORE I CAN DO ANYTHING --
DO YOU SMELL THAT? WHAT --?!

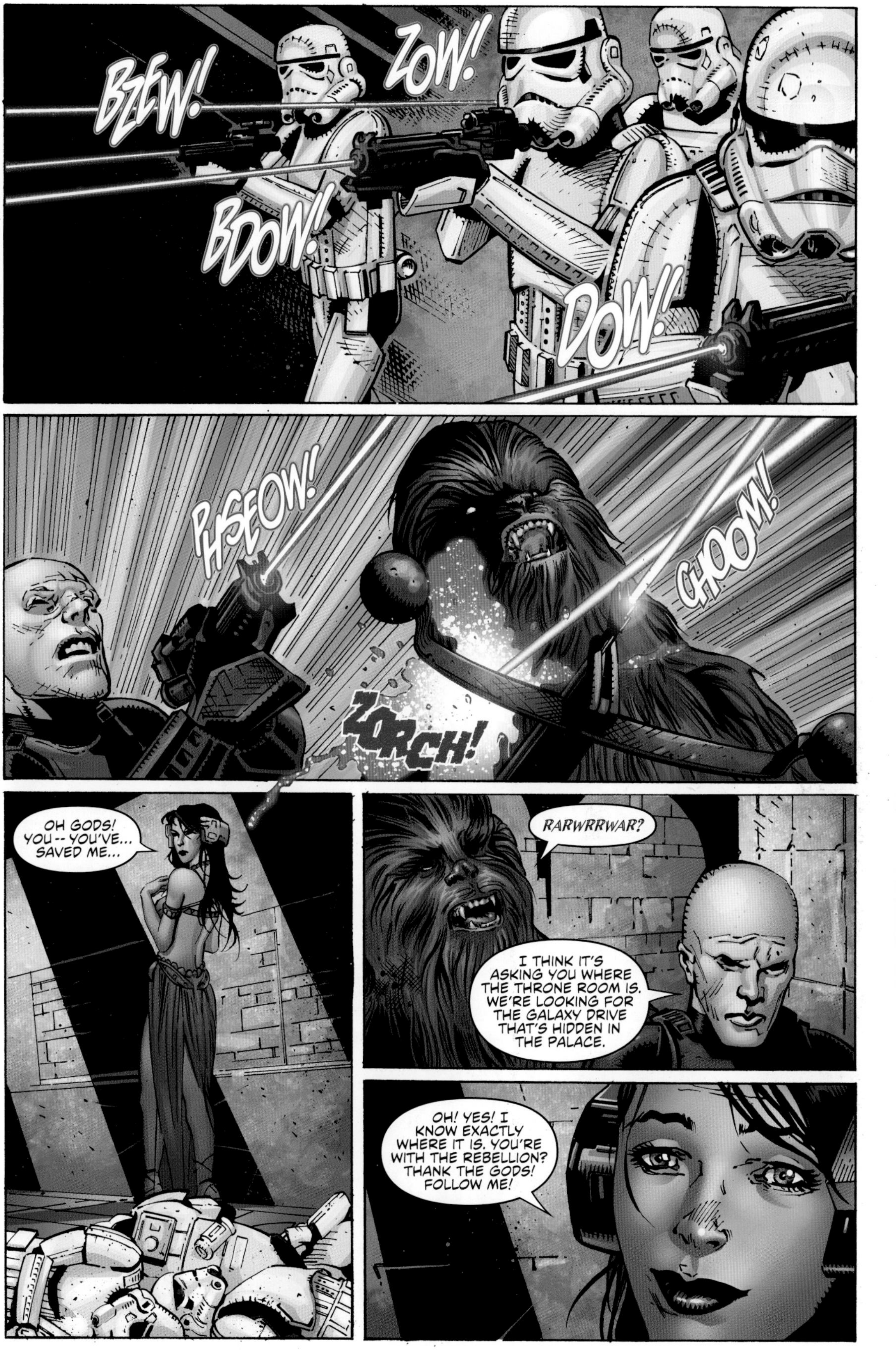
BZEW!
ZOW!
BDOW!
DOW!
PHSEOW!
CHOOM!
ZORCH!
OH GODS! YOU -- YOU'VE... SAVED ME...
RARWRRWAR?
I THINK IT'S ASKING YOU WHERE THE THRONE ROOM IS. WE'RE LOOKING FOR THE GALAXY DRIVE THAT'S HIDDEN IN THE PALACE.
OH! YES! I KNOW EXACTLY WHERE IT IS. YOU'RE WITH THE REBELLION? THANK THE GODS! FOLLOW ME!

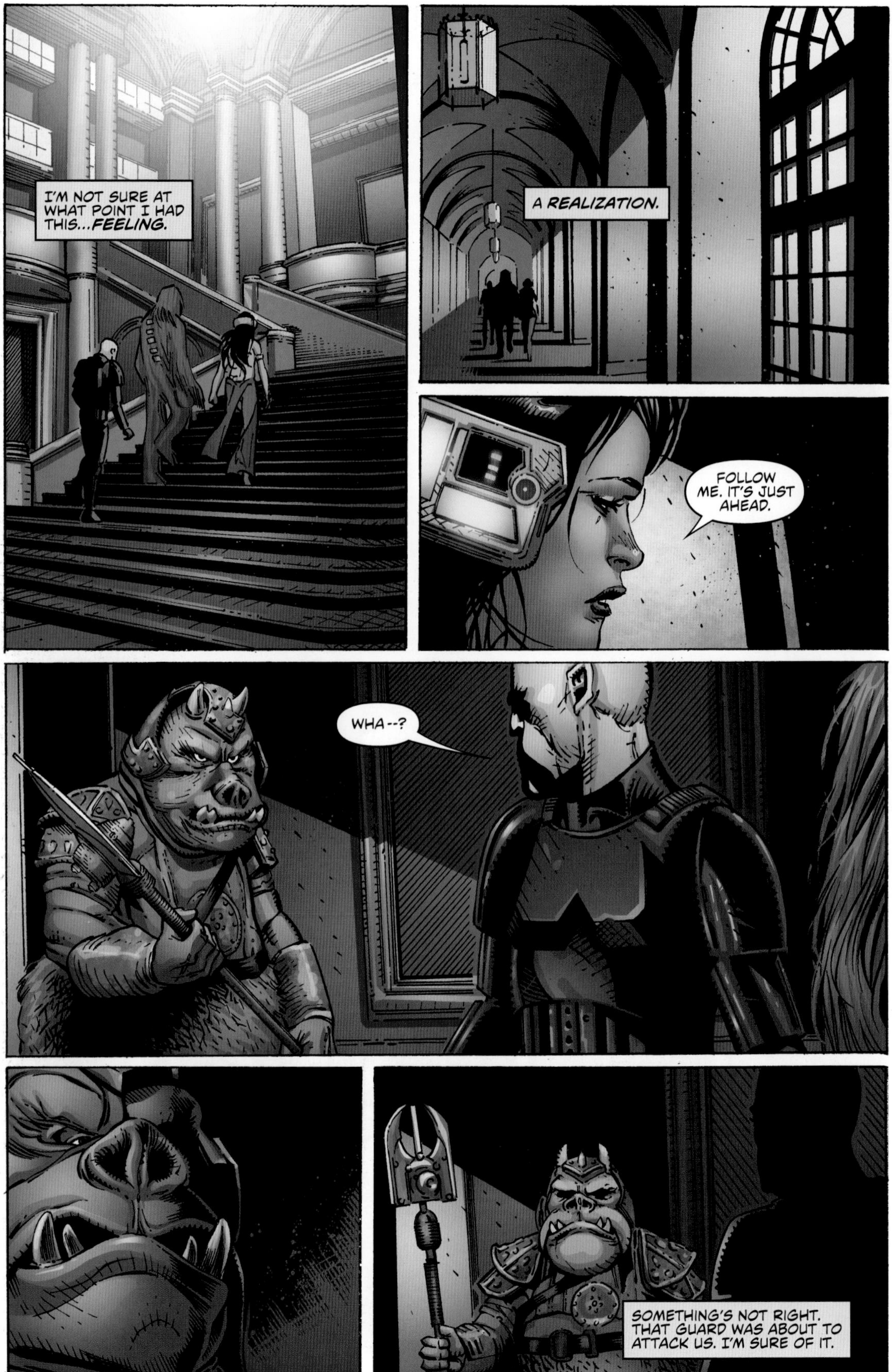
I'M NOT SURE AT WHAT POINT I HAD THIS...FEELING.
A REALIZATION.
FOLLOW ME. IT'S JUST AHEAD.
WHA--?
SOMETHING'S NOT RIGHT. THAT GUARD WAS ABOUT TO ATTACK US. I'M SURE OF IT.

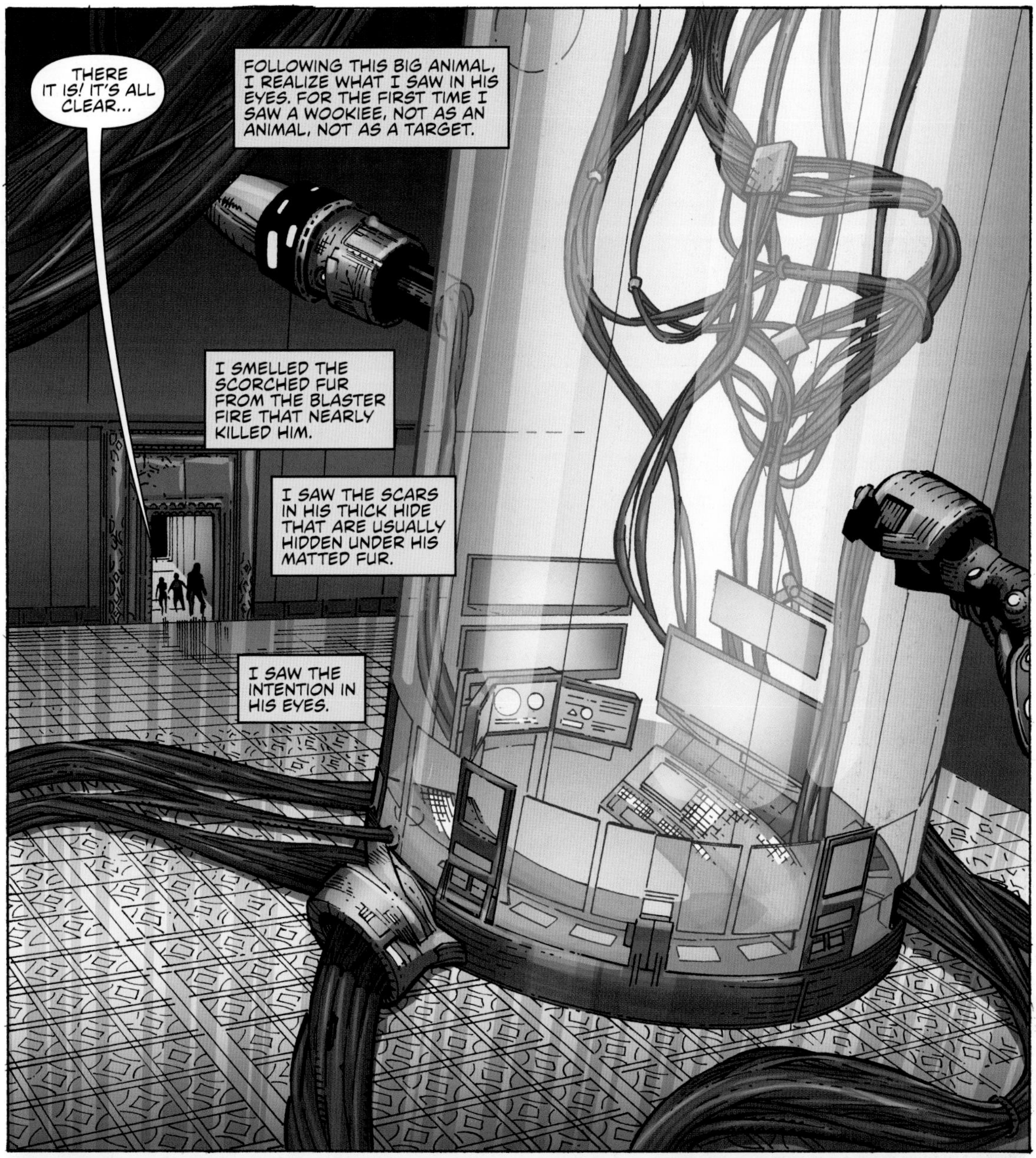
THERE IT IS! IT'S ALL CLEAR...
FOLLOWING THIS BIG ANIMAL, I REALIZE WHAT I SAW IN HIS EYES. FOR THE FIRST TIME I SAW A WOOKIEE, NOT AS AN ANIMAL, NOT AS A TARGET.
I SMELLED THE SCORCHED FUR FROM THE BLASTER FIRE THAT NEARLY KILLED HIM.
I SAW THE SCARS IN HIS THICK HIDE THAT ARE USUALLY HIDDEN UNDER HIS MATTED FUR.
I SAW THE INTENTION IN HIS EYES.

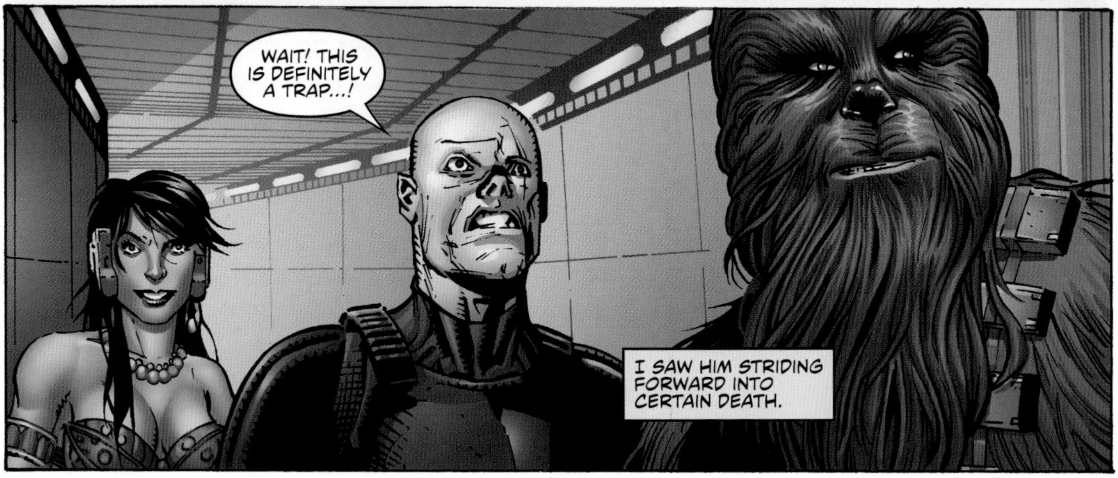
WAIT! THIS IS DEFINITELY A TRAP...!
I SAW HIM STRIDING FORWARD INTO CERTAIN DEATH.

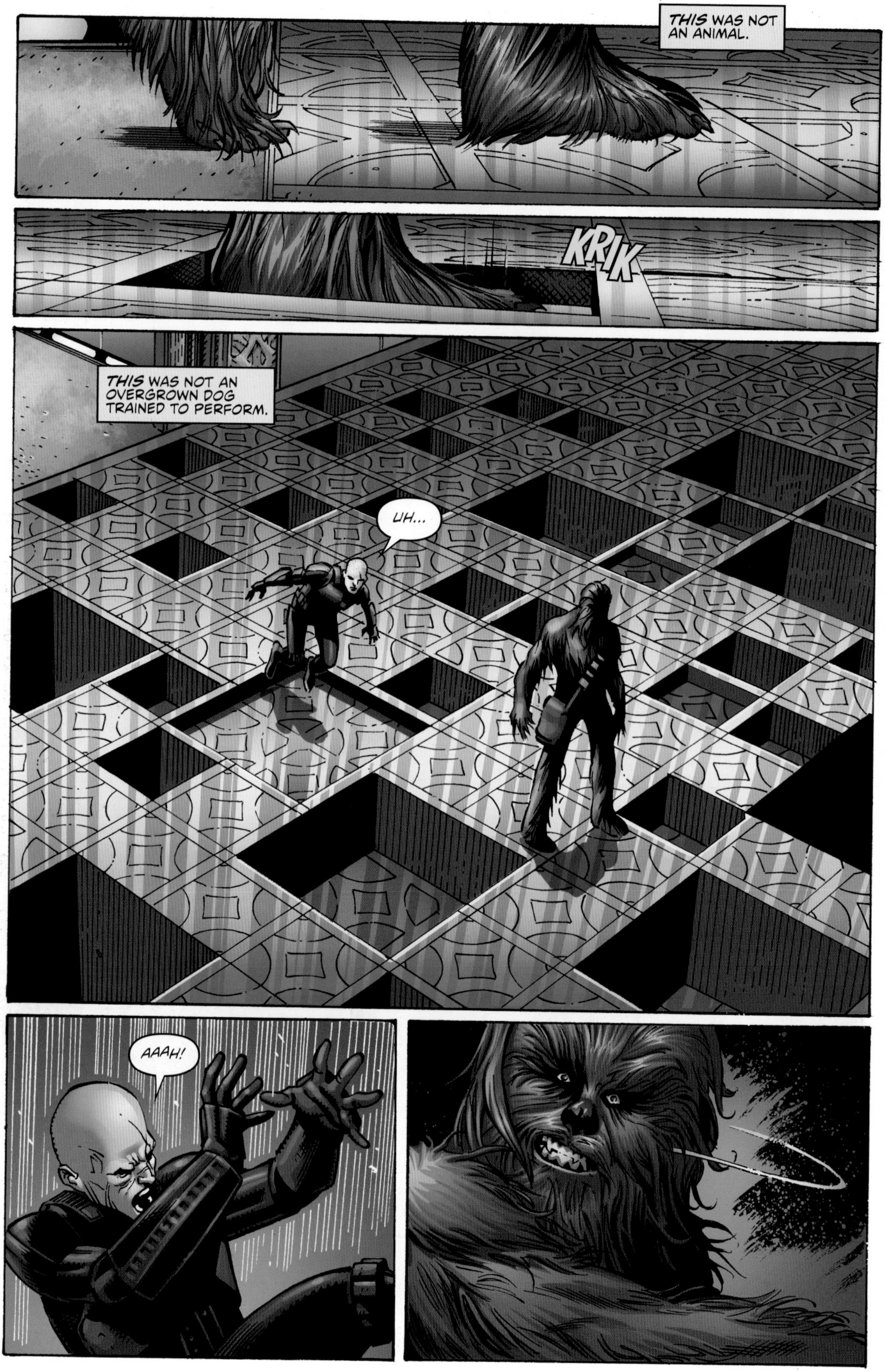
THIS WAS NOT AN ANIMAL.
KRIK
THIS WAS NOT AN OVERGROWN DOG TRAINED TO PERFORM.
UH...
AAAH!

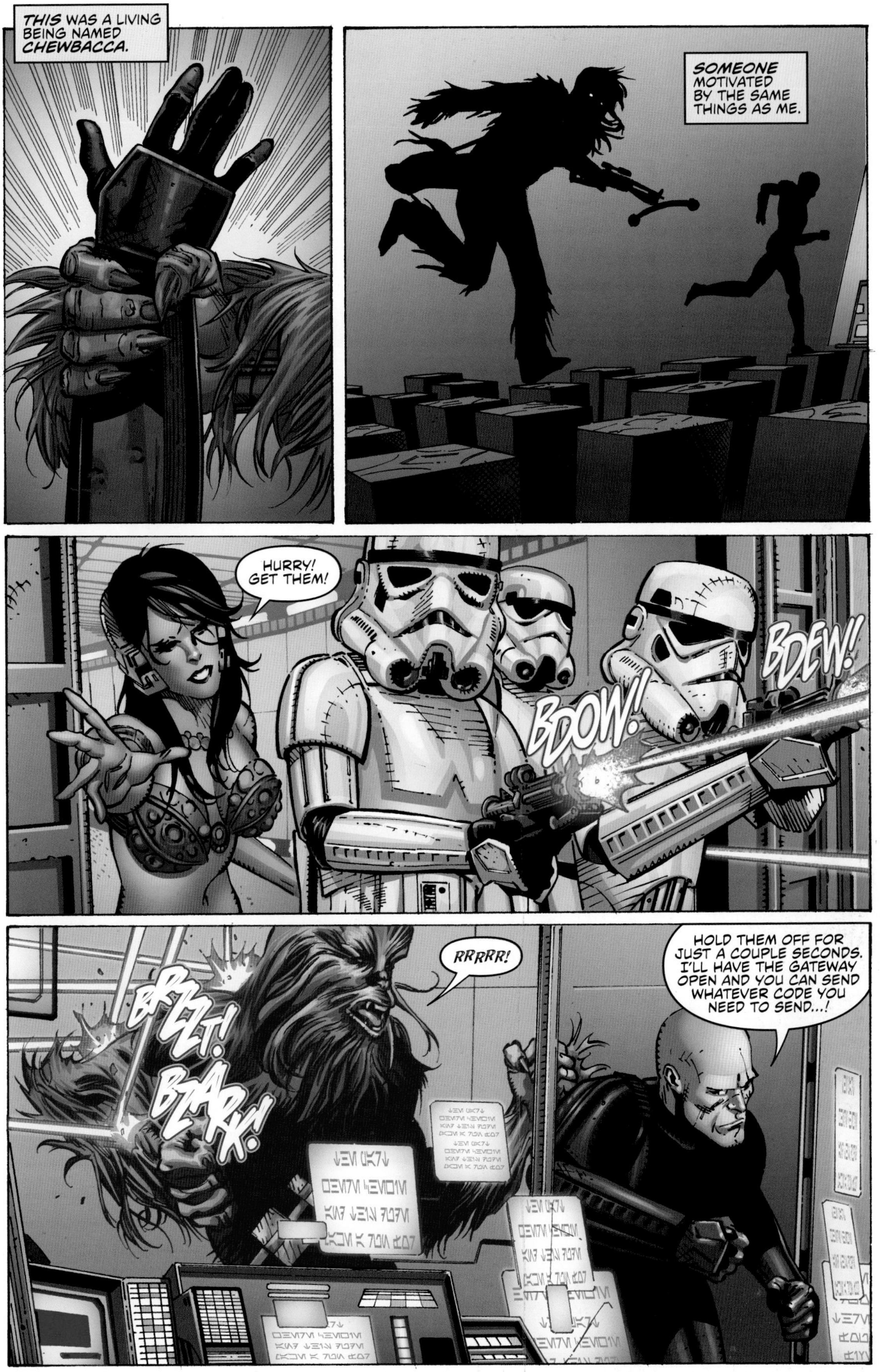
THIS WAS A LIVING BEING NAMED CHEWBACCA.
SOMEONE MOTIVATED BY THE SAME THINGS AS ME.
HURRY! GET THEM!
BDOW!
BDEW!
BRZZT!
BZARK!
RRRRR!
HOLD THEM OFF FOR JUST A COUPLE SECONDS. I'LL HAVE THE GATEWAY OPEN AND YOU CAN SEND WHATEVER CODE YOU NEED TO SEND...!

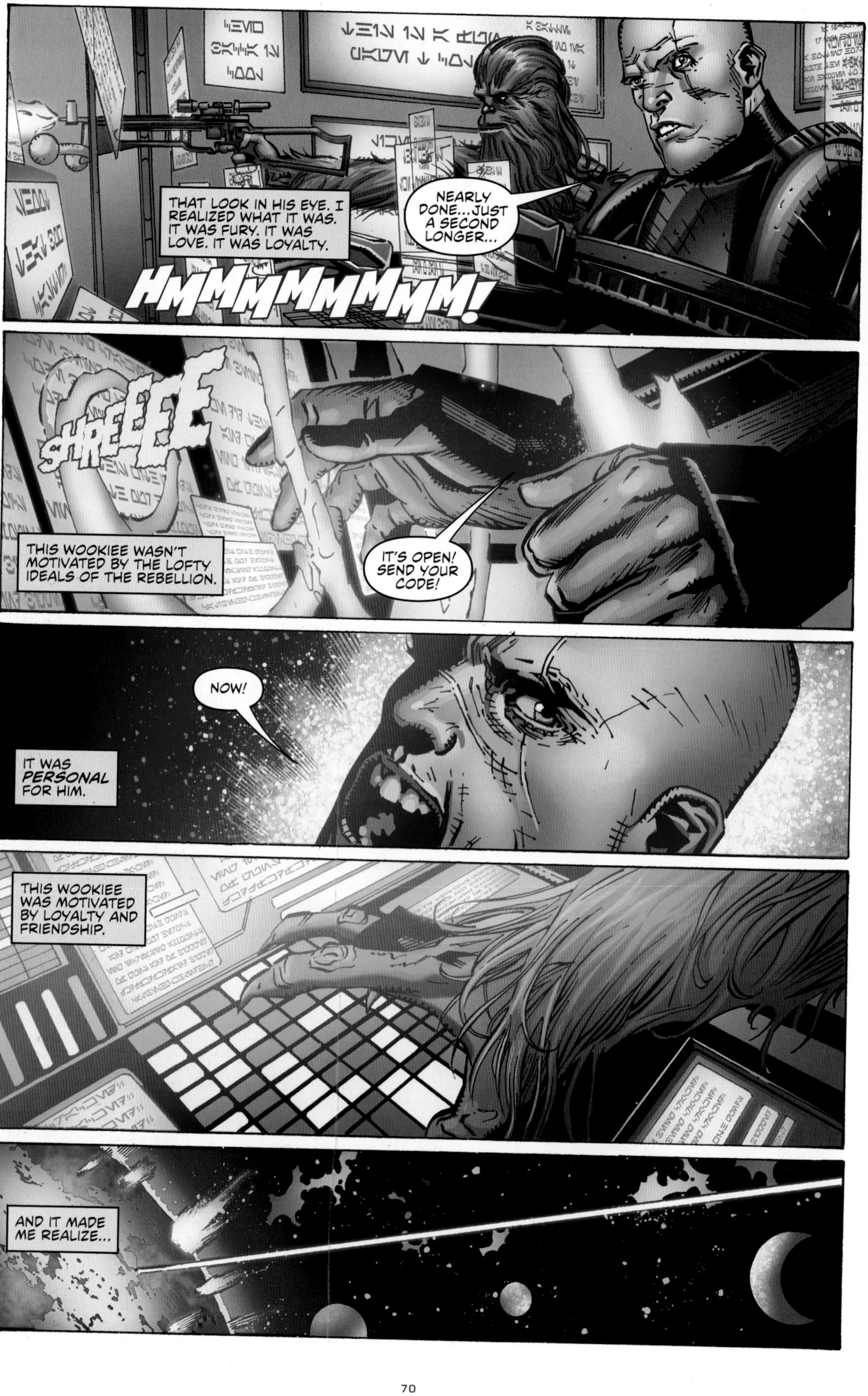

THAT LOOK IN HIS EYE. I REALIZED WHAT IT WAS. IT WAS FURY. IT WAS LOVE. IT WAS LOYALTY.
NEARLY DONE...JUST A SECOND LONGER...
HMMMMMMMMMM!
SHREEEE
THIS WOOKIEE WASN'T MOTIVATED BY THE LOFTY IDEALS OF THE REBELLION.
IT'S OPEN! SEND YOUR CODE!
IT WAS *PERSONAL* FOR HIM.
NOW!
THIS WOOKIEE WAS MOTIVATED BY LOYALTY AND FRIENDSHIP.
AND IT MADE ME REALIZE...

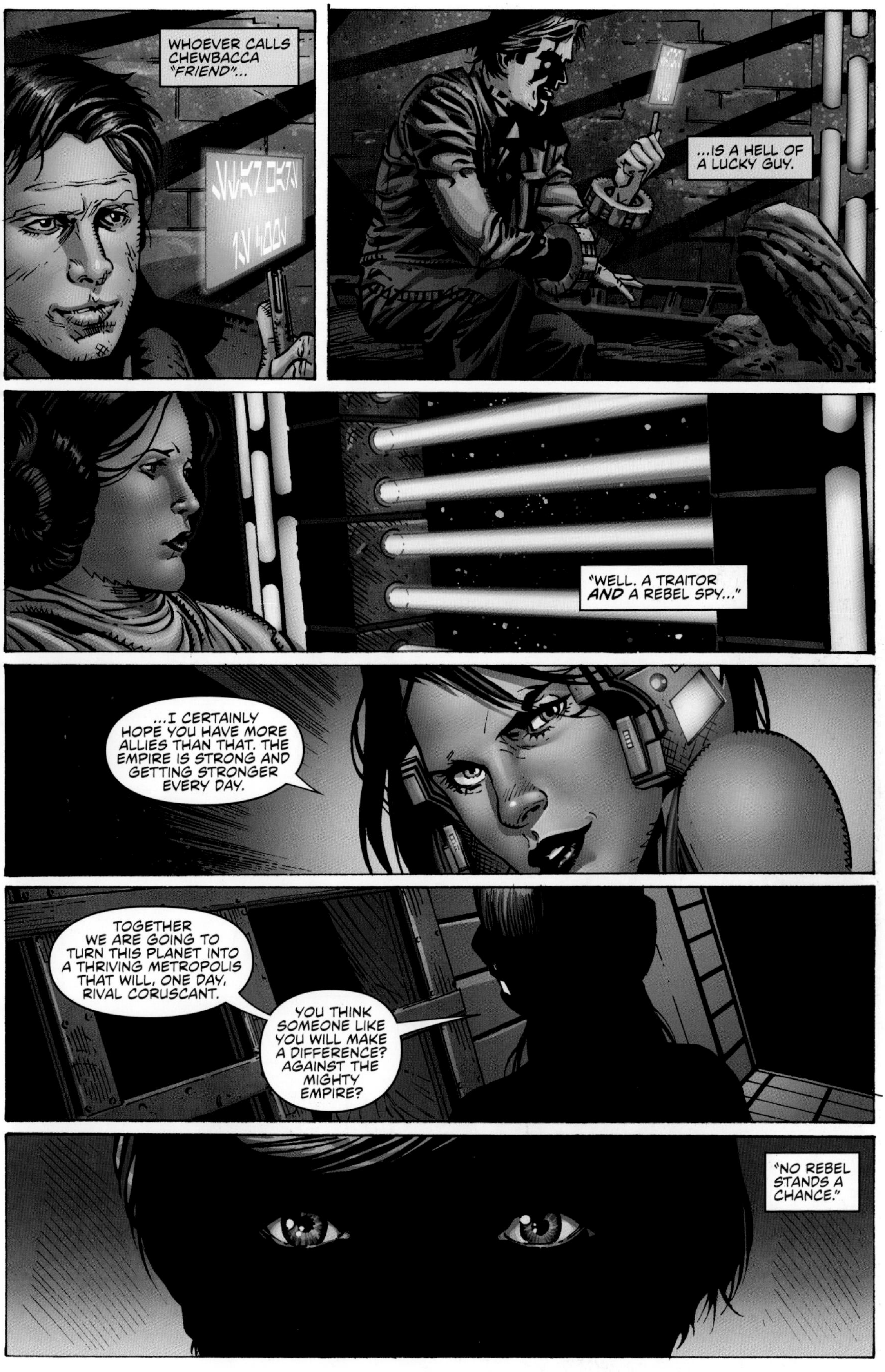

WHOEVER CALLS CHEWBACCA "FRIEND"...
...IS A HELL OF A LUCKY GUY.
"WELL, A TRAITOR AND A REBEL SPY..."
...I CERTAINLY HOPE YOU HAVE MORE ALLIES THAN THAT. THE EMPIRE IS STRONG AND GETTING STRONGER EVERY DAY.
TOGETHER WE ARE GOING TO TURN THIS PLANET INTO A THRIVING METROPOLIS THAT WILL, ONE DAY, RIVAL CORUSCANT.
YOU THINK SOMEONE LIKE YOU WILL MAKE A DIFFERENCE? AGAINST THE MIGHTY EMPIRE?
"NO REBEL STANDS A CHANCE."

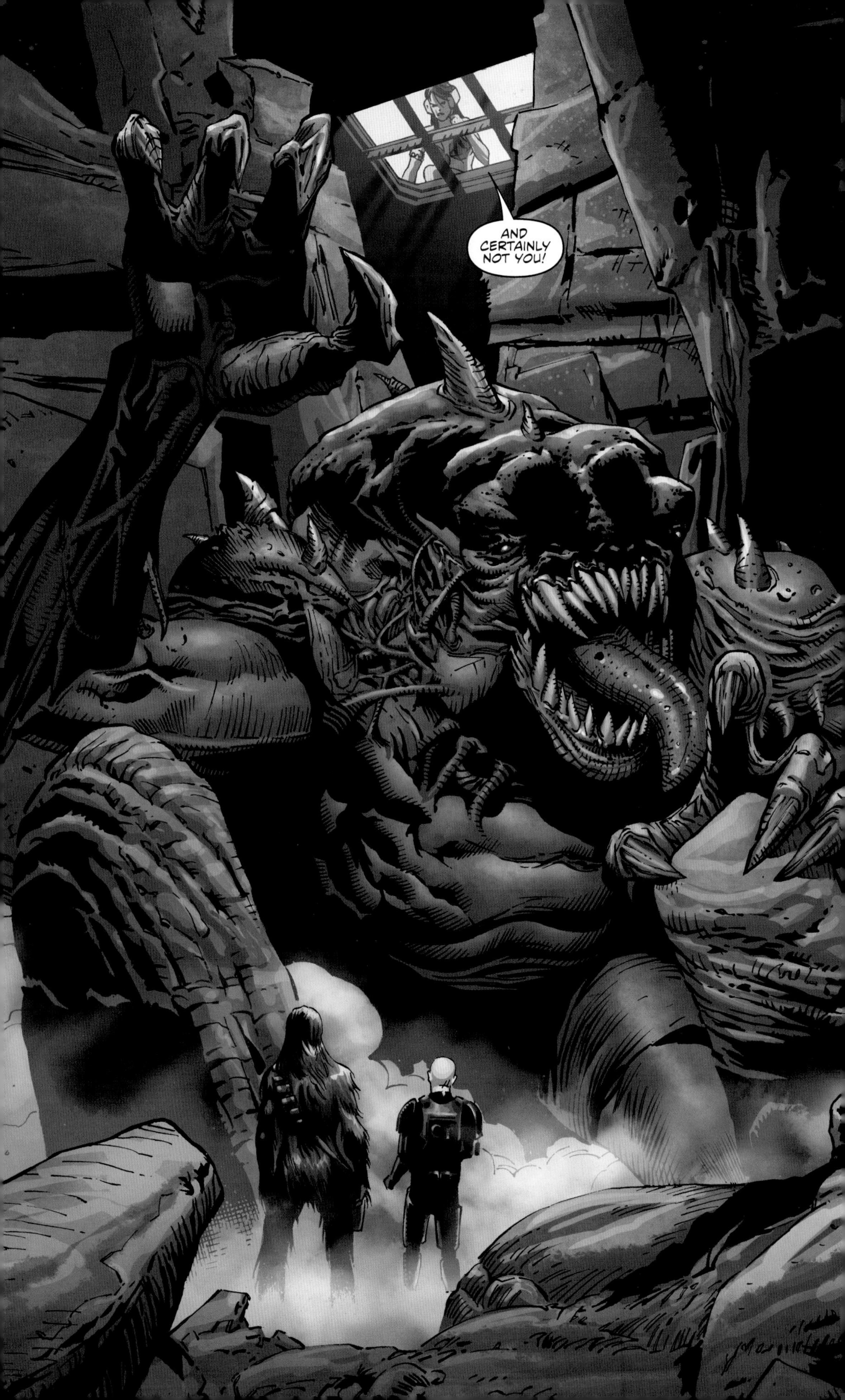
AND CERTAINLY NOT YOU!

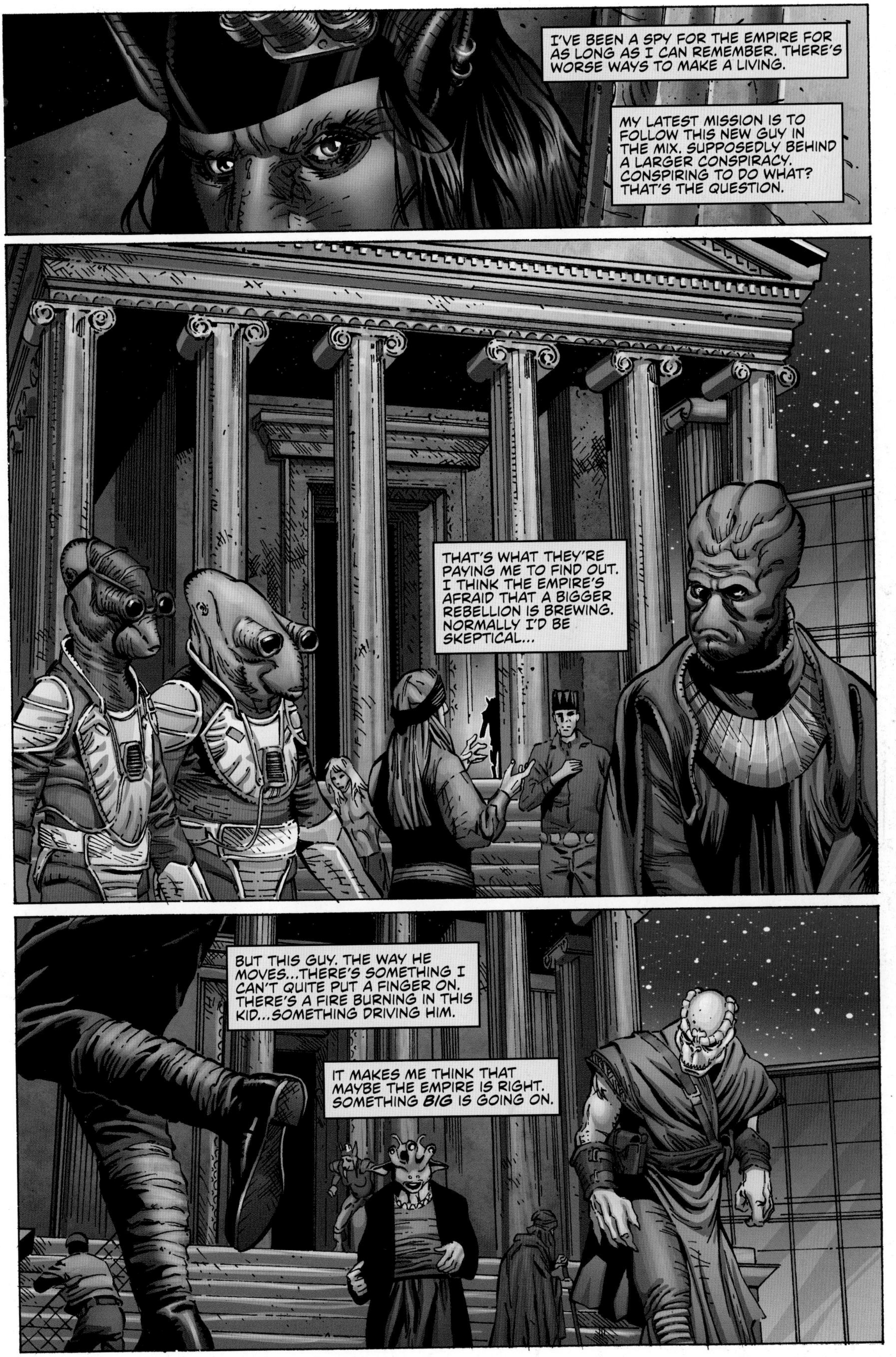
I'VE BEEN A SPY FOR THE EMPIRE FOR AS LONG AS I CAN REMEMBER. THERE'S WORSE WAYS TO MAKE A LIVING.
MY LATEST MISSION IS TO FOLLOW THIS NEW GUY IN THE MIX. SUPPOSEDLY BEHIND A LARGER CONSPIRACY. CONSPIRING TO DO WHAT? THAT'S THE QUESTION.
THAT'S WHAT THEY'RE PAYING ME TO FIND OUT. I THINK THE EMPIRE'S AFRAID THAT A BIGGER REBELLION IS BREWING. NORMALLY I'D BE SKEPTICAL...
BUT THIS GUY. THE WAY HE MOVES...THERE'S SOMETHING I CAN'T QUITE PUT A FINGER ON. THERE'S A FIRE BURNING IN THIS KID...SOMETHING DRIVING HIM.
IT MAKES ME THINK THAT MAYBE THE EMPIRE IS RIGHT. SOMETHING *BIG* IS GOING ON.

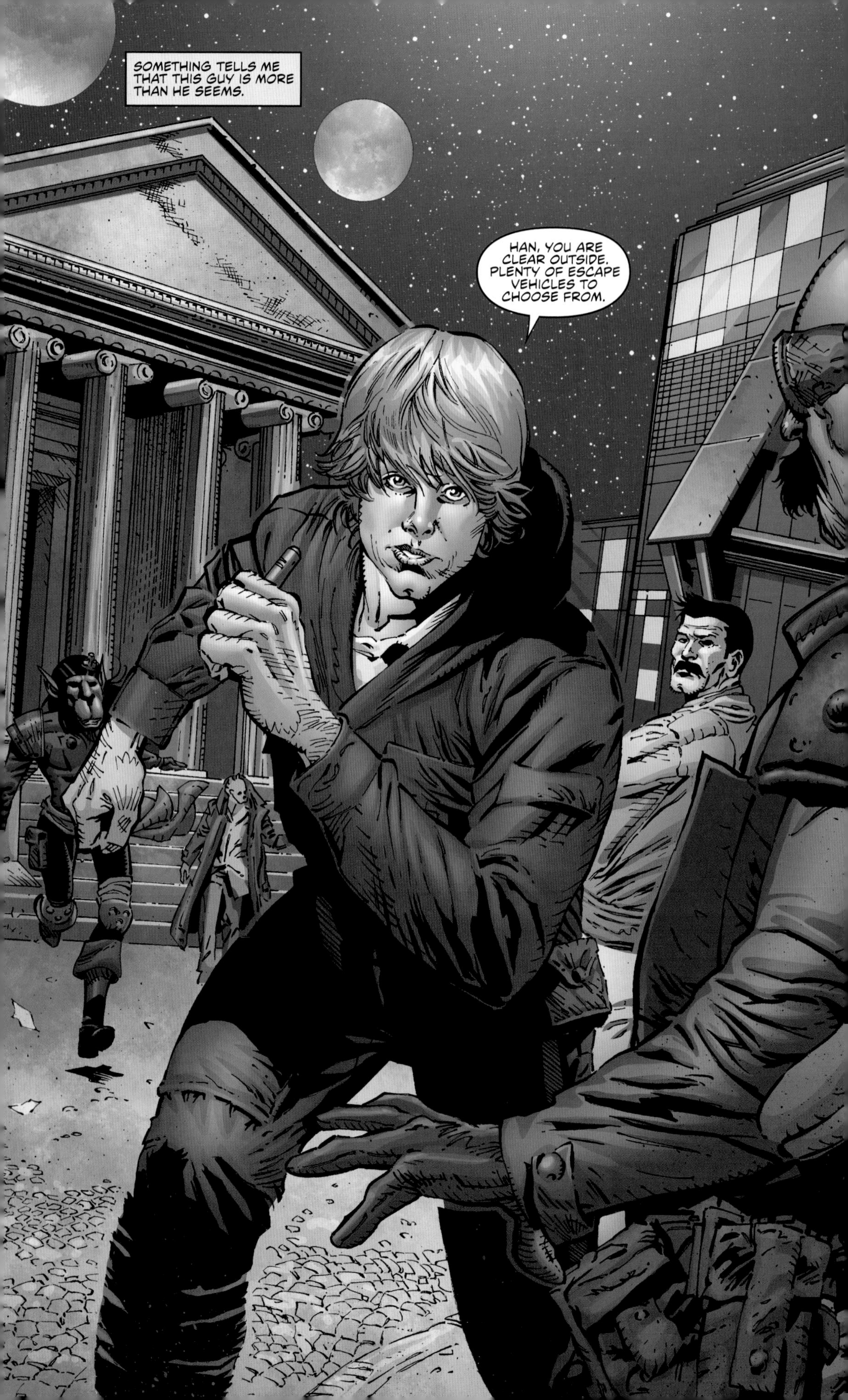
SOMETHING TELLS ME THAT THIS GUY IS MORE THAN HE SEEMS.
HAN, YOU ARE CLEAR OUTSIDE. PLENTY OF ESCAPE VEHICLES TO CHOOSE FROM.

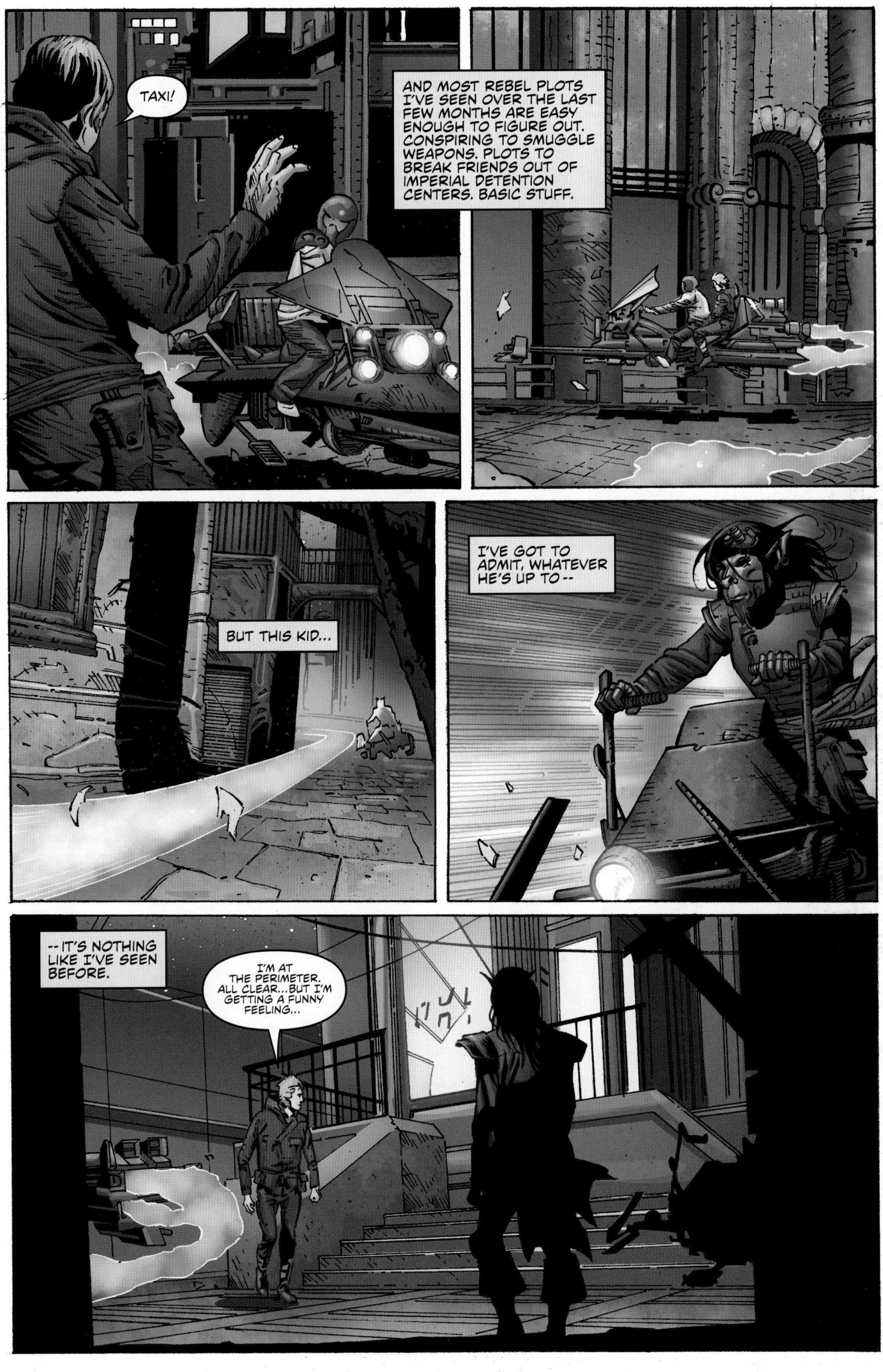
TAXI!
AND MOST REBEL PLOTS I'VE SEEN OVER THE LAST FEW MONTHS ARE EASY ENOUGH TO FIGURE OUT. CONSPIRING TO SMUGGLE WEAPONS. PLOTS TO BREAK FRIENDS OUT OF IMPERIAL DETENTION CENTERS. BASIC STUFF.
BUT THIS KID...
I'VE GOT TO ADMIT, WHATEVER HE'S UP TO--
--IT'S NOTHING LIKE I'VE SEEN BEFORE.
I'M AT THE PERIMETER. ALL CLEAR...BUT I'M GETTING A FUNNY FEELING...

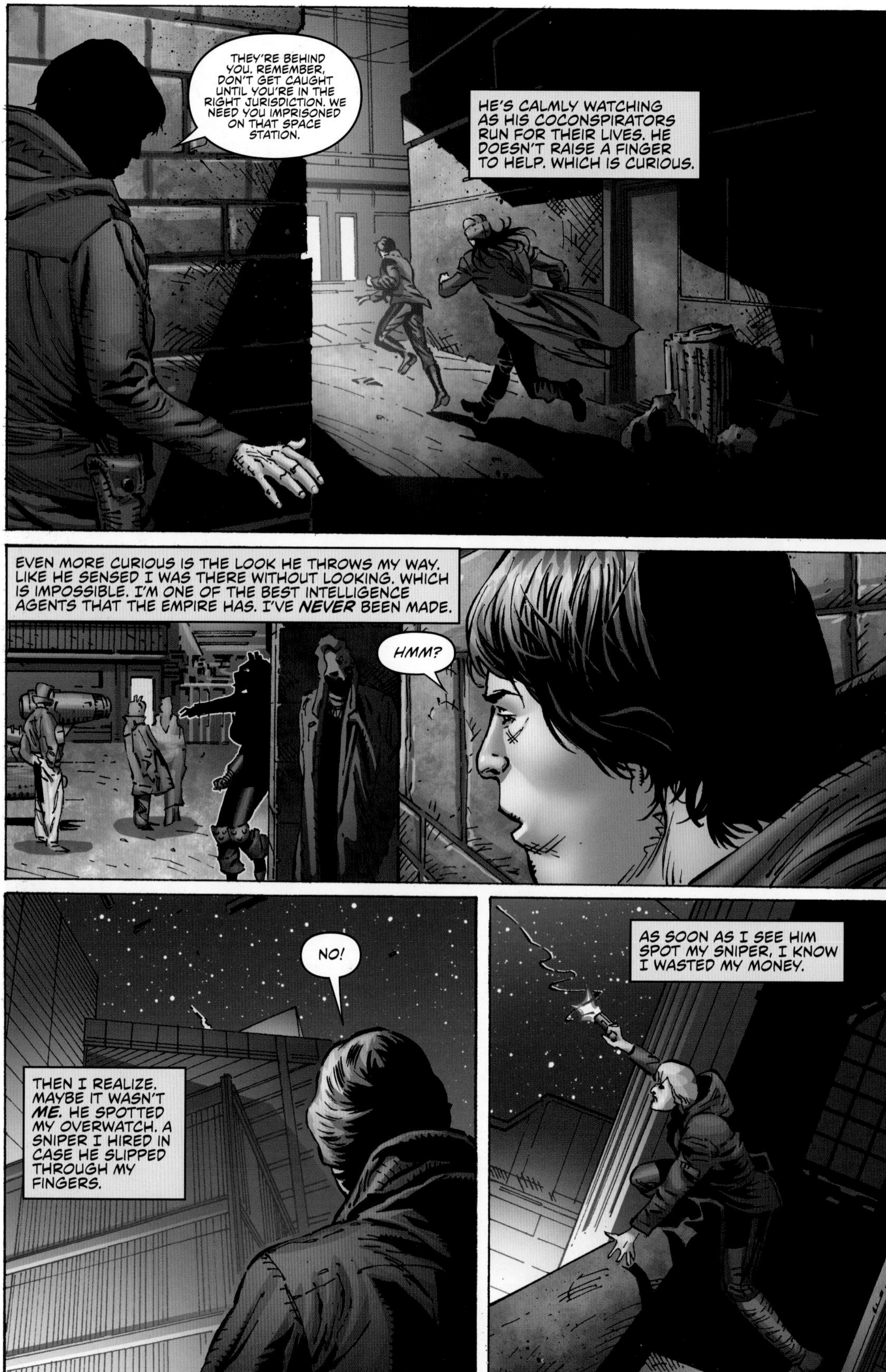
THEY'RE BEHIND YOU. REMEMBER, DON'T GET CAUGHT UNTIL YOU'RE IN THE RIGHT JURISDICTION. WE NEED YOU IMPRISONED ON THAT SPACE STATION.
HE'S CALMLY WATCHING AS HIS COCONSPIRATORS RUN FOR THEIR LIVES. HE DOESN'T RAISE A FINGER TO HELP. WHICH IS CURIOUS.
EVEN MORE CURIOUS IS THE LOOK HE THROWS MY WAY. LIKE HE SENSED I WAS THERE WITHOUT LOOKING. WHICH IS IMPOSSIBLE. I'M ONE OF THE BEST INTELLIGENCE AGENTS THAT THE EMPIRE HAS. I'VE ***NEVER*** BEEN MADE.
HMM?
NO!
THEN I REALIZE. MAYBE IT WASN'T ***ME.*** HE SPOTTED MY OVERWATCH. A SNIPER I HIRED IN CASE HE SLIPPED THROUGH MY FINGERS.
AS SOON AS I SEE HIM SPOT MY SNIPER, I KNOW I WASTED MY MONEY.

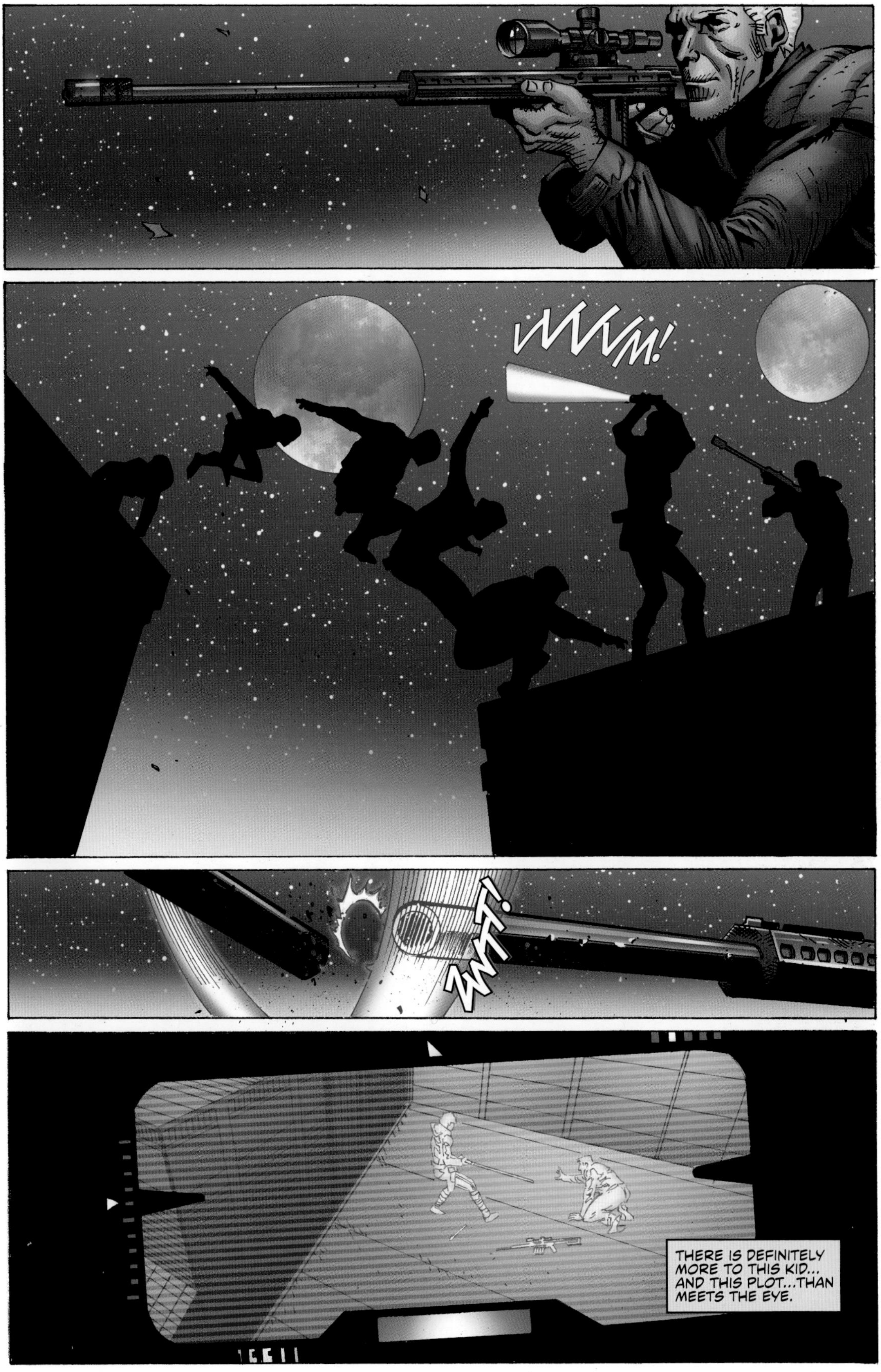
VVVVM!
ZWTT!
THERE IS DEFINITELY MORE TO THIS KID... AND THIS PLOT...THAN MEETS THE EYE.

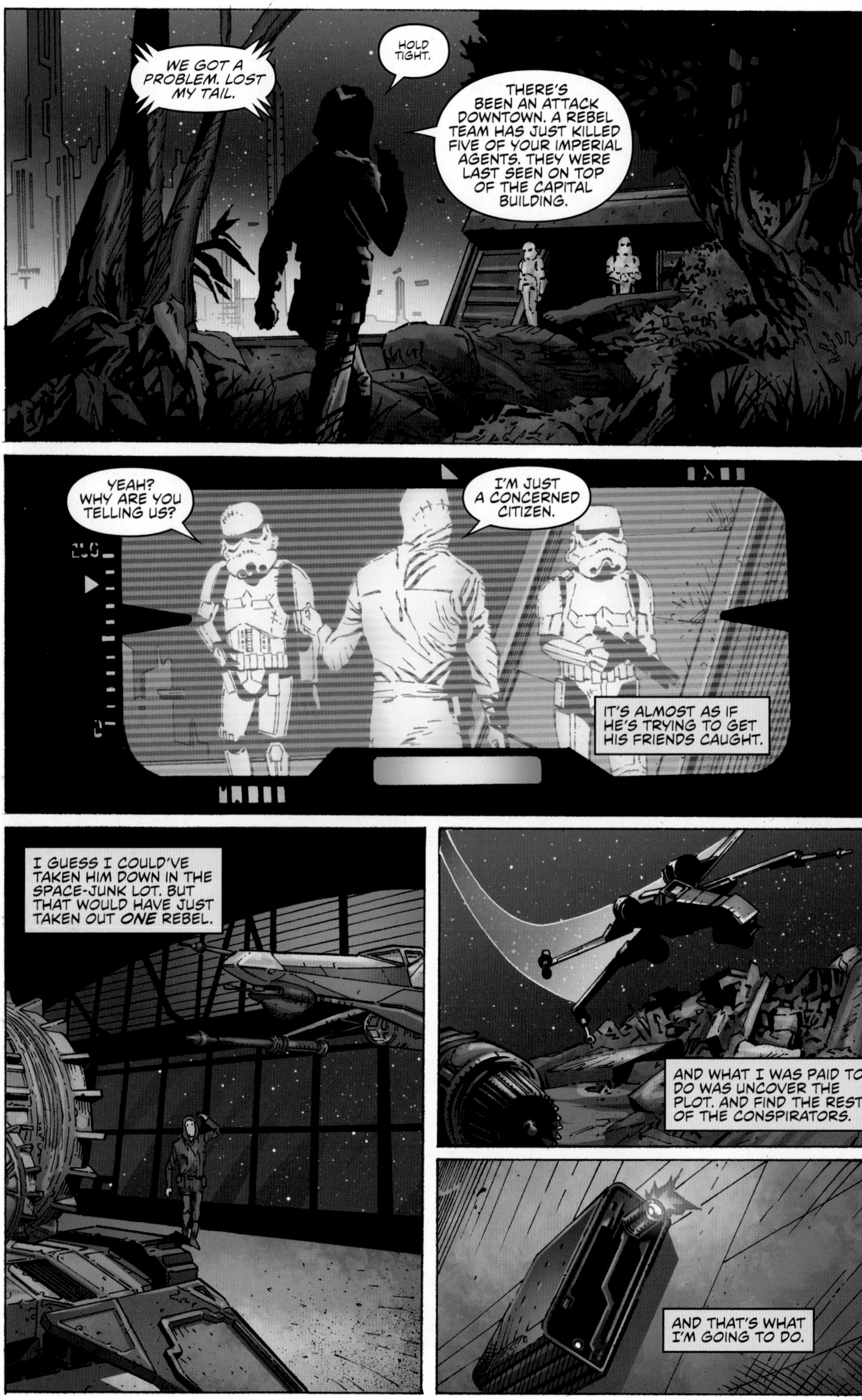
WE GOT A PROBLEM. LOST MY TAIL.
HOLD TIGHT.
THERE'S BEEN AN ATTACK DOWNTOWN. A REBEL TEAM HAS JUST KILLED FIVE OF YOUR IMPERIAL AGENTS. THEY WERE LAST SEEN ON TOP OF THE CAPITAL BUILDING.
YEAH? WHY ARE YOU TELLING US?
I'M JUST A CONCERNED CITIZEN.
IT'S ALMOST AS IF HE'S TRYING TO GET HIS FRIENDS CAUGHT.
I GUESS I COULD'VE TAKEN HIM DOWN IN THE SPACE-JUNK LOT. BUT THAT WOULD HAVE JUST TAKEN OUT ONE REBEL.
AND WHAT I WAS PAID TO DO WAS UNCOVER THE PLOT. AND FIND THE REST OF THE CONSPIRATORS.
AND THAT'S WHAT I'M GOING TO DO.

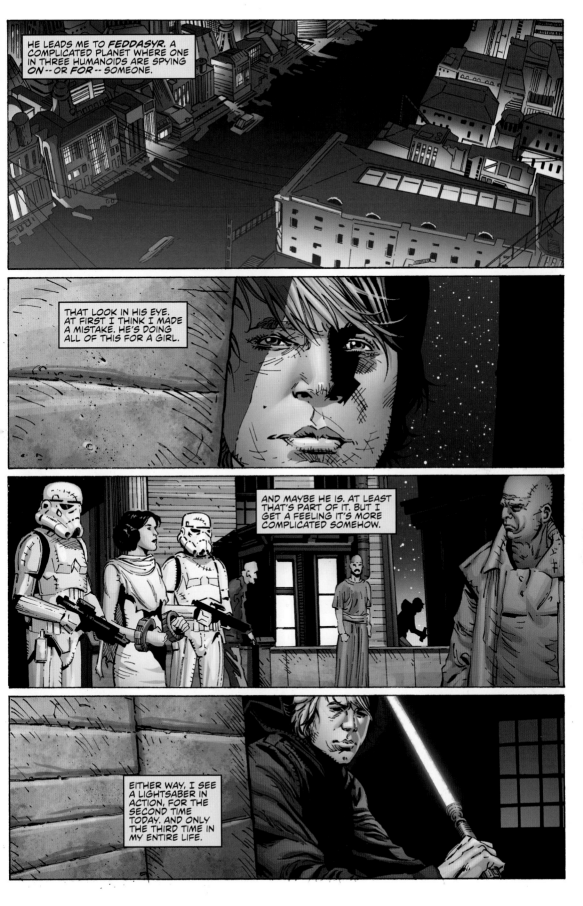

HE LEADS ME TO *FEDDASYR.* A COMPLICATED PLANET WHERE ONE IN THREE HUMANOIDS ARE SPYING ON -- OR *FOR* -- SOMEONE.

THAT LOOK IN HIS EYE. AT FIRST I THINK I MADE A MISTAKE. HE'S DOING ALL OF THIS FOR A GIRL.

AND MAYBE HE IS. AT LEAST THAT'S PART OF IT. BUT I GET A FEELING IT'S MORE COMPLICATED SOMEHOW.

EITHER WAY, I SEE A LIGHTSABER IN ACTION, FOR THE SECOND TIME TODAY. AND ONLY THE THIRD TIME IN MY ENTIRE LIFE.

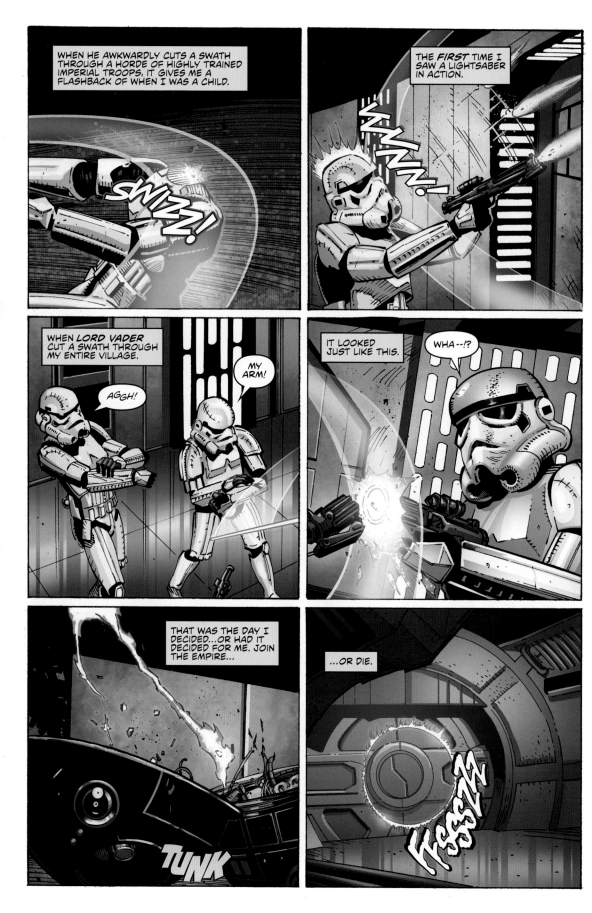

WHEN HE AWKWARDLY CUTS A SWATH THROUGH A HORDE OF HIGHLY TRAINED IMPERIAL TROOPS, IT GIVES ME A FLASHBACK OF WHEN I WAS A CHILD.

SWIZZ!

THE *FIRST* TIME I SAW A LIGHTSABER IN ACTION.

WNNN!

WHEN *LORD VADER* CUT A SWATH THROUGH MY ENTIRE VILLAGE.

AGGH!

MY ARM!

IT LOOKED JUST LIKE THIS.

WHA--!?

THAT WAS THE DAY I DECIDED...OR HAD IT DECIDED FOR ME. JOIN THE EMPIRE...

...OR DIE.

TUNK

FFSSSZZ

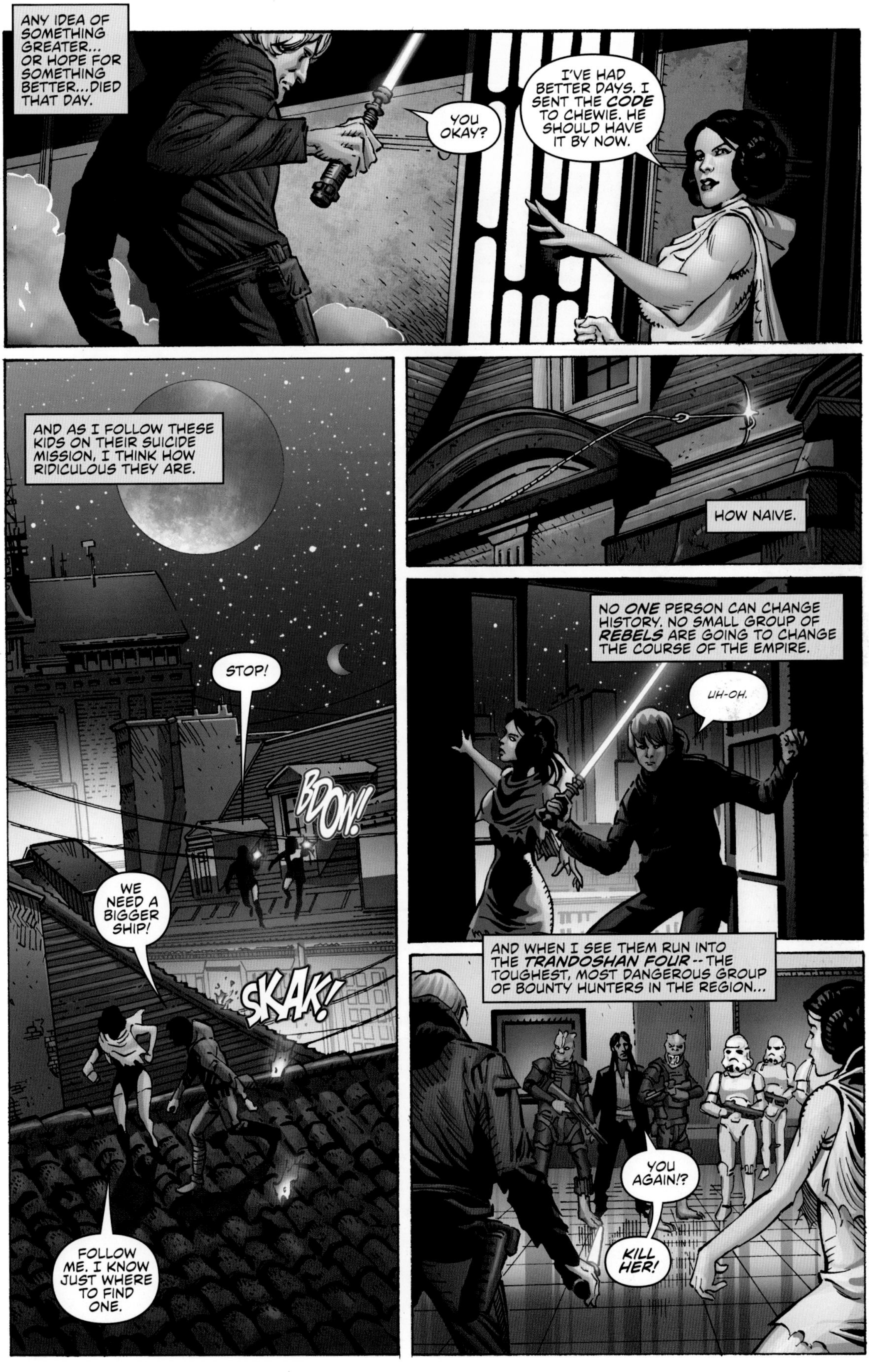
ANY IDEA OF SOMETHING GREATER... OR HOPE FOR SOMETHING BETTER...DIED THAT DAY.
YOU OKAY?
I'VE HAD BETTER DAYS. I SENT THE CODE TO CHEWIE. HE SHOULD HAVE IT BY NOW.
AND AS I FOLLOW THESE KIDS ON THEIR SUICIDE MISSION, I THINK HOW RIDICULOUS THEY ARE.
STOP!
BDOW!
WE NEED A BIGGER SHIP!
SKAK!
FOLLOW ME. I KNOW JUST WHERE TO FIND ONE.
HOW NAIVE.
NO ONE PERSON CAN CHANGE HISTORY. NO SMALL GROUP OF REBELS ARE GOING TO CHANGE THE COURSE OF THE EMPIRE.
UH-OH.
AND WHEN I SEE THEM RUN INTO THE TRANDOSHAN FOUR -- THE TOUGHEST, MOST DANGEROUS GROUP OF BOUNTY HUNTERS IN THE REGION...
YOU AGAIN!?
KILL HER!

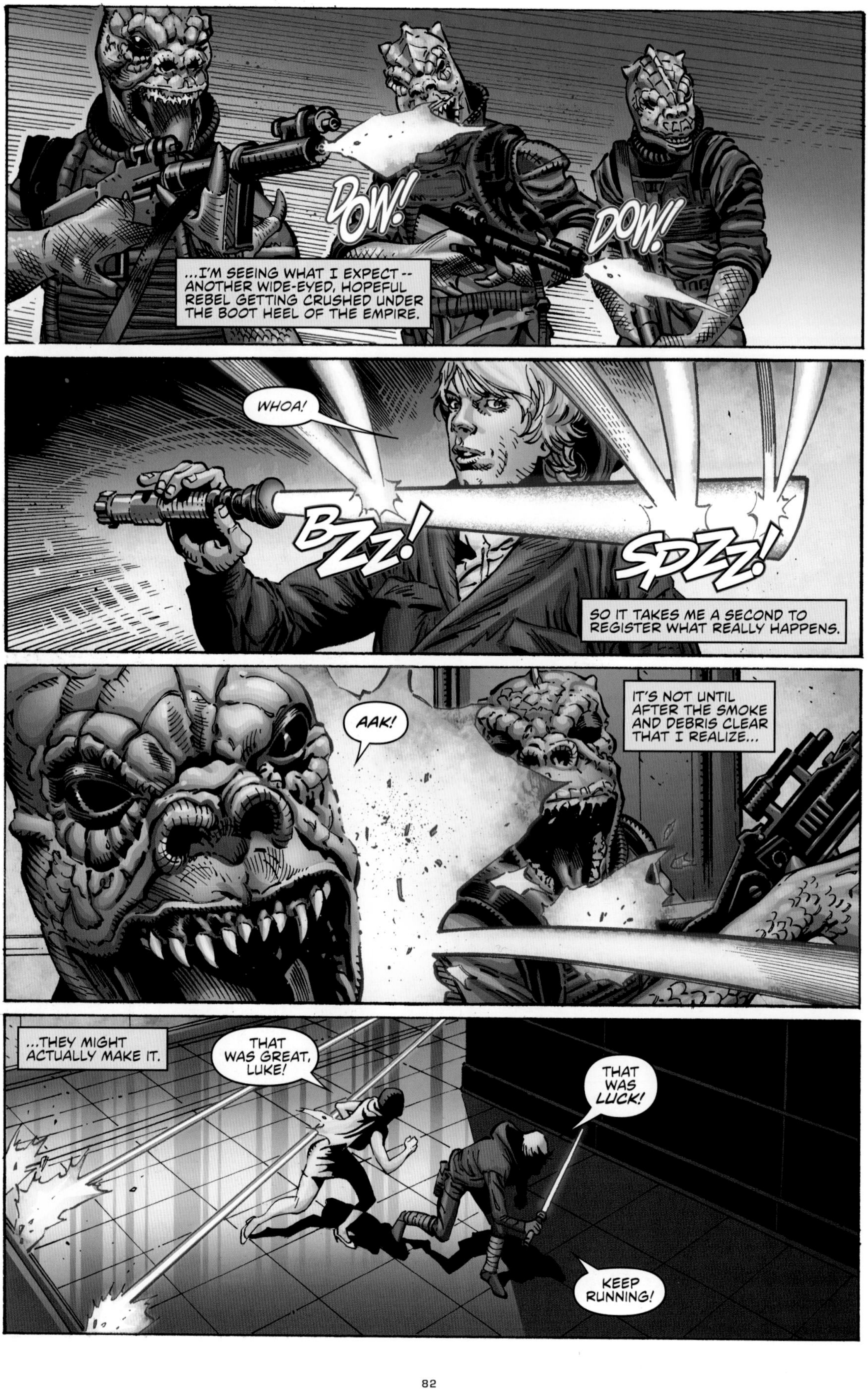
DOW!
DOW!
...I'M SEEING WHAT I EXPECT -- ANOTHER WIDE-EYED, HOPEFUL REBEL GETTING CRUSHED UNDER THE BOOT HEEL OF THE EMPIRE.
WHOA!
BZZ!
SPZZ!
SO IT TAKES ME A SECOND TO REGISTER WHAT REALLY HAPPENS.
AAK!
IT'S NOT UNTIL AFTER THE SMOKE AND DEBRIS CLEAR THAT I REALIZE...
...THEY MIGHT ACTUALLY MAKE IT.
THAT WAS GREAT, LUKE!
THAT WAS LUCK!
KEEP RUNNING!

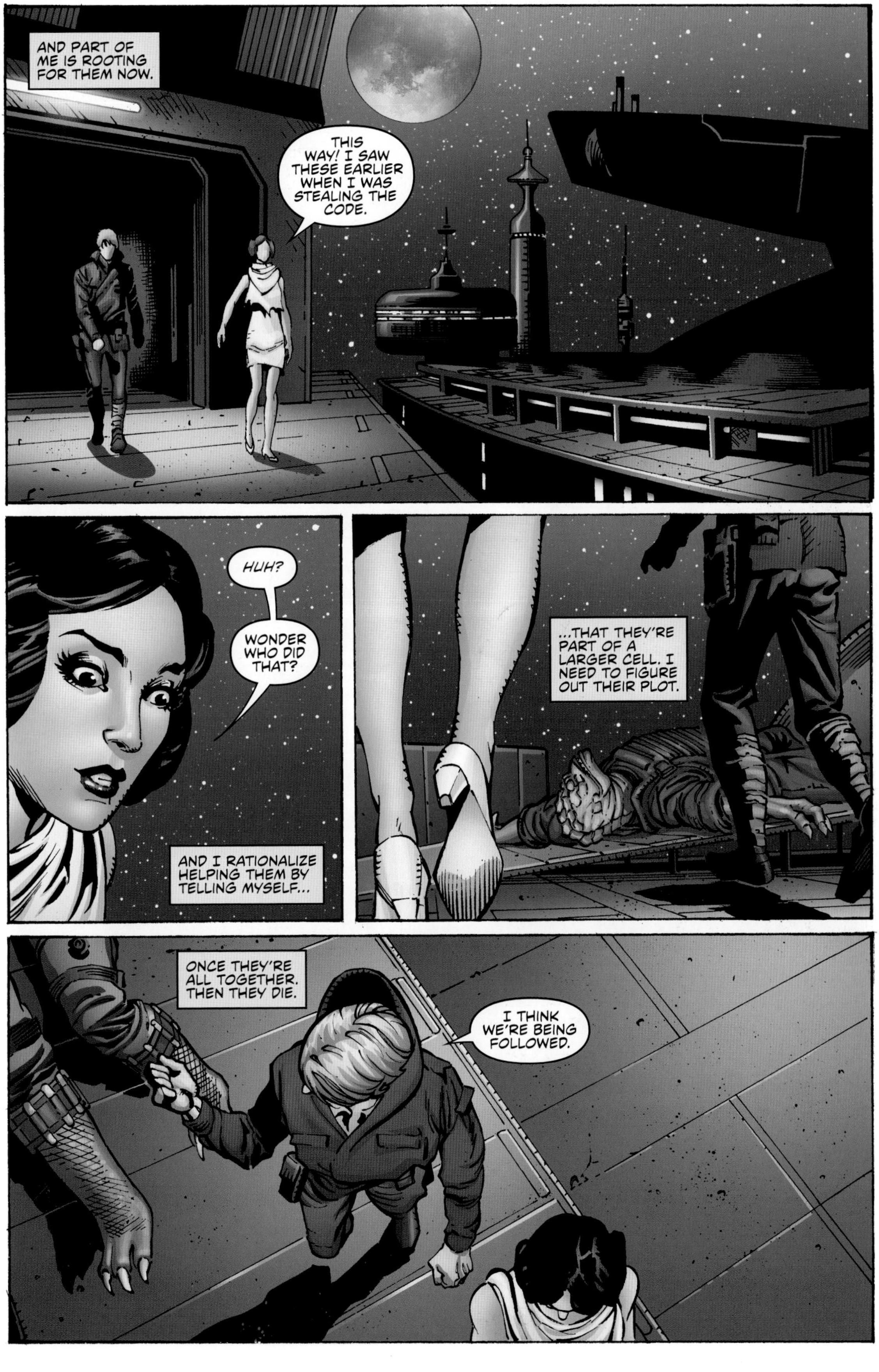
AND PART OF ME IS ROOTING FOR THEM NOW.
THIS WAY! I SAW THESE EARLIER WHEN I WAS STEALING THE CODE.
HUH?
WONDER WHO DID THAT?
AND I RATIONALIZE HELPING THEM BY TELLING MYSELF...
...THAT THEY'RE PART OF A LARGER CELL. I NEED TO FIGURE OUT THEIR PLOT.
ONCE THEY'RE ALL TOGETHER. THEN THEY DIE.
I THINK WE'RE BEING FOLLOWED.

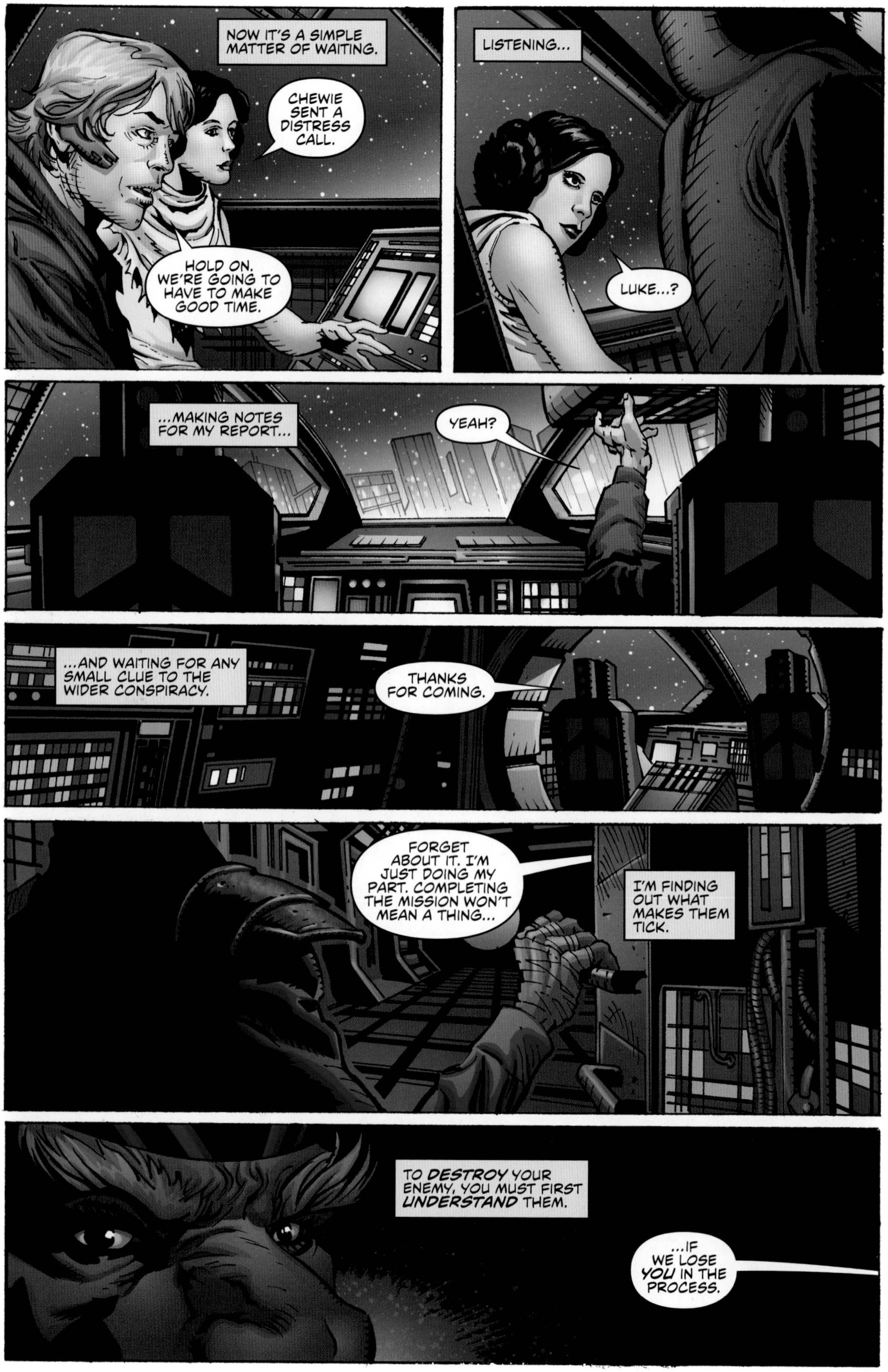
NOW IT'S A SIMPLE MATTER OF WAITING.
CHEWIE SENT A DISTRESS CALL.
HOLD ON. WE'RE GOING TO HAVE TO MAKE GOOD TIME.
LISTENING...
LUKE...?
...MAKING NOTES FOR MY REPORT...
YEAH?
...AND WAITING FOR ANY SMALL CLUE TO THE WIDER CONSPIRACY.
THANKS FOR COMING.
FORGET ABOUT IT. I'M JUST DOING MY PART. COMPLETING THE MISSION WON'T MEAN A THING...
I'M FINDING OUT WHAT MAKES THEM TICK.
TO *DESTROY* YOUR ENEMY, YOU MUST FIRST *UNDERSTAND* THEM.
...IF WE LOSE *YOU* IN THE PROCESS.

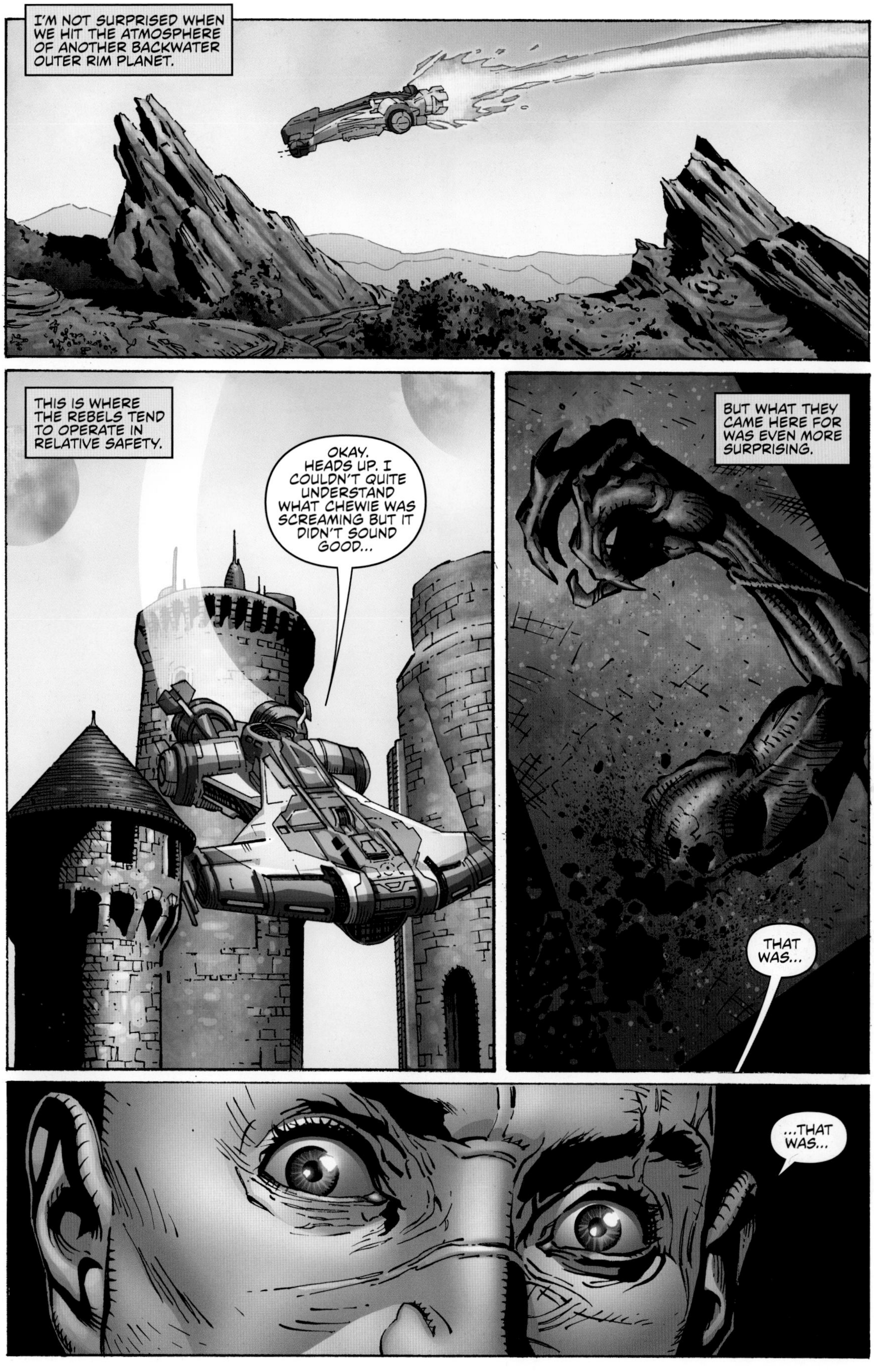
I'M NOT SURPRISED WHEN WE HIT THE ATMOSPHERE OF ANOTHER BACKWATER OUTER RIM PLANET.
THIS IS WHERE THE REBELS TEND TO OPERATE IN RELATIVE SAFETY.
OKAY. HEADS UP. I COULDN'T QUITE UNDERSTAND WHAT CHEWIE WAS SCREAMING BUT IT DIDN'T SOUND GOOD...
BUT WHAT THEY CAME HERE FOR WAS EVEN MORE SURPRISING.
THAT WAS...
...THAT WAS...

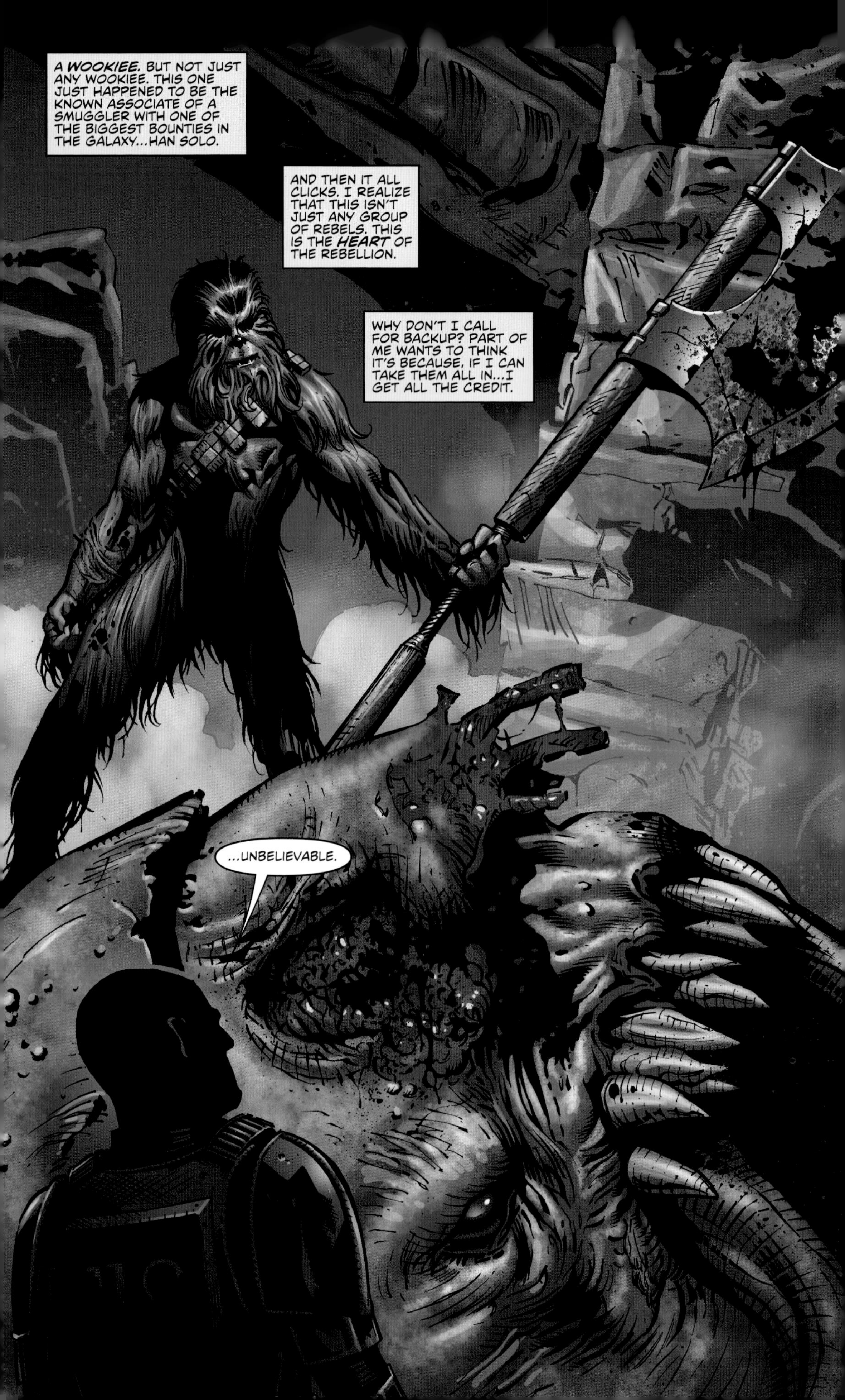
A WOOKIEE. BUT NOT JUST ANY WOOKIEE. THIS ONE JUST HAPPENED TO BE THE KNOWN ASSOCIATE OF A SMUGGLER WITH ONE OF THE BIGGEST BOUNTIES IN THE GALAXY...HAN SOLO.
AND THEN IT ALL CLICKS. I REALIZE THAT THIS ISN'T JUST ANY GROUP OF REBELS. THIS IS THE HEART OF THE REBELLION.
WHY DON'T I CALL FOR BACKUP? PART OF ME WANTS TO THINK IT'S BECAUSE, IF I CAN TAKE THEM ALL IN...I GET ALL THE CREDIT.
...UNBELIEVABLE.

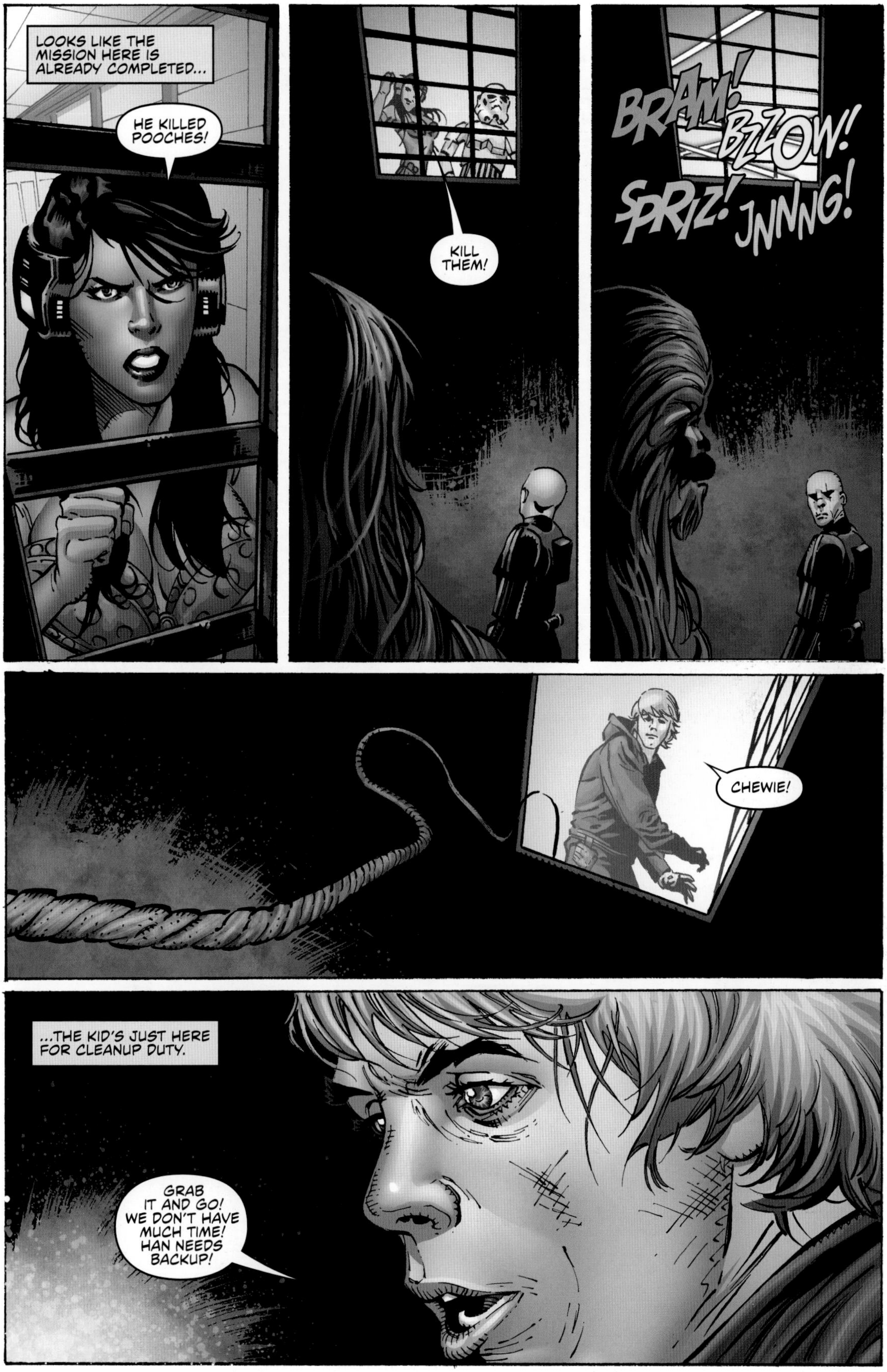
LOOKS LIKE THE MISSION HERE IS ALREADY COMPLETED...
HE KILLED POOCHES!
KILL THEM!
BRAM!
BZZOW!
SPRIZ!
JNNNG!
CHEWIE!
...THE KID'S JUST HERE FOR CLEANUP DUTY.
GRAB IT AND GO! WE DON'T HAVE MUCH TIME! HAN NEEDS BACKUP!

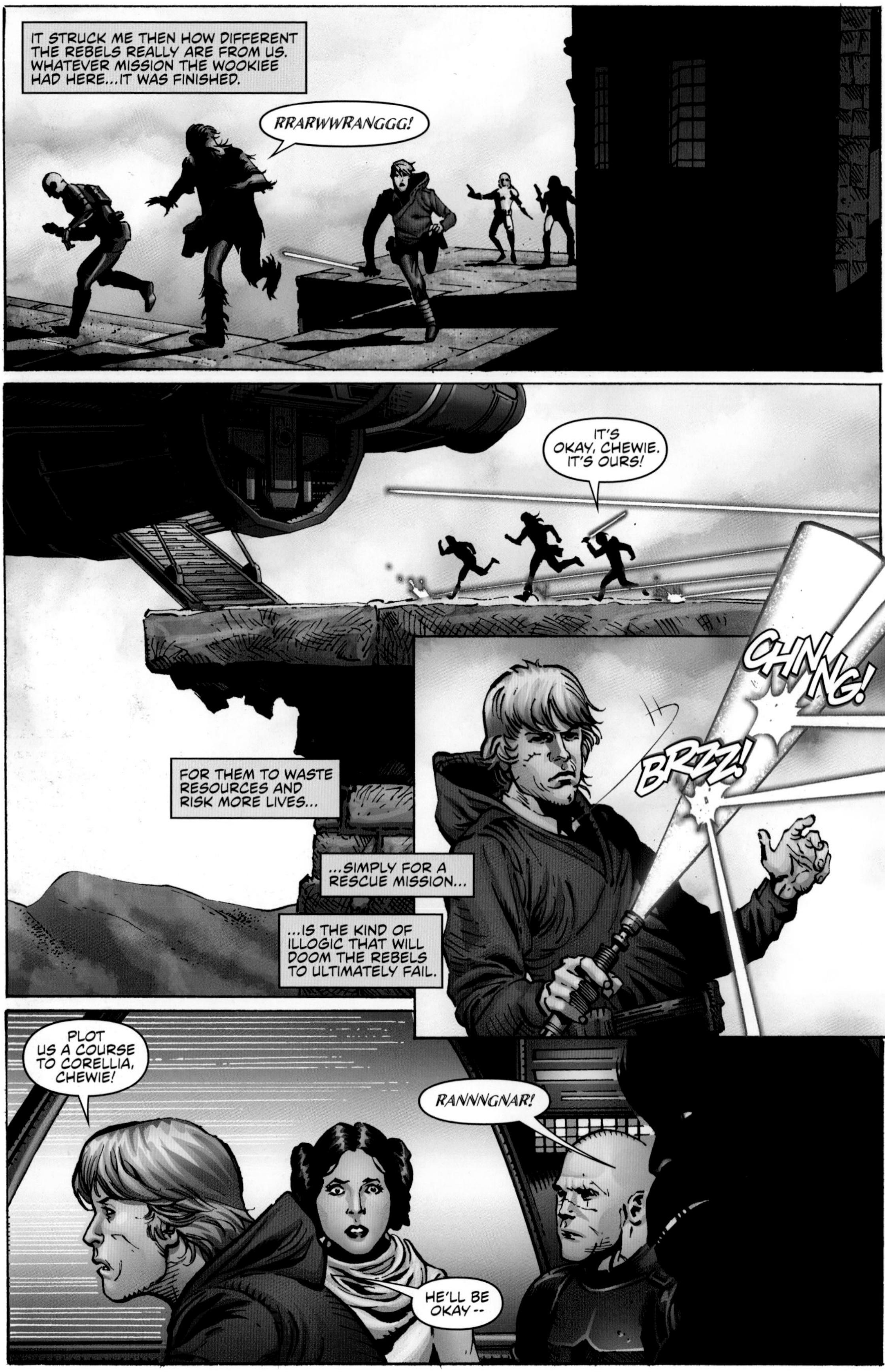
IT STRUCK ME THEN HOW DIFFERENT THE REBELS REALLY ARE FROM US. WHATEVER MISSION THE WOOKIEE HAD HERE...IT WAS FINISHED.
RRARWWRANGGG!
IT'S OKAY, CHEWIE. IT'S OURS!
FOR THEM TO WASTE RESOURCES AND RISK MORE LIVES...
...SIMPLY FOR A RESCUE MISSION...
...IS THE KIND OF ILLOGIC THAT WILL DOOM THE REBELS TO ULTIMATELY FAIL.
CHINNG!
BRZZ!
PLOT US A COURSE TO CORELLIA, CHEWIE!
RANNNGNAR!
HE'LL BE OKAY --

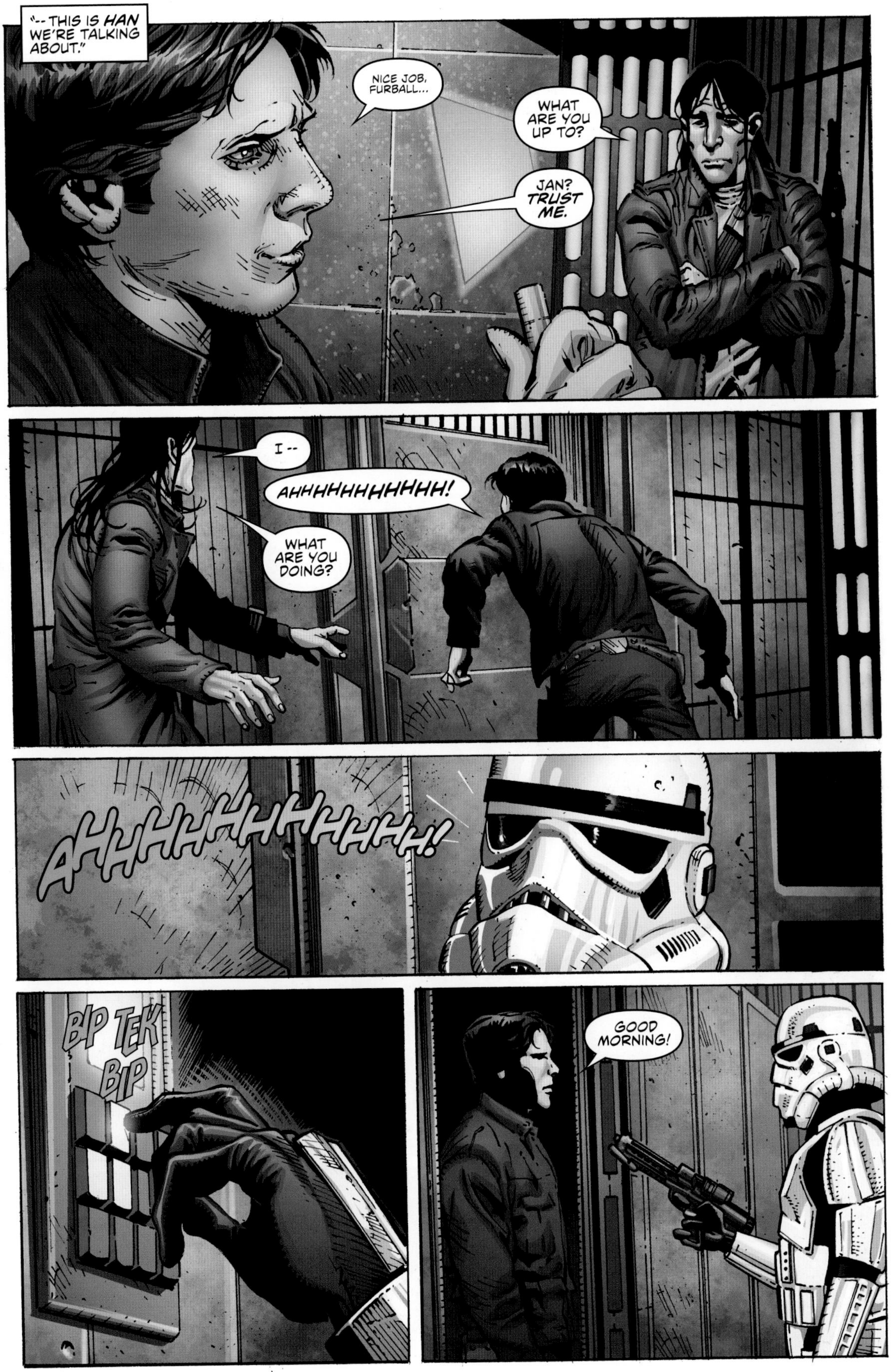
"-- THIS IS HAN WE'RE TALKING ABOUT."
NICE JOB, FURBALL...
WHAT ARE YOU UP TO?
JAN? TRUST ME.
I --
AHHHHHHHHHH!
WHAT ARE YOU DOING?
AHHHHHHHHHHH!
BIP TEK BIP
GOOD MORNING!

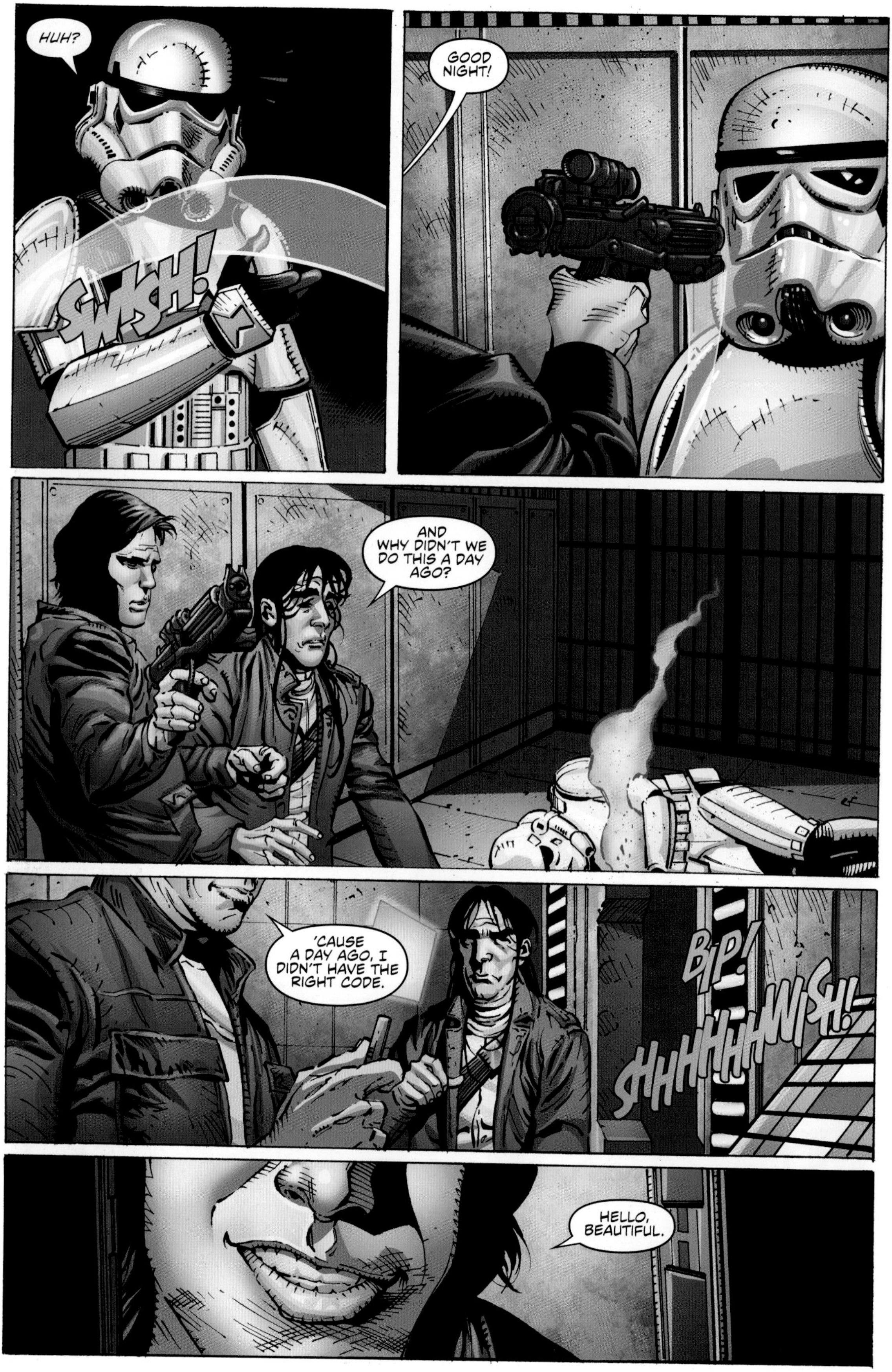
HUH?
SWISH!
GOOD NIGHT!
AND WHY DIDN'T WE DO THIS A DAY AGO?
'CAUSE A DAY AGO, I DIDN'T HAVE THE RIGHT CODE.
BIP!
SHHHHHHWISH!
HELLO, BEAUTIFUL.

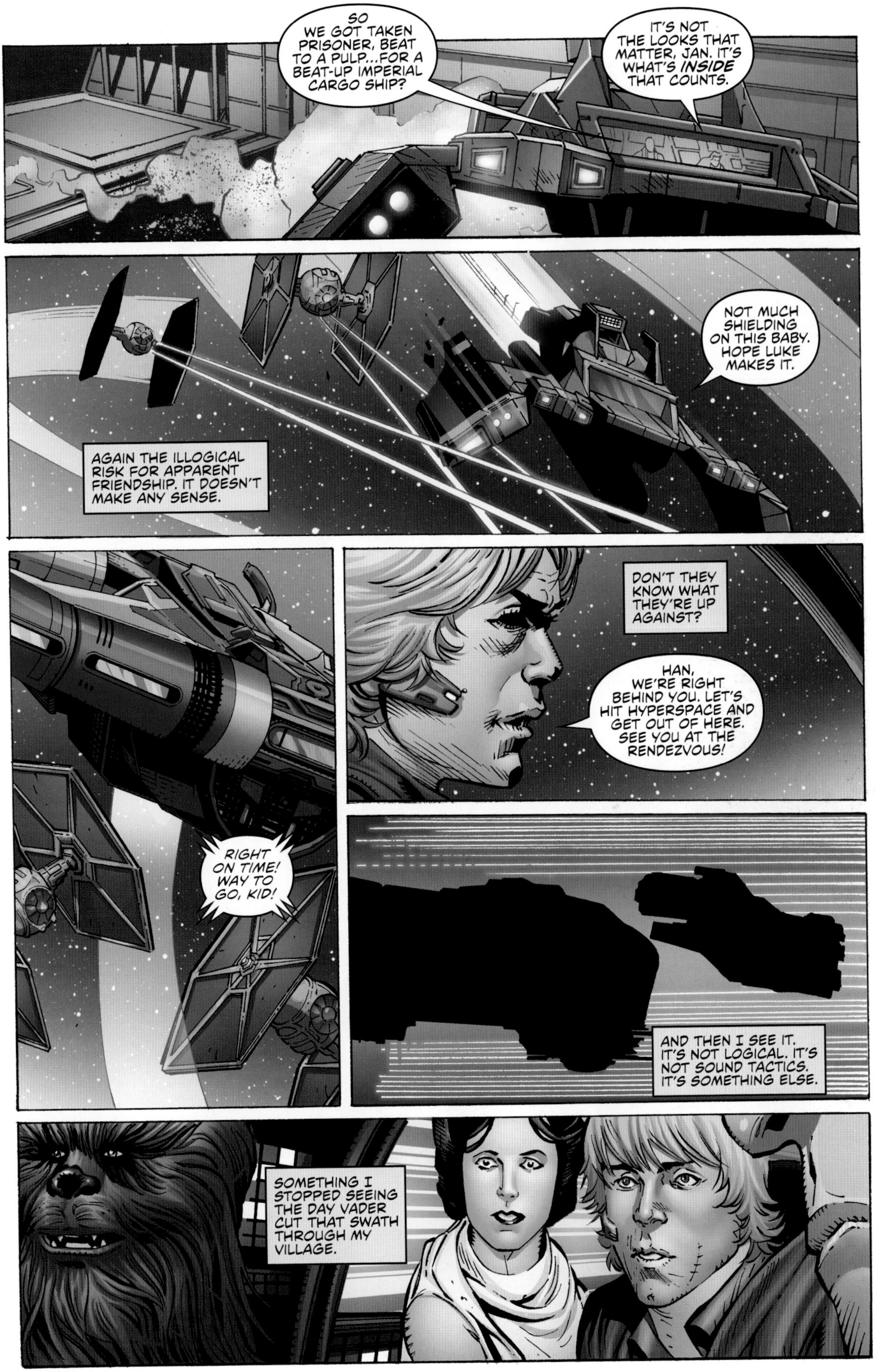
SO WE GOT TAKEN PRISONER, BEAT TO A PULP...FOR A BEAT-UP IMPERIAL CARGO SHIP?
IT'S NOT THE LOOKS THAT MATTER, JAN. IT'S WHAT'S *INSIDE* THAT COUNTS.
NOT MUCH SHIELDING ON THIS BABY. HOPE LUKE MAKES IT.
AGAIN THE ILLOGICAL RISK FOR APPARENT FRIENDSHIP. IT DOESN'T MAKE ANY SENSE.
DON'T THEY KNOW WHAT THEY'RE UP AGAINST?
HAN, WE'RE RIGHT BEHIND YOU. LET'S HIT HYPERSPACE AND GET OUT OF HERE. SEE YOU AT THE RENDEZVOUS!
RIGHT ON TIME! WAY TO GO, KID!
AND THEN I SEE IT. IT'S NOT LOGICAL. IT'S NOT SOUND TACTICS. IT'S SOMETHING ELSE.
SOMETHING I STOPPED SEEING THE DAY VADER CUT THAT SWATH THROUGH MY VILLAGE.

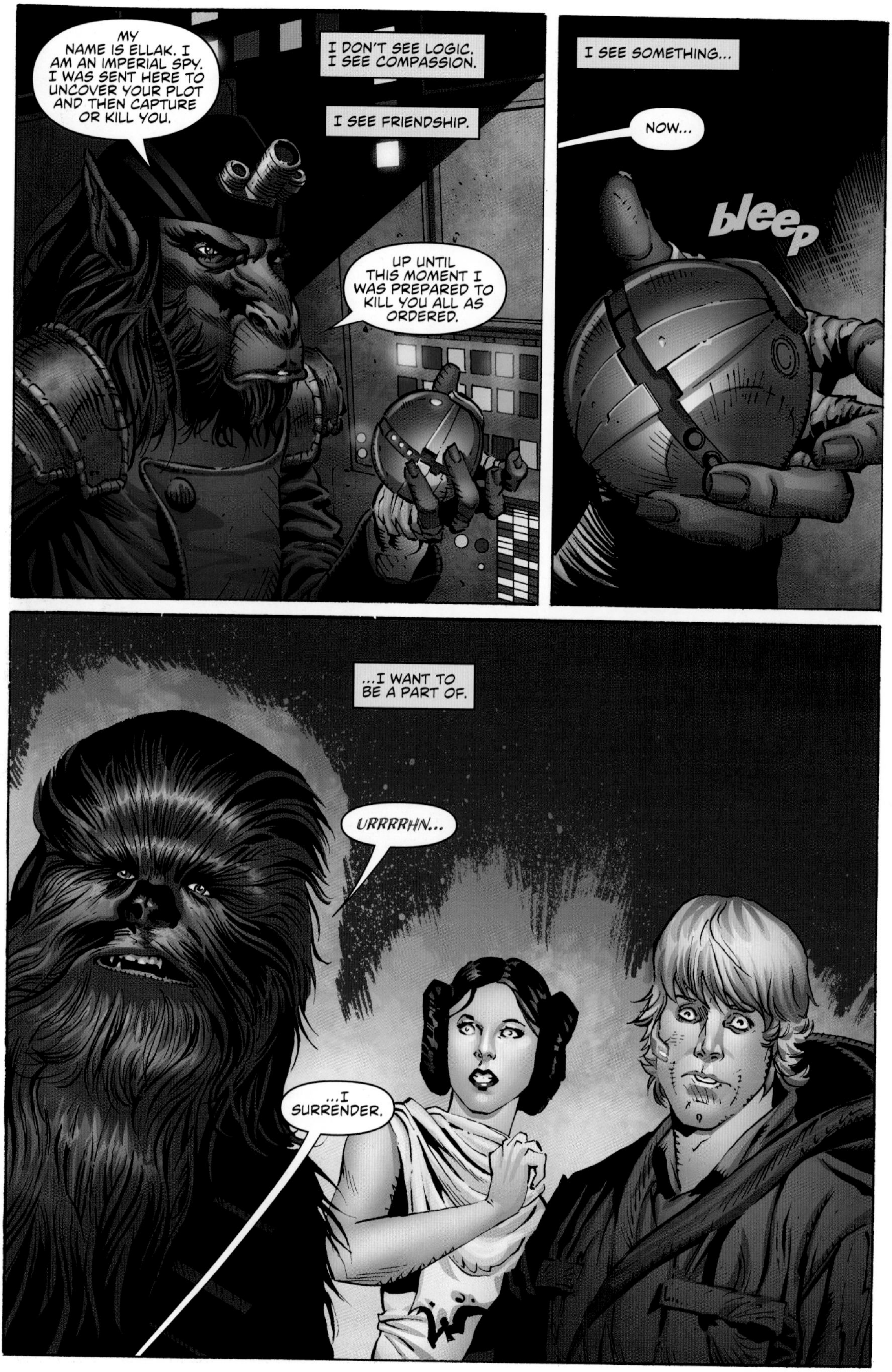
MY NAME IS ELLAK. I AM AN IMPERIAL SPY. I WAS SENT HERE TO UNCOVER YOUR PLOT AND THEN CAPTURE OR KILL YOU.
I DON'T SEE LOGIC. I SEE COMPASSION.
I SEE FRIENDSHIP.
UP UNTIL THIS MOMENT I WAS PREPARED TO KILL YOU ALL AS ORDERED.
I SEE SOMETHING...
NOW...
bleep
...I WANT TO BE A PART OF.
URRRRHN...
...I SURRENDER.

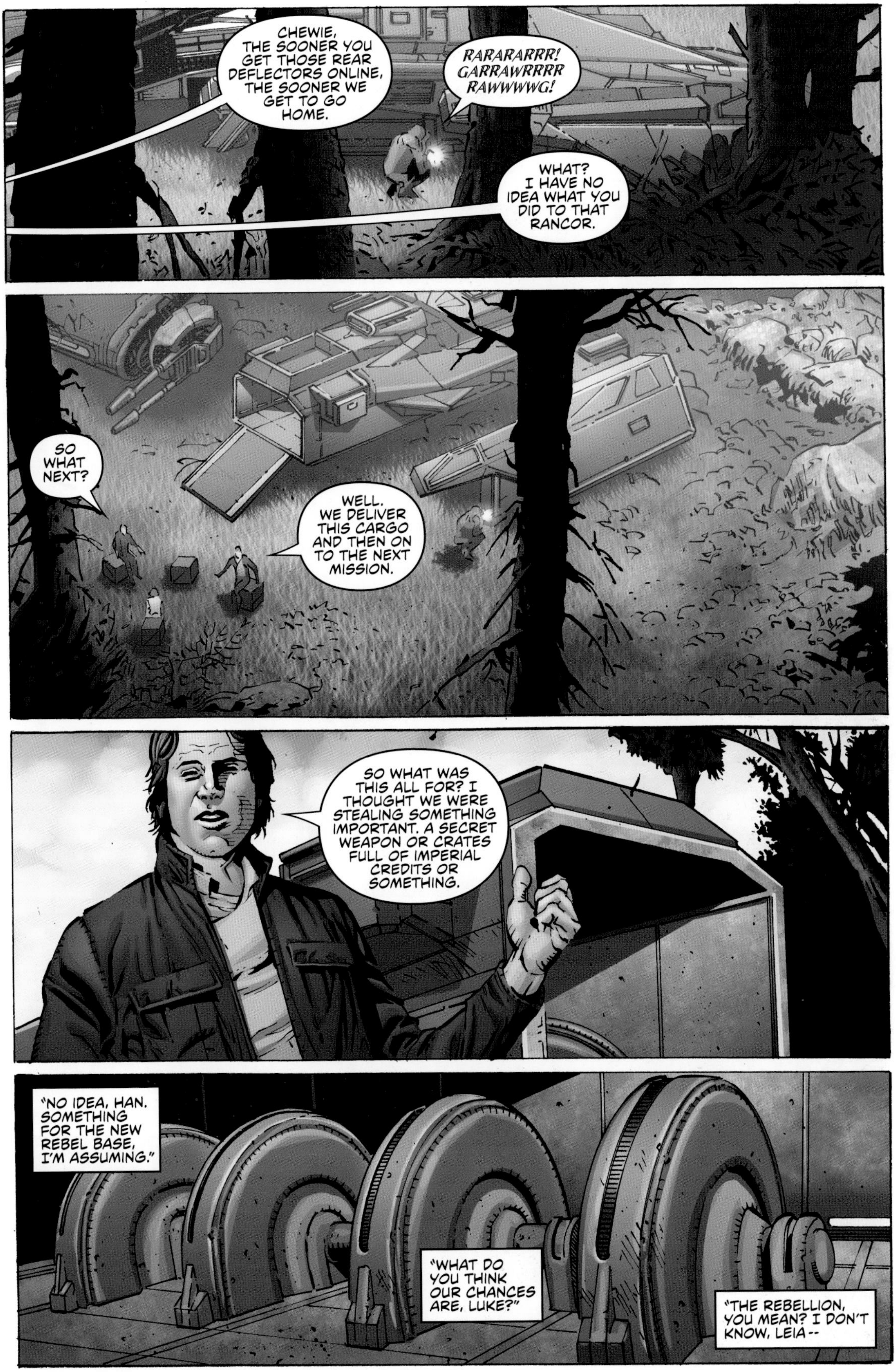
CHEWIE, THE SOONER YOU GET THOSE REAR DEFLECTORS ONLINE, THE SOONER WE GET TO GO HOME.
RARARARRR! GARRAWRRRR RAWWWWG!
WHAT? I HAVE NO IDEA WHAT YOU DID TO THAT RANCOR.
SO WHAT NEXT?
WELL. WE DELIVER THIS CARGO AND THEN ON TO THE NEXT MISSION.
SO WHAT WAS THIS ALL FOR? I THOUGHT WE WERE STEALING SOMETHING IMPORTANT. A SECRET WEAPON OR CRATES FULL OF IMPERIAL CREDITS OR SOMETHING.
"NO IDEA, HAN. SOMETHING FOR THE NEW REBEL BASE, I'M ASSUMING."
"WHAT DO YOU THINK OUR CHANCES ARE, LUKE?"
"THE REBELLION, YOU MEAN? I DON'T KNOW, LEIA --

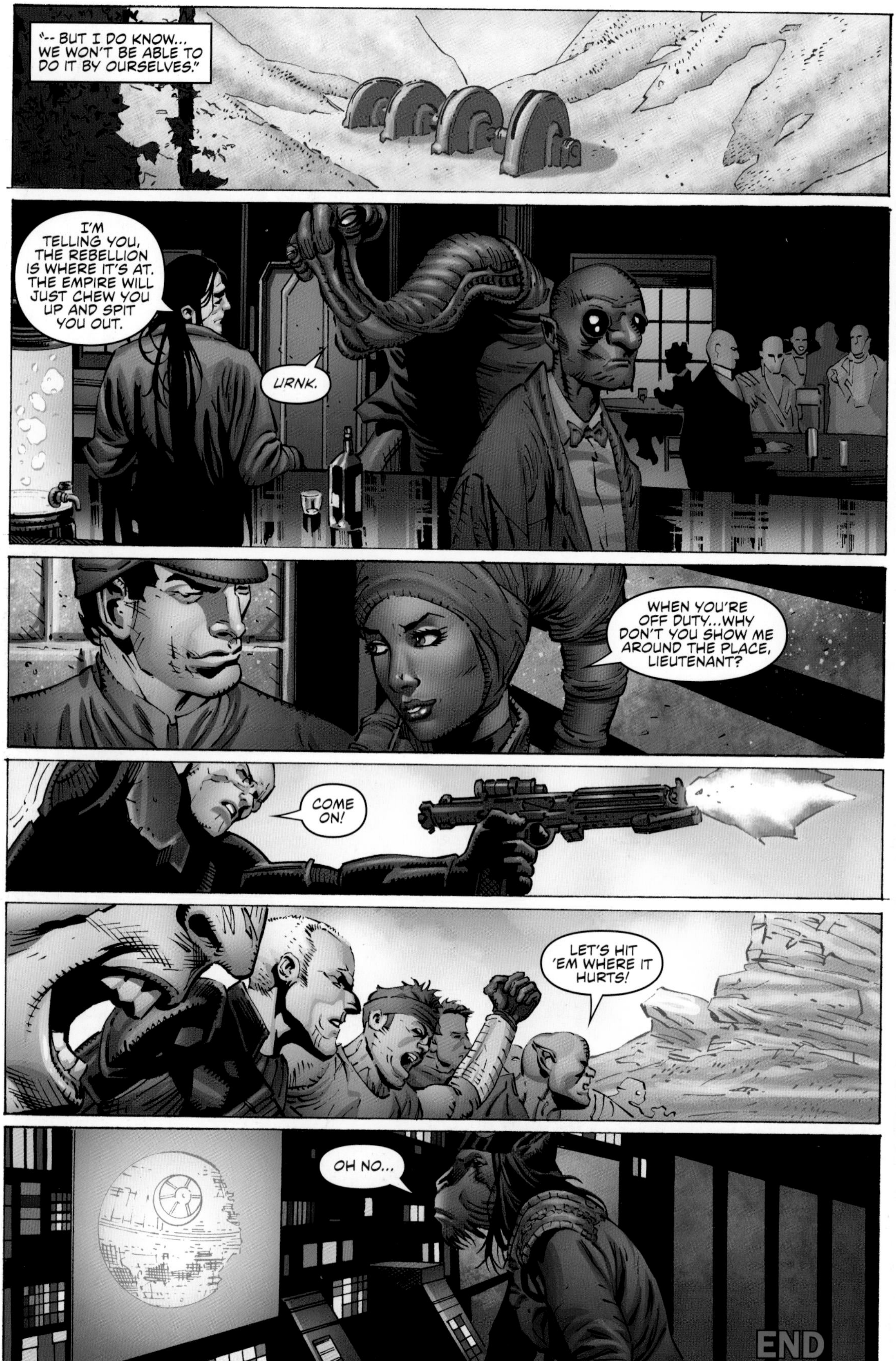
"-- BUT I DO KNOW... WE WON'T BE ABLE TO DO IT BY OURSELVES."
I'M TELLING YOU, THE REBELLION IS WHERE IT'S AT. THE EMPIRE WILL JUST CHEW YOU UP AND SPIT YOU OUT.
URNK.
WHEN YOU'RE OFF DUTY...WHY DON'T YOU SHOW ME AROUND THE PLACE, LIEUTENANT?
COME ON!
LET'S HIT 'EM WHERE IT HURTS!
OH NO...
END

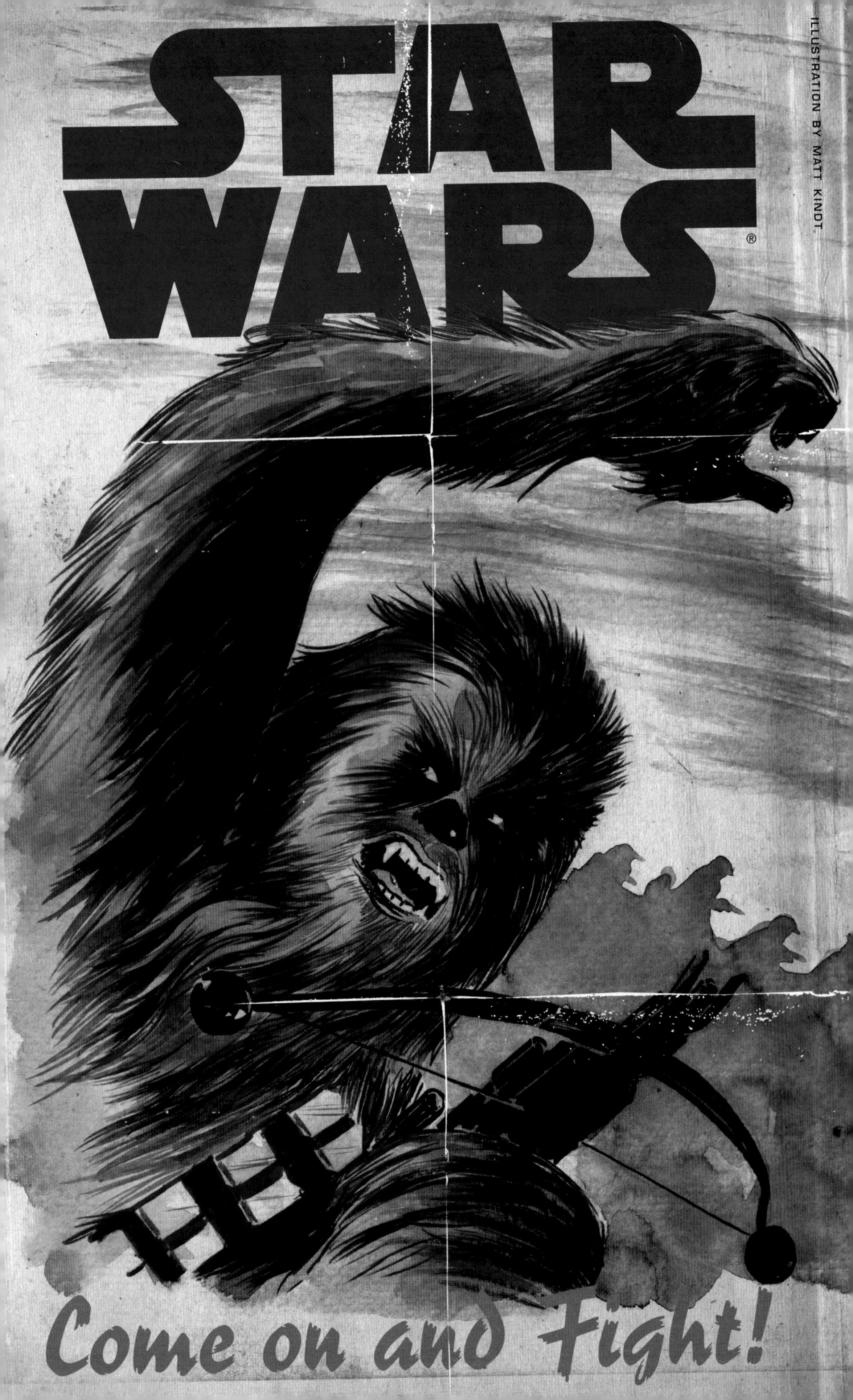
STAR WARS®
ILLUSTRATION BY MATT KINDT
Come on and fight!

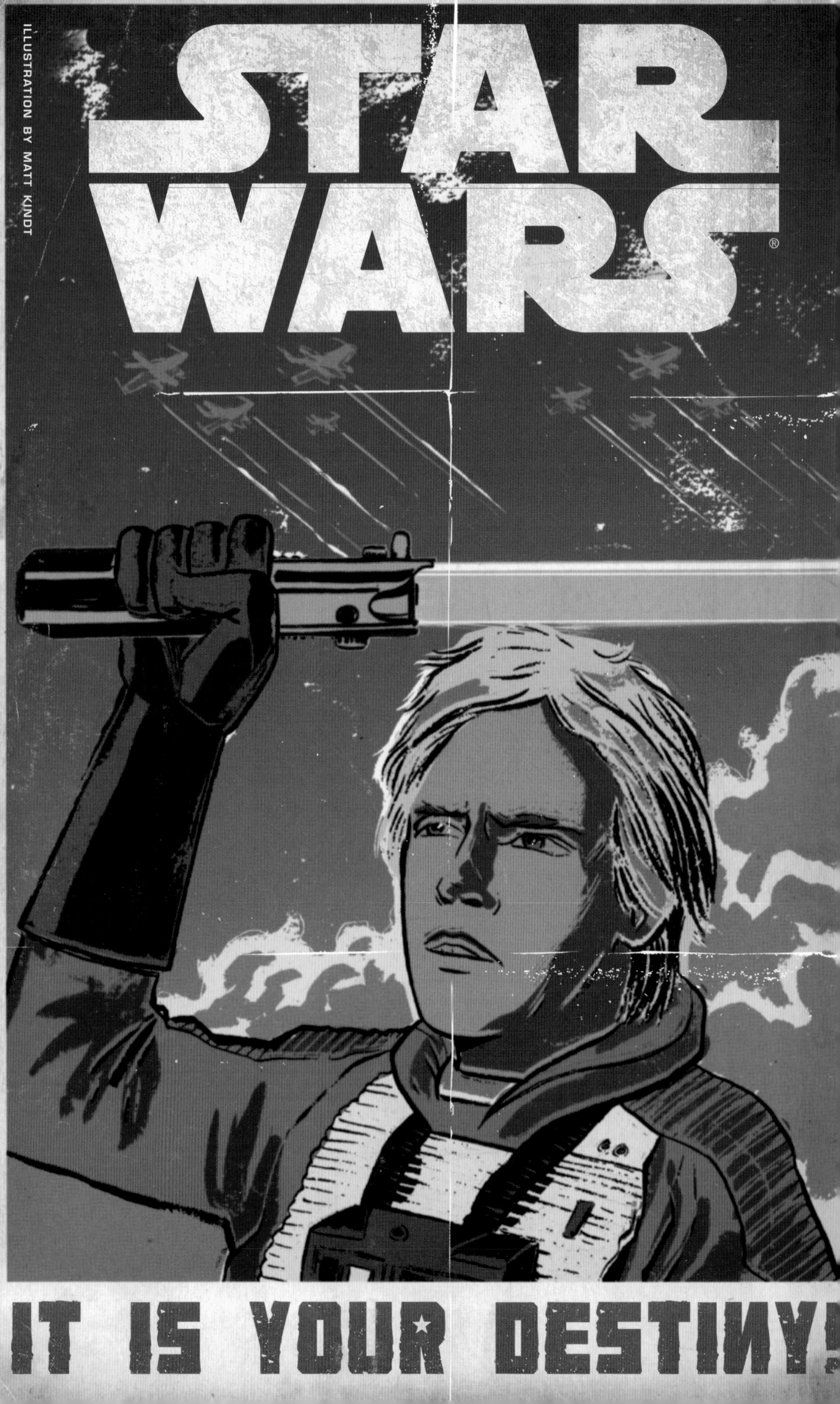

ILLUSTRATION BY MATT KINDT
STAR WARS®
IT IS YOUR DESTINY!